SOUTH-WESTERN

Pre•GED

WRITING SKILLS

Reviewer Team

Mary Ann Christensten
Butler County
Community College
Eldorado, KS

Mary Ann Corley
Maryland State Department
of Education
Columbia, MD

Ellen Carley Frechette
Boston, MA

Barbara Goodridge
Lowell Adult Center
Arlington, MA

Lynn Malachowski
Richland Community
College
Decatur, IL

Molly Milner
Los Angeles
Unified School District
Los Angeles, CA

Susan Nicoles
Winterstein Adult Center
Sacramento, CA

Ruth Schwendeman
Quinsigamond
Community College
Worcester, MA

Robbie Thomas
Cincinnati Public Schools
Adult Division
Cincinnati, OH

Diane Trimble
Expanded Special
Educational Agricultural
Lab (E-SEAL)
Pensacola, FL

South-Western Educational Publishing

Betty B. Schechter, Publisher
Barbara K. Baker, Marketing Manager
Mark Linton, Developmental Editor
Martha Conway, Production Editor
Kimberlee Kusnerak, Production Editor
Gayle Statman, Production Editor
Devore Nixon, Photography Coordinator
Elaine St. John-Lagenaur, Senior Designer
Sheila Puckett, Quality Assurance Specialist
Karen Roberts, Team Leader, Production Coordinator

ISBN: 0-538-63988-1

Library of Congress Cataloging-in-Publication Data
South-Western pre-GED writing skills.
p. 320 cm.
Includes index.
ISBN 0-538-63988-1 (alk. paper)
1. English language—Composition and exercises—Study and teaching (Secondary)—United States—Problems, exercises, etc. 2. General educational development tests. I. South-Western Educational Publishing.
LB1631.S659 1996
808'.042'0712—dc20 95-16115
CIP

1 2 3 4 5 6 7 8 PR 99 98 97 96 95

Printed in the United States of America

I(T)P International Thomson Publishing Company

South-Western Educational Publishing is an ITP Company.
The ITP trademark is used under license.

This book is printed on recycled, acid-free paper that meets Environmental Protection Agency standards.

TABLE OF CONTENTS

Pre-GED Writing Skills

WRITING SKILLS LESSONS 138

CONNECTIONS

INTRODUCTION

Congratulations on beginning your preparation for the GED Tests! This South-Western *Pre-GED Writing Skills* book is designed to make it easier for you to build your skills in preparation for taking the GED Writing Skills Test.

The Pre-GED Series focuses mainly on developing critical-thinking and problem-solving skills. You will need these foundation skills to complete the questions on the GED Tests. In addition, this series will help you develop content knowledge in the different subject areas.

WHAT ARE THE GED TESTS?

There are five separate GED Tests: Writing Skills, Social Studies, Science, Interpreting Literature and the Arts, and Mathematics. To receive a GED certificate or diploma, you must obtain a passing score based on the results of all five tests.

Questions on the GED Tests are multiple choice, with the exception of one essay question on the Writing Skills Test. Five possible answers are given for each multiple-choice question. To select the best answer, you must be able to understand and apply the given information.

WHAT IS THE GED PREPARATION SYSTEM?

South-Western's GED Preparation System includes test preparation books, exercises books, and state-of-the-art interactive software. Each of these learning tools is available at two levels—Pre-GED and GED.

The Pre-GED Series is the entry level of the South-Western GED Preparation System. The Pre-GED Series provides the same instructional approach as South-Western's GED Series. However, the Pre-GED Series focuses more on developing the critical-thinking skills you will need to answer GED questions correctly. You can move easily and with confidence into the GED Series once you have mastered the Pre-GED Series.

PRE-GED TEST PREPARATION BOOKS

The Pre-GED Series includes one test preparation book for each of the five GED Tests. Section 1 of each book explains how to use the book most effectively and includes a pretest. Section 2 presents the foundation skills needed to pass the GED. Lessons in Section 3 provide instruction and practice. A posttest is included at the end of Section 3.

A unique, full-color section called CONNECTIONS appears at the back of the book. The CONNECTIONS themes and activities connect the information you are learning with your everyday life.

PRE-GED EXERCISE BOOKS

An exercise book complements each test preparation book. The organization of the exercise book corresponds to the lesson organization in Section 3 of the main book. The exercises provide additional opportunities to work in the content areas and apply the foundation skills. A posttest is included at the end of the book.

PRE-GED ADVANTAGE SOFTWARE

South-Western's Pre-GED Advantage software is as easy-to-use and engaging as South-Western's GED Advantage software! It follows the same structure used throughout the GED Preparation System. South-Western's Pre-GED Advantage is available for DOS or Macintosh standalone or networked computers.

Individual lessons are filled with abundant instruction and practice. You will focus on gaining both the foundation skills and content knowledge needed for success on the GED Tests. Colorful graphics, animations, electronic mail, and personalized recommended "Action Plans" will help to enhance your learning.

HOW WILL THE GED PREPARATION SYSTEM HELP YOU?

Studies show that GED test-takers have two difficulties. First, they often do not have the basic skills needed to answer the questions. Section 2 of the Pre-GED preparation books will help you develop the basic thinking skills needed for each GED Test. The exercise books will give you additional practice using these key skills.

Second, some test-takers do not have enough general subject knowledge. Section 3 of the Pre-GED preparation books provides subject area information, instruction, and practice. The exercise books provide you with additional practice answering questions in the subject areas.

As you work through the materials in this Pre-GED Series, you will gain an increased ability to comprehend and apply the information you read, which is your *connection to success* on the GED Tests.

Introducing the Book

Start your work by turning to page 2 and reading How to Use This Book. It will help you work more effectively and efficiently. Then do the Writing Skills Preview.

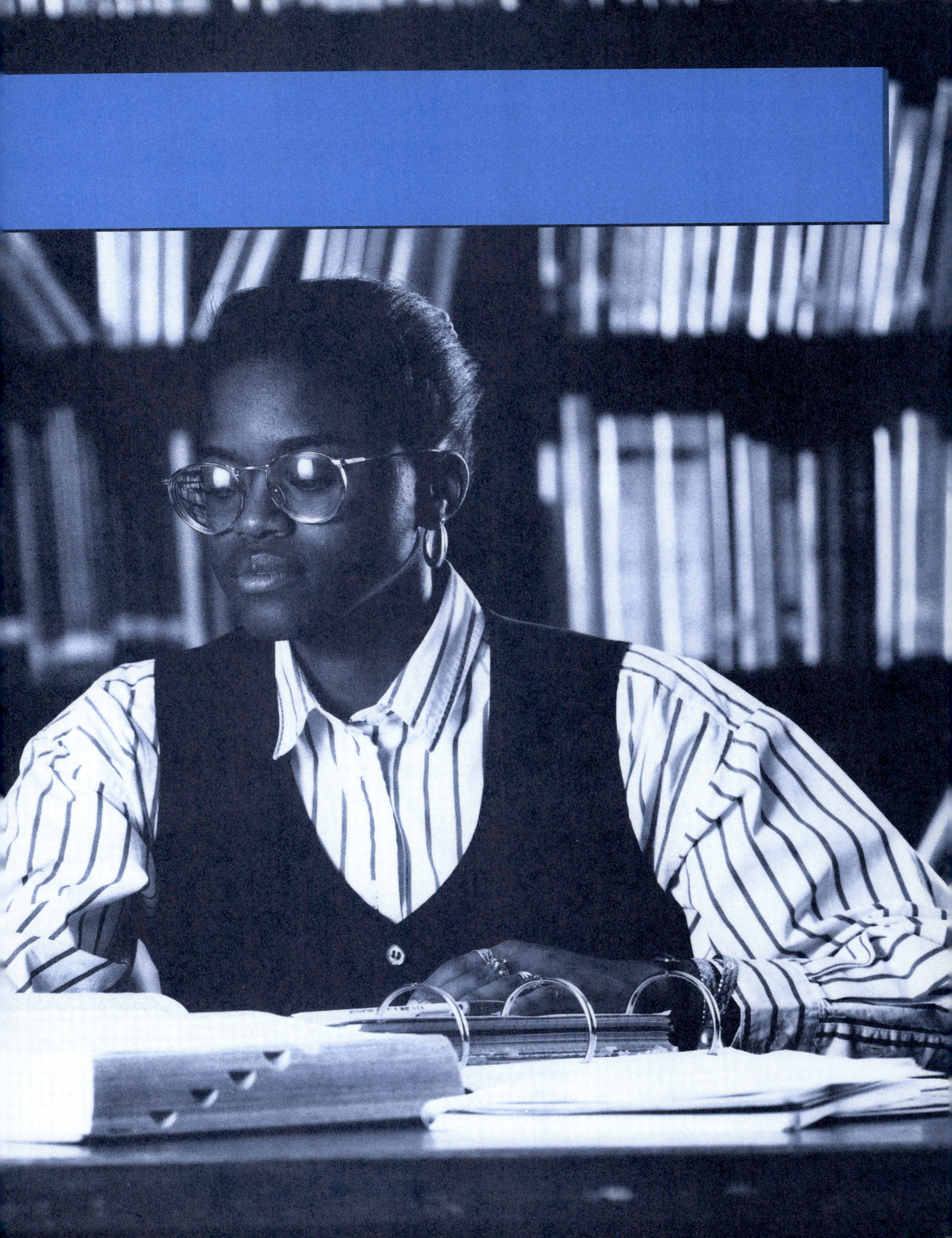

How to Use This Book

South-Western's *Pre-GED Writing Skills* book will help you begin your preparation for passing the GED Tests. Understanding how this book is organized will enable you to use each section to your advantage.

HOW IS THIS BOOK ORGANIZED?

This *Pre-GED Writing Skills* book is part of the South-Western GED Preparation System. Like its corresponding *GED Writing Skills* book, it is divided into four distinct sections. Each one is easy to find and easy to use.

- **SECTION 1** Right now you are in Section 1. It will get you started in your pre-GED study. Section 1 pages are identified by the rectangle-shaped thumb-tabs.
- **SECTION 2** Section 2 contains lessons that cover the writing process. Section 2 pages are identified by the half-circle thumb-tabs.
- **SECTION 3** Writing Skills lessons in Section 3 reinforce the skills you learned in Section 2 while presenting instruction and practice on the kinds of exercises you will find on the GED Writing Skills Test. Section 3 pages are identified by the triangle-shaped thumb-tabs.
- **CONNECTIONS** This full-color section of exciting theme pages is found at the back of this book.

Finding answers and explanations to your work is easy, too. Sections 1, 2, and 3 end with Answers and Explanations. The Posttest Answers and Explanations appear after the test. The CONNECTIONS Answer Guide for activities on the theme pages appears just before CONNECTIONS.

WHAT IS IN EACH SECTION?

Preparing to pass the GED Tests is not always easy, but you can do it. To help you, here is more about what you will find in each section of this book.

Section 1: Introducing the Book

Use the Skills Preview in Section 1 to find out what you already know and what skills you need to practice. It has two parts: questions in several formats (such as true/false or short answer) and items in GED format (multiple choice). Test-taking tips are provided on page 6. These tips will help you when you complete the Skills Preview and when you take any other test in the book.

Section 2: Foundation Skills

Skills in this section provide you with instruction and practice in the writing process. In each Foundation Skill, you will practice thinking about what to write and organizing, drafting, revising, and editing your writing. You will use these skills in the GED Writing Skills Test, Part 2, which is writing an essay.

Section 2 contains many special features. To help build your reading comprehension, difficult words are in bold type and are defined for you in the margins. Here are some of the other features.

TRY IT! When you see a Try It! exercise following an instructional passage, you will find an opportunity to practice the skill you are learning. The answer to the exercise follows immediately. Make sure you complete the exercise before you read the answer. By comparing your work to the answer given, you can check your understanding of the skill being presented.

PRACTICE EXERCISES Each Foundation Skill contains two or more Practice exercises. The Answers and Explanations at the end of Section 2 let you check your answers after you complete each Practice. This way you will know immediately what you have mastered and what you should review.

TIPS Each tip box gives hints for mastering the skill. Use it as a quick reference.

> ***Journal Writing***
>
> The Journal Writing feature provides you with further opportunities to practice the skills you have learned. It suggests topics for you to write about in your journal.

WORKING TOGETHER This feature provides an opportunity for group problem solving on topics related to the information being presented.

CHECKLIST Each checklist box provides a list of items to keep in mind for each step of the writing process. Use it for quick checkups when proofing and revising your work.

SKILL CHECKUP

SKILL CHECKUP Each Foundation Skill ends with a Skill Checkup. These questions are in the same format as those on the GED.

At the end of Section 2, you will find a comprehensive review that checks your understanding of all the Foundation Skills. These questions are in the same format as the GED. You can use the Referral Chart at the end of the Section 2 Answers and Explanations to evaluate your performance.

Section 3: Writing Skills Lessons

The GED Writing Skills Test, Part 1, is almost evenly divided among questions on usage, sentence structure, and mechanics. Section 3 presents one unit of instruction on each of these content areas covered on the GED Writing Skills Test.

As in Section 2, difficult words are defined in the margins to provide vocabulary assistance. Some other key features are listed below.

RULE BOX This feature provides rules and examples for mastering specific writing skills.

EDITING PRACTICE

EDITING PRACTICE Each lesson provides one exercise to practice your editing skills. To edit, you search for and correct errors in a longer passage by applying what you have learned in each lesson.

FOCUS This feature provides specific instruction on a special writing skill.

CONNECTIONS Each lesson in Section 3 provides you with an activity that "connects" information in the lesson to one of the CONNECTIONS theme pages at the end of the book. You can read more about the CONNECTIONS theme pages on the next page.

PRE-GED PRACTICE

PRE-GED PRACTICE Each lesson ends with a GED-style practice. These practice exercises help you prepare for the GED Writing Skills Test in two ways. They provide practice answering GED-style questions. They also allow you to apply what you learned in the Foundation Skills to writing skills passages. This is exactly what you will have to do on the GED Writing Skills Test.

At the end of Section 3, you will find a comprehensive review that checks your understanding of the Writing Skills lessons. These questions are in the same format as the GED. You can use the Referral Chart found in the Section 3 Answers and Explanations to evaluate your performance.

Connections

This high-interest, full-color section is at the end of the book. It contains information and activities that relate to current issues in our society. You are challenged to "make the connection" between the information presented and your daily life. The activities on the theme pages will help you develop your thinking, writing, and problem-solving skills. Also, every theme has a "Working World" box with employment information.

Posttest

After completing Sections 2 and 3, you can take the Writing Skills Posttest. It is about half the length of the GED Writing Skills Test, Part 1, and contains GED-style questions. You will see areas where you have improved your skills. You also will be able to identify areas where you need to pay special attention as you take your next step—South-Western's *GED Writing Skills* book.

LET'S GET STARTED!

Follow these steps to progress toward your goal—successful completion of the GED Tests.

1. Be certain you read the Introduction on page *vi* and all of the information in How to Use This Book in Section 1, pages 2–5.
2. Complete the Skills Preview, which begins on page 6. Follow the directions carefully. Be certain you read the test-taking tips. Use them for the Skills Preview and for any other test in the book.
3. Go to Section 2. Work carefully through the Foundation Skills. Remember, all the exercises and features are designed to help prepare you for the GED Tests. When you complete each Practice exercise and Skill Checkup, check your answers before continuing.
4. Complete the Section 2 Review. Use the Referral Chart at the end of the Section 2 Answers and Explanations to check your success.
5. Work carefully through the Writing Skills lessons in Section 3. Always check your answers before moving on to the next exercise.
6. Do the exercises in South-Western's *Pre-GED Writing Skills Exercises* book to reinforce the skills and content presented in Section 3.
7. Complete the Section 3 Writing Skills Review. Then use the Referral Chart at the end of the Section 3 Answers and Explanations to see how well you understand the content you studied.
8. Try CONNECTIONS. Read the information on each theme. Work through the related problem-solving and writing activities. Be sure also to read the employment information.
9. Review the test-taking tips on page 6. Take the Posttest. Check your answers and then complete the Referral Chart.
10. Congratulate yourself! At this point, you will be ready for the South-Western *GED Writing Skills* book.

Writing Skills Preview

As an adult learner, you bring your life experience to the Pre-GED program. You probably have more writing skills than you realize. You may have written letters, kept a journal or diary, or filled out a job application. As you read, you will find other writing skills that you already know something about.

The Skills Preview that follows is a pretest that lets you practice answering writing skills questions. This will help you discover what you already know and what you need to study before you take the GED Writing Skills Test. All the information you need to answer each item is given. The Preview is not scored. Its purpose is to help you identify your areas of strength and areas where you need additional practice. Remember, for the Preview, *how many* you get right or wrong is not important. *Which ones* you get right or wrong is very important.

The Preview is divided into two parts. Part I contains questions presented in several styles. Part II contains multiple-choice questions similar to those on the GED test. Both Part I and Part II test your ability to understand and apply what you read in three content areas of writing: usage, sentence structure, and mechanics.

TEST-TAKING TIPS

The following steps will help you do your best on the Preview. They also will help you work successfully in Sections 2 and 3.

- Set aside a time period when you know you will not be disturbed.
- Sit in a quiet place with a comfortable chair and good lighting.
- Do anything you need to do—get a drink of water or go to the rest room—*before* you start the test. Once you have started, continue until you are finished. Take as much time as you need.
- Complete Part I, and take a break before starting Part II. Or, take the two parts on different days as two separate tests.
- Relax. Remember, there is no "passing" or "not passing" score.
- When you have finished the Preview, check your answers against the Answers and Explanations on pages 16 and 17.
- Use the Referral Charts on pages 18 and 19 to help you analyze your performance.

Part I

***Items 1 to 9** contain errors in grammar, usage, punctuation, or spelling. If you think the sentence is correct, write a C in the space provided. Otherwise, edit the sentence by crossing out any errors and writing your corrections above.*

_____ **1.** In the 1980s, homelessness became a huge problem in citys all across the United States.

_____ **2.** Although homelessness had existed before the 1980s, they became more widespread and more visible during this decade.

_____ **3.** In many American cities, individuals, couples, and families struggled to survive on the streets.

_____ **4.** Since then, many citizens and civic leaders has tried to ignore the problem.

_____ **5.** Police officers sometimes are criticized, for mistreating homeless people in some cities.

_____ **6.** Attempts to get people off the streets and into beds in shelters not always successful.

_____ **7.** For instance, many homeless people feel that shelters run by the city are more dangerous than the streets.

_____ **8.** Some urban residents are afraid of homeless people.

_____ **9.** However, most homeless people are most vulnerable than they are dangerous.

Items 10 to 16 *contain errors in grammar, usage, punctuation, or spelling. If you think the sentence is correct, write a* C *in the space provided. Otherwise, edit the sentence by crossing out any errors and writing your corrections above.*

_____ **10.** Its been months since I've heard from my friend Helen.

_____ **11.** Believe it or not, that is just about normal for the two of we old friends.

_____ **12.** Our friendship is a good example of how staying in touch is necessary to keep a relationship fresh.

_____ **13.** Since I moved far away from where she lives, it have been vital to stay in touch.

_____ **14.** Easier than it sounds, however!

_____ **15.** It seems like less and less individuals write letters anymore and the telephone can get pretty expensive.

_____ **16.** However, if you leave a relationship alone to long, it seems to lose some of its life.

Item 17 *contains sensory details the writer uses to create a picture in the reader's mind. Underline all the sensory details in the descriptive paragraph.*

17. The Lincoln School has a handsome brick face. The school was built in 1924, and it features separate entrances for boys and girls. Inside there are small classrooms filled with old wooden desks and chairs. Because of the building's age, handrails, stairs, the edges of desks, and windowsills are worn smooth.

Items 18 to 24 *contain errors in grammar, usage, punctuation, or spelling. If you think the sentence is correct, write a* C *in the space provided. Otherwise, edit the sentence by crossing out any errors and writing your corrections above.*

_____ **18.** Americans—perhaps more than people in any other country in the world—take physical fitness very seriously.

_____ **19.** Hundreds of thousands of Americans of all ages participates in some form of physical exercise.

_____ **20.** For many people, "keeping in shape" means running, jogging, or a walk around the block.

_____ **21.** Others exercise together or individual at a fitness center.

_____ **22.** Americans are also keenly aware of how diet affects health?

_____ **23.** In the late 1980s, anti-smoking laws were passed.

_____ **24.** However, here people are most interested in public health than in smokers' rights.

In ***Items 25 to 27****, verbs are written in the passive voice. Rewrite these sentences to change the verbs into the active voice.*

25. A variety of wildflowers were picked by Paula and me.

____

26. The car was driven by me as the roadside was watched by Paula.

____

27. Queen Anne's lace and clover were seen by her beside the gravel.

____

Items 28 to 35 *contain errors in grammar, usage, punctuation, or spelling. If you think the sentence is correct, write a C in the space provided. Otherwise, edit the sentence by crossing out any errors and writing your corrections above.*

_____ **28.** Some people Iv'e known for years hardly ever read; however, I find it quite enjoyable.

_____ **29.** My friend Robert read three pages of *the Autobiography of Malcolm X* and then stopped.

_____ **30.** To me this is nearly unbelievable.

_____ **31.** After reading the first paragraph of that book; I couldn't put it down until I finished.

_____ **32.** My husband reads alot for a month or two and then doesn't read at all for several weeks.

_____ **33.** This Summer, he read every book published by Chester Himes, for example.

_____ **34.** My husbands favorite author is Raymond Chandler, I'd guess.

_____ **35.** Mine own reading taste includes stories and biographies.

In ***Items 36 to 39****, there are errors in subject-verb agreement. Revise each sentence by changing the form of any verbs that do not agree with their subjects. Write the correct verb above the incorrect one.*

36. Do Herb or Mr. Graham ever talk about getting another dog?

37. We is thinking of giving them a puppy.

38. The dog is sweet and he seem healthy.

39. We wonder if they misses their old dog too much to want a new one.

▶ *Answers begin on page 16.*

Part II

Choose the ***one best answer*** *for each item.* ***Items 1 to 5*** *refer to the following paragraph.*

(1)As a friend and I were crossing the Verrazano-Narrows Bridge, I wondered out loud if it was the longest bridge in the world. (2)She said really annoyingly "it can't be," but I disagreed and asked her if she had ever been across a longer one. (3)She claimed that both the George Washington Bridge and the Golden Gate Bridge were longest. (4)After I told her that she was wrong, I decided to do a little research on the subject of bridges. (5)In addition to the answer to our dispute, I learned a lot about some of the world's most famous structures. (6)In fact, the Humber Bridge in Hull, England, is the longest bridge anywhere. (7)About four hundred feet shorter (but still 4,260 feet long) is the Verrazano-Narrows Bridge. (8)The third longest bridge in the world; the Golden Gate Bridge in San Francisco is only sixty feet shorter than the Verrazano.

1. Which type of writing is this passage an example of?
(1) explanatory
(2) persuasive
(3) descriptive
(4) narrative
(5) contemplative

2. Sentence 2: She said really annoyingly "it can't be," but I disagreed and asked her if she had ever been across a longer one.

Which of the following is the best way to write the underlined portion of this sentence? If you think the original is the best way, choose (1).
(1) "it can't be,"
(2) "it cant be,"
(3) "it can't be;"
(4) "It cant be,"
(5) "It can't be,"

3. Sentence 3: She claimed that both the George Washington Bridge and the Golden Gate Bridge were longest.

Which of the following is the best way to write the underlined portion of this sentence? If you think the original is the best way, choose (1).
(1) were longest.
(2) were longer.
(3) was longest.
(4) was longer.
(5) we're longer.

4. Sentence 4: After I told her that she was wrong, I decided to do a little research on the subject of bridges.

Which of the following is the best way to write the underlined portion of this sentence? If you think the original is the best way, choose (1).
(1) After I told her that she was wrong,
(2) After I told her that she was wrong;
(3) If I told her that she was wrong,
(4) After I told her that she's was wrong
(5) After I told her that she was wrong

5. Sentence 7: About four hundred feet shorter (but still 4,260 feet long) is the Verrazano-Narrows Bridge.

Which of the following is the best way to write the underlined portion of this sentence? If you think the original is the best way, choose (1).
(1) is the Verrazano-Narrows Bridge.
(2) is, the Verrazano-Narrows Bridge.
(3) are the Verrazano-Narrows Bridge.
(4) are the verrazano-narrows bridge.
(5) was the verrazano-narrows bridge.

***Items 6 to 14** refer to the following paragraph.*

(1)Apparently, my Great-Great Grandfather was an artist, as well as a poor farmer. (2)Of course, he never was going to school to learn how to draw or paint. (3)He did, however, make colorful paintings on pieces of wood; I found three of these paintings in my aunts cellar. (4)Noone in my family ever told me about this ancestor of mine. (5)I guess that says something about how little value people in my family has put on art over the years. (6)The paintings, two landscapes and a portrait (perhaps a self-portrait). (7)In the portrait, a man, which looks tired, grim, and intelligent, is holding a tool. (8)One of the landscapes shows the harbor at Cutler, the other landscape shows the meadow where so many of my people were buried. (9)These three items will be treasured by me for the rest of my life.

6. Sentence 1: Apparently, my Great-Great Grandfather was an artist, as well as a poor farmer.

Which of the following is the best way to write the underlined portion of this sentence? If you think the original is the best way, choose (1).

(1) my Great-Great Grandfather was an artist,
(2) my Great-Great Grandfather was an artist
(3) my great-great grandfather was an artist,
(4) my great-great grandfather was an artist
(5) my Great-Great Grandfather were an artist

7. Sentence 2: Of course, he never was going to school to learn how to draw or paint.

What correction should be made to this sentence?

(1) change *never was* to *was not*
(2) change *was going* to *is going*
(3) change *was going* to *was attending*
(4) change *was going* to *went*
(5) remove the comma after *course*

8. Sentence 3: He did, however, make colorful paintings on pieces of wood; I found three of these paintings in my aunts cellar.

Which of the following is the best way to write the underlined portion of this sentence? If you think the original is the best way, choose (1).

(1) in my aunts cellar.
(2) in my Aunts cellar?
(3) in my Aunts cellar.
(4) in my aunt's cellar.
(5) on my aunts cellar.

9. Sentence 4: Noone in my family ever told me about this ancestor of mine.

Which of the following is the best way to write the underlined portion of this sentence? If you think the original is the best way, choose (1).

(1) Noone
(2) No one
(3) No-one
(4) No One
(5) Noonne

10. Sentence 5: I guess that says something about how little value people in my family has put on art over the years.

What correction should be made to this sentence?
(1) change *guess* to *suppose*
(2) change *guess* to *guessed*
(3) change *says* to *say*
(4) change *says* to *said*
(5) change *has* to *have*

11. Sentence 6: The paintings, two landscapes and a portrait (perhaps a self-portrait).

Which of the following is the best way to write the underlined portion of this sentence? If you think the original is the best way, choose (1).
(1) The paintings, two landscapes
(2) The paintings, too landscapes
(3) The paintings were two landscapes
(4) The paintings, were two landscapes
(5) The paintings was two landscapes

12. Sentence 7: In the portrait, a man, which looks tired, grim, and intelligent, is holding a tool.

Which of the following is the best way to write the underlined portion of this sentence? If you think the original is the best way, choose (1).
(1) which
(2) whose
(3) who
(4) whom
(5) what

13. Sentence 8: One of the landscapes shows the harbor at Cutler, the other landscape shows the meadow where so many of my people were buried.

Which of the following is the best way to write the underlined portion of this sentence? If you think the original is the best way, choose (1).
(1) Cutler, the
(2) cutler, the
(3) Cutler the
(4) Cutler; the
(5) cutler; the

14. Sentence 9: These three items will be treasured by me for the rest of my life.

Which of the following is the best way to write the underlined portion of this sentence? If you think the original is the best way, choose (1).
(1) These three items will be treasured by me
(2) These three items will be treasured by I
(3) I will treasure these three items
(4) I will treasured these three items
(5) I will be treasured by these three items

Items 15 to 25 *refer to the following paragraphs.*

(1)Although a majority of people get their news from television or radio, newspapers are a far superior source of information.

(2)A good newspaper usually has between one and two dozen full-length stories about local, national, and international events. (3)Each of these stories are at least several paragraphs long. (4)In contrast, most half-hour television news broadcasts devote approximately 16 minutes to news! (5)The remaining time is given to sports, weather, and advertising. (6)As these facts show, newspapers typically cover more news than other media do.

(7)Since they do not rely on pictures to convey meaning, newspapers spend less space on sensational stories. (8)For the same reason (because it relies on printed words and not momentary images), newspapers offer the luxury of time. (9)A reader can read the paper according to his or her own needs and desires. (10)One can read slowly or quickly, reflect on a story and reread part or all of it, or read a story in bits and pieces during the course of a day.

(11)Newspapers are the more thorough, interesting, and adaptable sources of news that we have.

15. What is the main idea of this essay?
- (1) Newspapers are a better news source than television and radio.
- (2) Good newspapers contain at least a dozen full-length news stories.
- (3) Newspapers typically cover more news than other media do.
- (4) Newspapers are not as sensational as television news is.
- (5) A person can adapt a newspaper to his or her own needs and desires.

16. What is the purpose of this essay?
- (1) to explain or inform the reader about a topic
- (2) to persuade the reader to take an action or hold an opinion
- (3) to entertain or amuse the reader
- (4) to describe a person, place, or event
- (5) to relate a story

17. How many paragraphs does this essay include?
- (1) one
- (2) eleven
- (3) four
- (4) two
- (5) three

18. Sentence 3: Each of these stories are at least several paragraphs long.

What correction should be made to this sentence?
- (1) change *Each* to *each*
- (2) change *stories* to *storys*
- (3) change *stories* to *story's*
- (4) change *are* to *were*
- (5) change *are* to *is*

19. How does the writer support the main idea of the essay?
- (1) by identifying the audience of the essay
- (2) by using facts to compare and contrast two or more things
- (3) by using sensory details
- (4) by narrowing the topic
- (5) by brainstorming

20. Which paragraph or paragraphs make up the body of this essay?
- (1) paragraphs one and four
- (2) paragraphs one and two
- (3) paragraphs one, two, three, and four
- (4) paragraph four
- (5) paragraphs two and three

21. Sentence 4: In contrast, most half-hour television news broadcasts devote approximately 16 minutes to news!

What type of sentence is this?
(1) question
(2) exclamation
(3) compound sentence
(4) statement
(5) command

22. Sentence 7: Since they do not rely on pictures to convey meaning, newspapers spend less space on sensational stories.

What is the connecting word that links the two clauses in this sentence?
(1) *newspapers*
(2) *convey*
(3) *meaning*
(4) *Since*
(5) *they*

23. Sentence 8: For the same reason (because it relies on printed words and not momentary images), newspapers offer the luxury of time.

Which of the following is the best way to write the underlined portion of this sentence? If you think the original is the best way, choose (1).
(1) it relies
(2) it rely
(3) they relies
(4) they rely
(5) they'll rely

24. Sentence 11: Newspapers are the more thorough, interesting, and adaptable sources of news that we have.

What correction should be made to this sentence?
(1) change *Newspapers* to *News papers*
(2) change *are* to *were*
(3) change *are* to *is*
(4) change *more* to *most*
(5) change *thorough* to *through*

25. According to the writer, why do newspapers "offer the luxury of time"?
(1) Readers can read newspapers whenever they want.
(2) Readers can enjoy sensational stories.
(3) Newspapers have between one and two dozen full-length stories.
(4) Newspapers are a superior news source.
(5) Television news broadcasts contain 16 minutes of news.

► *Answers begin on page 17.*

SKILLS PREVIEW • Answers and Explanations

Part I, pages 7–10

1. In the 1980s, homelessness became a huge problem in ~~citys~~ *cities* all across the United States.
2. Although homelessness had existed before the 1980s, ~~they~~ *it* became more widespread and more visible during this decade.
3. C
4. Since then, many citizens and civic leaders ~~has~~ *have* tried to ignore the problem.
5. Police officers sometimes are criticized~~,~~ for mistreating homeless people in some cities.
6. Attempts to get people off the streets and into beds in shelters ^*are* not always successful.
7. C
8. C
9. However, most homeless people are ~~most~~ *more* vulnerable than they are dangerous.
10. ~~Its~~ *It's* been months since I've heard from my friend Helen.
11. Believe it or not, that is just about normal for the two of ~~we~~ *us* old friends.
12. C
13. Since I moved far away from where she lives, it ~~have~~ *has* been vital to stay in touch.
14. ^*It is (or That is)* ~~E~~easier than it sounds, however!
15. It seems like ~~less~~ *fewer* and ~~less~~ *fewer* individuals write letters anymore and the telephone can get pretty expensive.
16. However, if you leave a relationship alone ~~to~~ *too* long, it seems to lose some of its life.
17. handsome brick face, separate entrances, small classrooms, old wooden desks and chairs, handrails, stairs, the edges of desks, and windowsills
18. C
19. Hundreds of thousands of Americans of all ages participate~~s~~ in some form of physical exercise.
20. For many people, "keeping in shape" means running, jogging, or ~~a walk~~ *walking* around the block.
21. Others exercise together or ~~individual~~ *individually* at a fitness center.
22. Americans are also keenly aware of how diet affects health~~?~~*.*
23. C
24. However, here people are ~~most~~ *more* interested in public health than in smokers' rights.
25. Paula and I picked a variety of wildflowers.
26. I drove the car while Paula watched the roadside.
27. She saw Queen Anne's lace and clover beside the gravel.
28. Some people ~~Iv'e~~ *I've* known for years hardly ever read; however, I find it quite enjoyable.
29. My friend Robert read three pages of ~~the~~ *The* *Autobiography of Malcolm X* and then stopped.

30. C

31. After reading the first paragraph of that book~~.~~,

I couldn't put it down until I finished.

32. My husband reads ~~alot~~ a lot for a month or two and

then doesn't read at all for several weeks.

33. This ~~S~~ummer, he read every book published by

Chester Himes, for example.

34. My husband's favorite author is Raymond

Chandler, I'd guess.

35. ~~Mine~~ My own reading taste includes stories and

biographies.

36. C

37. We ~~is~~ are thinking of giving them a puppy.

38. The dog is sweet and he ~~seem~~ seems healthy.

39. We wonder if they ~~misses~~ miss their old dog too

much to want a new one.

Part II, pages 11–15

1. (4) The passage is an example of *narrative writing*, writing that tells a story.
2. (5) The quotation (since it is a complete sentence) should begin with an initial capital letter. It also contains the contraction *can't*.
3. (2) The nouns *George Washington Bridge* and *Golden Gate Bridge* form a compound subject. They take the plural verb *were*. The comparative adjective *longer* is correct.
4. (1) The comma is necessary to separate the two clauses. *She* is the correct pronoun form.
5. (1) This sentence needs no comma except in the numeral. The proper noun *Verrazano-Narrows Bridge* should be capitalized and agrees in number with the singular verb *is*.
6. (3) The words *great-great* and *grandfather* should not be capitalized. A comma does not follow *artist*. *Was* agrees with the subject.
7. (4) The simple past tense form *went* is correct.
8. (4) This statement should end in a period. The possessive word *aunt's* is spelled with an apostrophe. It is not capitalized.
9. (2) *No one* is correctly spelled as two words.
10. (5) The plural subject *people* must agree with the plural form of the verb *have*.
11. (3) The sentence as written is a fragment. The verb *were* agrees with the subject *paintings* and makes the sentence complete. No comma is necessary.
12. (3) The pronoun *who* is the correct choice to agree with the antecedent *man*.
13. (4) This compound sentence should be joined by a semicolon. *Cutler* is a proper noun and must be capitalized.
14. (3) The original sentence was written in the passive voice; the active voice is better.
15. (1) Each of the other answers are supporting details, not the main idea.
16. (2) The writer is attempting to persuade the reader of the newspaper's superiority.
17. (3) The essay contains four paragraphs.
18. (5) The subject of the sentence is *each*, so the singular verb *is* is correct. Choice (1) would create a capitalization error. Choices (2) and (3) would create spelling errors. Choice (4) would create a grammatical mistake.
19. (2) The writer contrasts newspapers with television and radio as sources of news. The author uses no sensory details of note. Choices (1) and (4) do not help the writer support the idea. Choice (5), brainstorming, is not a method of support.
20. (5) Paragraph one is the introduction, and Paragraph four is the conclusion.
21. (2) The sentence expresses surprise or strong emotion and ends with an exclamation point.
22. (4) The connecting word *Since* connects the dependent clause *Since they do not rely on pictures to convey meaning* to the independent clause.
23. (4) The subject of this sentence is the plural noun *newspapers*. The plural pronoun *they* agrees with it in number. The verb then must be changed to the plural form *rely* to agree with its subject, *they*.
24. (4) More than two things are being compared, so *most* is the correct adjective.
25. (1) The writer says that a reader can read newspapers according to her or his own desires.

SKILLS PREVIEW REFERRAL CHARTS

When you have completed Parts I and II of the Writing Skills Preview, check your answers against the Answers and Explanations beginning on page 16. On the following charts, circle the items you answered correctly.

Use this first chart to help you determine your areas of strength and identify the areas where your skills are less developed. Notice that each item is related to a specific skill in Section 2: Foundation Skills in this book. Section 2: Foundation Skills introduces you to the writing process.

SECTION 2: FOUNDATION SKILLS		PART I	PART II
Foundation Skill 1:	Beginning to Write (pp. 22–31)	1, 10, 16, 30, 34	6, 8, 9
Foundation Skill 2:	Writing Sentences (pp. 32–41)	22, 31	11, 13, 21, 22
Foundation Skill 3:	Journal Writing (pp. 42–51)	11, 35	4, 12
Foundation Skill 4:	Identifying Purpose and Audience (pp. 52–61)	14	16
Foundation Skill 5:	Writing a Paragraph (pp. 62–71)		17
Foundation Skill 6:	Writing to Narrate (pp. 72–81)	3, 12	1, 2, 7
Foundation Skill 7:	Writing to Explain (pp. 82–91)	25, 26, 27	14, 25
Foundation Skill 8:	Writing to Describe (pp. 92–101)	9, 15, 17, 21, 24	3, 24
Foundation Skill 9:	Writing to Persuade (pp. 102–111)	2, 4, 7, 8, 13, 18, 19, 36, 37, 38, 39	5, 10, 18, 19, 23
Foundation Skill 10:	Writing an Essay (pp. 112–121)	5, 6, 20, 23, 28, 29, 32, 33	15, 20

Use this second chart in the same way you used the chart on page 18. Determine your areas of strength and identify areas where you need further development by circling the items you answered correctly.

SECTION 3: WRITING SKILLS LESSONS	PART I	PART II
Unit 1: Usage (pp. 140–201)	1, 2, 3, 4, 7, 8, 9, 10, 11, 12, 13, 17, 19, 22, 24, 25, 26, 27, 34, 35, 36, 37, 38, 39	1, 3, 5, 7, 10, 12, 14, 18, 19, 23, 24, 25
Unit 2: Sentence Structure (pp. 202–221)	6, 14, 20, 21, 31	11, 13, 17, 20, 22
Unit 3: Mechanics (pp. 222–253)	5, 15, 16, 18, 23, 28, 29, 30, 32, 33	2, 4, 6, 8, 9, 15, 16, 21

Do you notice any patterns in the items you did not circle? Try to identify areas where you need more practice. Then pay special attention to those areas as you work in Sections 2 and 3 of this book. For additional practice, you also can use South-Western's *Pre-GED Writing Skills Exercises* book.

Foundation Skills

These 10 Foundation Skills are the skills most frequently identified as needed for success on the GED Writing Skills Test. Each skill is presented through explanations, examples, and exercises.

Beginning to Write

You don't have to be the greatest writer in the world to begin writing. You don't even have to be able to write sentences to get started. The ideas are what is most important. So begin by finding and building up your ideas.

THINKING: BRAINSTORM IDEAS

grammar: the rules for putting words together to form sentences

Nobody can write a good essay (or even a good letter or paragraph) without thinking about it first. Brainstorming can help you get your ideas flowing freely. When you brainstorm, you think intensely about a subject and then jot down your ideas. The most important part of brainstorming is thinking, not writing, so don't worry about making mistakes in spelling, punctuation, or **grammar.** Just concentrate on the ideas that you think are important. At this stage, don't worry if your ideas are good or bad. Just get them on paper!

If you are beginning a writing assignment, brainstorming is a good way to decide what you want to write. Below is a writing topic and an example of one writer's brainstorming notes.

TOPIC A: Write a paragraph describing something you think is beautiful.

summer nights	*tall pine trees*	*horses running*	*Golden Gate Bridge*
Grand Canyon	*long hair—blond*	*my wife*	*Goose Rocks Beach*
antique chairs	*old green bottles*	*ocean*	*people singing*
snowy night	*baby Julia's face*	*rivers*	*sunset*

Practice your brainstorming skills. Take out a pen or pencil. Relax as you reread Topic A. Then think freely about the topic. Jot down your ideas. When you run out of ideas, take a look at your notes. Decide which idea you like best. Then brainstorm another list of ideas about the beauty of the subject you chose.

____

____

Brainstorming notes show many of the different things the writer considers beautiful. After making a list, you should read it over to see which idea you like the best. This writer liked the idea of Goose Rocks Beach the best. Here's a brainstorming list about that subject.

dunes	*ocean colors*	*terns & gulls*	*people swimming*
tidal pools	*warm & breezy*	*shells & stones*	*hot tar parking lot*
rocks	*sun all day!*	*cozy cove*	*horseshoe shaped beach*
cool water	*suntan lotion*	*frisbee*	*smell of salt air*

PRACTICE • 1

■ Answer the questions below.

1. What is brainstorming?

____

____

2. Why is it useful?

____

____

Journal Writing

Brainstorm a list of your favorite places. Then choose one of these places, and brainstorm as many ideas as you can about it.

BRAINSTORMING

If you run out of ideas, it helps to ask yourself questions about a topic. For example, as you brainstorm about a favorite place, ask yourself: What else did I see? What did I smell? What did I hear? How did I feel? How does the place change? Who else likes the place? Why? Asking questions can help you discover more ideas.

▶ *Answers begin on page 127.*

ORGANIZING: GROUP IDEAS INTO LISTS

Brainstorming is an "unorganized" activity. You list ideas in whatever order they come to you. However, this is probably not the best order in which to present your ideas when you write. After brainstorming ideas about a writing topic, you need to organize them.

You can do this by grouping the ideas. Look at the words and phrases you've written. In a general way, all of them are related because they all say something about the same topic. Now try to discover how the ideas are different from one another. Sometimes it helps to "step back" for a second and think about your topic again. Does your topic have different parts or sections? If so, are there ideas that describe these different parts? Divide your ideas into two or more groups.

As you make these new groups, think about a way to name each one. Giving each group a heading will help you see clearly what the ideas in each group have in common. Sometimes naming a group of ideas actually helps you come up with a few new ideas. Organizing your ideas also gives you a chance to see if there are any you should leave out when you write.

Below is a model of an organized list of ideas. Notice how the ideas are divided into groups. Compare this organized list with the unorganized list on page 23.

SIGHTS:

tidal pools *rocks* *shells & stones* *cozy cove*

terns & gulls *ocean colors* *horseshoe shaped beach* *dunes*

OTHER SENSES:

sun all day! *warm & breezy* *cool water* *smell of salt air*

~~*hot tar parking lot*~~

PEOPLE:

people swimming *frisbee* *suntan lotion* *sand castles*

The writer saw a pattern in the original list. There were a lot of words and phrases that described things a person sees looking around Goose Rocks Beach. Then there were several ideas that had to do with the sense of smell and the sense of touch. There were also a few ideas about what people do on the beach. The writer divided the ideas into groups, named the groups, added one idea (sand castles), and decided to cross out one idea (hot tar parking lot).

There is always a way to organize the different ideas you brainstorm. For example, brainstorming notes about a person could be organized into groups such as "personality," "appearance," and "memories."

Practice your organizing skills. Reread your brainstorming notes about Topic A on page 22. Think about ways you could organize your notes.

On a separate sheet, rewrite your brainstorming ideas into two or three groups. Give each group a heading that tells what ties the ideas in that group together. ■

PRACTICE • 2

■ Think about the writing topic below.

TOPIC B: Describe a friend of yours.

Now choose a friend to write about. Then brainstorm ideas for a paragraph on this topic. After you've listed as many ideas as you can, organize your list. Use the Organizing Checklist to help you.

ORGANIZING CHECKLIST

- ✔ Focus on the writing topic.
- ✔ Look at your list of ideas.
- ✔ Arrange the ideas into groups and name these groups.
- ✔ Add any ideas that occur to you.
- ✔ Cross out ideas that aren't important to your subject.

ORGANIZING YOUR IDEAS

Be sure to group your ideas under useful headings. Let the organizing help you bring your ideas into focus. Create groups that will allow you to describe your friend in a clear, detailed way.

► *Answers begin on page 127.*

DRAFTING: TURN IDEAS INTO SENTENCES

Once you have brainstormed and organized a list of ideas, you are ready to begin writing sentences. Up until this point you have been expressing ideas in words and phrases. At this stage of the writing process you will focus on turning those words and phrases into complete thoughts. It's a good idea to look back at your topic to refresh your memory.

TOPIC A: Write a paragraph describing something you think is beautiful.

Now look at the brainstorming notes you organized into groups. Which group do you think would be the best place to start a description of your topic? You might choose the group that is most important to you or the group you think will be easiest to write about. Choose one group and one particular idea with which to begin. Then tell something about that idea in a sentence. Don't worry about correct punctuation or spelling at this point. Drafting should be *creative.* Your goal is to get your thoughts flowing so that the words and phrases you have and new ideas become sentences that move from your mind onto the sheet of paper. You may even find that you want to join two or more ideas in one sentence, or one idea may lead to several sentences.

The writer describing Goose Rocks Beach decided to begin with the group of details called "sights." The phrase "ocean colors" became part of the first sentence:

At Goose Rocks Beach the ocean turns many different colors during the day.

Then the writer decided to say something more specific about the "ocean colors":

Most of the time the ocean at Goose Rocks Beach is dark blue. Sometimes, however, the ocean can be light blue, silver, gold, or gray.

Next, the writer moved on to other ideas in that group. Here is the first attempt at sentences about those ideas. At this stage, the writer has not worried about sentence structure. This will be corrected in a later step.

The beach has a horseshoe shape, and huge rocks make a cozy cove at one end of Goose Rocks beach. walk along the beach and you will find shells, stones, and tidal pools. Terns and gulls fly overhead.

After using all the ideas in the first group, the writer wrote sentences about the other groups of ideas:

One thing I love is feeling the warm sun. The thing I love the most is the smell of salt air. It smells like vacation. People have fun playing frisbee and making sandcastles.

Practice your drafting skills. Use your organized list about Topic A from the Try It! exercise on page 25 to help you write sentences. Choose one group from the list as a starting place. Then choose one word or phrase from that group and turn it into a sentence. Is there more you want to say about that idea? If so, write another sentence. Move on to the next idea in that group. Then write sentences for the ideas in your other groups. When you have written about all the ideas on your list, take a break. Congratulations on your first draft!

PRACTICE • 3

■ On page 25, you made an organized list about the topic below.

TOPIC B: Describe a friend of yours.

Look over your organized list. Choose a place to start, and then write sentences from your list of ideas. Refer back to the Drafting Checklist as you write your sentences.

____

____

____

____

____

____

____

____

____

DRAFTING CHECKLIST

- ✔ Reread the topic.
- ✔ Look over your prewriting notes and choose an idea.
- ✔ Turn the idea into a sentence.
- ✔ Is there more? Write another sentence.
- ✔ Go on to the next idea.
- ✔ Join two or more ideas when you can.

DRAFTING TIPS

When you are drafting sentences, try to relax and focus on your ideas. Think about what you ***want*** to say—not about what you think someone wants to read. Often writers find it helpful to think of writing as ***telling the truth*** about a subject. Thinking of writing as "truth-telling" can help you get at what is real, unusual, and interesting about a subject.

▶ *Answers begin on page 127.*

REVISING: TAKE OUT UNNECESSARY WORDS

Revising allows you to go back over your writing and look for ways to make it better. It is one of the most important steps in the writing process. It is also probably the most misunderstood step. Revising does *not* mean looking for errors in spelling and punctuation. It does *not* mean copying over your writing in neat handwriting. Both of those tasks are part of the editing stage of the writing process.

When you revise, you decide if you have put your thoughts down clearly and completely. You ask yourself questions like, "Will a reader be confused by anything in my writing?" and "Are there places where I could make the writing sharper or more interesting?"

If there are confusing passages in your writing, you need to revise them. Sometimes you can make something clearer by adding information. Other times just the opposite is true. In these cases, you can improve your writing by taking out things that aren't necessary. For instance, you may have repeated some unimportant word or phrase, or you may have a wordy sentence. The revising stage is the time to find ways to say something *better*. Better almost always means *clearer, tighter, truer,* and *more detailed.*

Below is a paragraph written in response to Topic A. Notice the way the writer revised the sentences in the first draft. The handwritten corrections are the revisions. Spelling and punctuation errors will be corrected on page 30 as part of the editing stage.

At Goose Rocks Beach the ocean turns many different colors during the day. Most of the time the ~~ocean at Goose Rocks Beach~~ water is dark blue. Sometimes, however, ~~the ocean~~ it can be light blue, silver, gold, or gray. The beach has a horshoe shape, and huge rocks make a cozy cove at one end of ~~Goose Rocks~~ the beach. walk along ~~the beach~~ clean, white sand and you will find shells, stones, and tidal pools. Terns and gulls fly overhead. ~~One thing~~ I loe ~~is~~ feeling the warm sun. ~~The thing~~ Most of all I love ~~the most is~~ the smell of salt air. It smells like vacation. Peple have fun playing frisbee and ~~people have fun~~ making sandcastles. ^Everybody seems to get along with each other.

Here are some of the revisions the writer made:

- Using the phrase *Goose Rocks Beach* three times was unnecessary. The writer removed the phrase from the second sentence and changed the phrase to *beach* in the fourth sentence.
- The word *ocean* appeared three times. The writer changed the word to the noun *water* in the second sentence and replaced the word with the pronoun *it* in the third sentence.
- The writer took out the unnecessary words *one thing* and *is* from the seventh sentence.
- The writer eliminated wordiness in the eighth sentence and the repetition of the phrase "people have fun" in the tenth sentence.The writer also improved these sentences by adding a few words in the fifth sentence *(clean white sand)* that gave more detail about the beach. The last sentence was also added because it seemed to grow out of the idea in the tenth sentence.

The things the writer took out and the few things the writer added made the picture of Goose Rocks Beach clearer and more vivid.

Review your notes and sentences about Topic A and Topic B. Choose one set to revise. Refer to the Revising Checklist as you work.

REVISING

As you revise, look for unnecessary repetition. Sometimes you will want to repeat a word or phrase to emphasize it. But most of the time repetition of words and phrases takes the energy out of writing. Look for opportunities to say things in new, fresh ways.

WORKING Together

Now practice your revising skills. Pair up with a classmate or a friend. You and your partner will give each other feedback on your sentences. Use the set of sentences that you did not revise in the Try It! exercise.

Read your partner's sentences as he or she reads yours. Refer to the Revising Checklist in order to evaluate the sentences. When you feel ready to share your responses, follow these guidelines:

1. Present your responses positively. Always make note of the good parts of the writing first.
2. Be as specific as you can about ways to make the writing better.

REVISING CHECKLIST

- ✔ Do all of your sentences have to do with the topic?
- ✔ Are any of your ideas unclear or incomplete?
- ✔ Can you add any information to make the writing clearer or more interesting?
- ✔ Can you take out unneces-sary words and repetition?

► *Answers begin on page 127.*

EDITING: CORRECT ERRORS AND MAKE HANDWRITING CLEAR

Editing is the final stage of the writing process. When you edit, you check your writing for errors in grammar, spelling, and punctuation. Look closely at all your sentences, punctuation, capital letters, and long or difficult words. Draw a line through any mistakes, and write the correct sentences or words above.

Now check your handwriting. What's the use of revising and editing if no one can read your words? Big or small, round or angular—there is no correct style of handwriting, but it should be clear.

The best way to develop clear handwriting is through concentration and practice. When you are writing, concentrate on the shape of each letter you make. When you have edited your grammar and spelling errors, look over the writing. Are any words hard to read? Draw a line through these words and write them more clearly above. Here's how one writer edited sentences from page 28 written in response to Topic A.

At Goose Rocks Beach the ocean turns many different colors during the day. Most of the time the water is dark blue. Sometimes, however, it can be light blue, silver, gold, or gray. The beach has a ~~horshoe~~ horseshoe shape, and huge rocks make a cozy cove at one end of the beach. ~~walk~~ W along the clean, white sand and you will find shells, stones, and tidal pools. Terns and gulls fly overhead. I ~~loe~~ love feeling the warm sun. Most of all I love the smell of salt air. ~~it~~ I smells like vacation. ~~Pepte~~ People have fun playing frisbee and making sandcastles. Everybody seems to get along with each other.

Practice your editing. Correct grammar and spelling errors in the sentences. Use the editing checklist to help you. Then copy the revised sentences you wrote for Topics A and B on clean pages. Concentrate on your handwriting. When you're done, read the sentences over and fix any words that are unclear. Then copy the sentences over again. Has your handwriting improved?

Try giving your writing to a friend to read. Ask your friend to point out any errors you missed or places where your handwriting isn't clear.

PRACTICE • 4

Edit the following sentences. Use the Editing Checklist to help you. When you are done, copy the sentences over. Concentrate on your handwriting.

Antonio and Rolanda wanted to hear music at a club last night. They tried the West End Lounge, but the West End Lounge was closed? For Renovations. rolanda suggested the Harborside Club. She said that hers friend Herb loves the atmosphere there. So, Rolanda and Antonio went there and listen to a salsa band. They did danced until 4:00 A.M.

EDITING CHECKLIST

- ✔ Is the grammar correct?
- ✔ Are the sentences punctuated correctly?
- ✔ Is the capitalization correct?
- ✔ Are words spelled correctly?
- ✔ Is my handwriting clear?

SKILL CHECKUP

Write several sentences about the following topic.

TOPIC C: Describe a responsibility that you take especially seriously.

Follow these steps in your writing:

1. Think: Brainstorm ideas about your topic.
2. Organize: Group your ideas and name each group.
3. Draft: Turn your ideas into sentences.
4. Revise: Check your sentences for unnecessary words or unclear thoughts.
5. Edit: Check your sentences for errors in grammar, spelling, and punctuation.

____

____

____

____

____

► *Answers begin on page 127.*

FOUNDATION SKILL 2

Writing Sentences

Every time you talk to a friend or listen to the radio, you probably hear sentences. Although people don't always use complete sentences when they talk, it's important to use complete sentences when you write.

THINKING: BRAINSTORM LISTS

Sentences are the building blocks of writing. All good writing is made up of series of sentences. Good sentences start with good ideas. As you already know from Lesson 1, the best way to come up with good ideas is to brainstorm. Here's a list of ideas one writer brainstormed about the topic below:

TOPIC A: Describe the things in life that are important to you.

my job

my husband

my kids

happiness

my home

my dog

my mom and my brothers

free time

exercising

This writer brainstormed ideas and then listed all the things she could think of that were important to her. Notice that the ideas on the list are not described or explained. It's not important to do that when you are brainstorming. What *is* important is to focus your thoughts on the topic and come up with a list of ideas, however general they might be.

TRY IT!

Practice your brainstorming skills. Brainstorm a list of ideas about the things in your life that are important to you.

______________________	______________________
______________________	______________________
______________________	______________________

PRACTICE • 1

■ Answer these questions about the list on page 32.

1. Why is the writer making this list?

____

____

2. Which of the following items *isn't* on the writer's list?

her job	her kids	her dog
exercising	her cat	free time

Journal Writing

Brainstorm a list of ideas about your idea of the perfect vacation. Then write a sentence about each of the ideas on your list.

BRAINSTORMING

Use a clean sheet of paper when you are making your list. List the items vertically instead of horizontally. This will make it easier for you to find a particular item later.

▶ *Answers begin on page 127.*

ORGANIZING: CLUSTER LIST ENTRIES

Prewriting activities like brainstorming are designed to get your ideas flowing. You write down words or phrases that come into your head in whatever order you think of them. When you brainstorm, you are not thinking about organizing your ideas. Once you finish brainstorming, it's time to organize your list.

One good way to organize a brainstorming list is to cluster together the items on the list that are related to each other. Then when you are creating sentences from these ideas, you may be able to combine several ideas in one sentence.

To cluster list entries, look at the list and try to come up with some ways the different entries might be related. Sometimes the ways entries are related won't be obvious at first. Try asking yourself questions about the entries such as: What items go together in everyday life? Which items have elements in common? How many clusters do I need? This can often help you see how different entries might relate to one another. Once you have found something that relates several entries, write it down on a sheet of paper and circle it. Then cluster the related entries around it.

Below is how one writer clustered her brainstorming list using Topic A from page 32. Notice how she added explanations and notes to her entries as she clustered them.

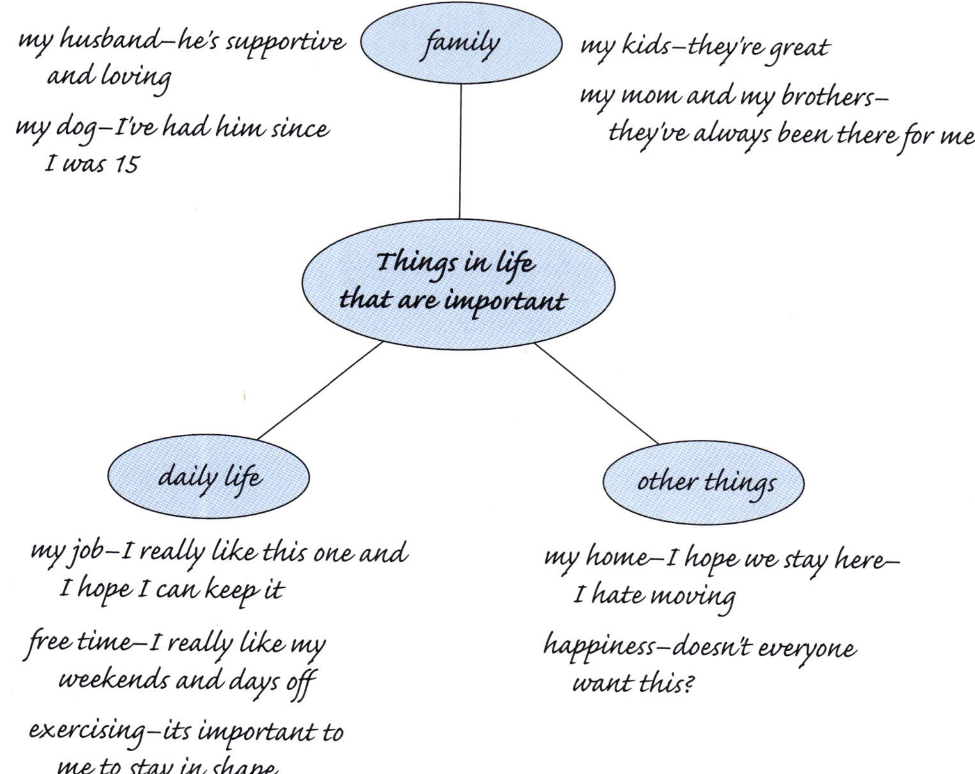
family
my husband–he's supportive and loving
my dog–I've had him since I was 15
my kids–they're great
my mom and my brothers–they've always been there for me
Things in life that are important
daily life
my job–I really like this one and I hope I can keep it
free time–I really like my weekends and days off
exercising–its important to me to stay in shape
other things
my home–I hope we stay here–I hate moving
happiness–doesn't everyone want this?

Now practice your organizing skills. Reread Topic A and your brainstorming list. Think about some ways the items on your list are related.

On a separate sheet of paper, make clusters with the entries on your list. Add notes, details, or explanations to each entry.

PRACTICE • 2

Now think about the topic below. Read and reflect on the topic and then follow the steps.

TOPIC B: Which TV shows do you like? Why?

1. Brainstorm a list of programs you like.

___

___

___

2. Think of ways to cluster the entries on your list.

3. Cluster the entries and then write brief notes, details, or explanations beside each one.

___

___

___

___

___

ORGANIZING CHECKLIST

- ✔ Focus on how your list entries might be related.
- ✔ Write down the different ways entries are related and circle these labels.
- ✔ Cluster the appropriate entries around each circle.
- ✔ Add brief notes, details, or explanations to each entry.

ORGANIZING

Don't try to make too many clusters, or you might end up with as many clusters as entries on your list! Really focus on how your entries can be related. If you still have too many, ask yourself whether two clusters are related and whether they can be combined to form one new cluster.

▶ *Answers begin on page 127.*

DRAFTING: WRITE THE FOUR TYPES OF SENTENCES

Once your ideas are organized, you can draft your words and phrases into sentences. A sentence must express a complete thought. It also must contain both a subject and a verb. All sentences begin with a capital letter and end with a punctuation mark.

There are four types of sentences: statements, commands, questions, and exclamations. Below are explanations of the four types of sentences and some examples.

1. A statement gives information. It ends with a period.

   The election is only a week away.

2. A command gives an order or makes a request. It ends with a period.

   Don't you dare close that door.

   Please, don't call me again.

3. A question asks something. It ends with a question mark.

   Is anyone going on vacation next month?

4. An exclamation expresses strong emotion. It ends with an exclamation point.

   That was an incredible fireworks display!

The writer of the clustered list on page 34 decided to turn her list entries into sentences. She thought of what she wanted to say about a particular entry and then wrote it out as a complete thought. The first draft of the sentences she wrote starts below. See if you can identify the different types of sentences she used.

Many things in my life are important to me. My family is the most important. My husband and kids are great! They are very supportive and loving. My mom and all my brothers are too. We're very close.

Certain daily activities are important to me as well. I really like my new job, so it's fun to go to work every day. I also enjoy exercising, running, bike riding, roller skating, and aerobics.

Other things also mean a lot to me—like being happy. Doesn't everyone feel this way? I also like my home a lot. I hope we don't have to move. I hate all the packing and unpacking!

In the sentences above, the writer used her cluster list to guide her. She wrote sentences using the ideas and the organization she had developed in her prewriting. She added a few new details that did not appear on her list. She also left out a few details.

Practice your drafting skills. On a separate sheet, write sentences based on the clustered list you made about Topic A on page 32. Before you begin, reread the topic and review your clustered list. Then focus on one idea, and write your first sentence. ■

PRACTICE • 3

■ On page 35, you made a clustered list on the topic below.

TOPIC B: Which TV shows do you like? Why?

Look over your clustered list. Then choose a place to start, and write sentences from your clusters of ideas. Refer to the Drafting Checklist on this page if you need to.

____

____

____

____

____

DRAFTING TIPS

When drafting sentences, think about expressing a complete thought. Sometimes it helps to identify the subject of the sentence (the person or thing doing the action) and the verb of the sentence (the action being done by the subject).

DRAFTING CHECKLIST

- ✔ Decide which idea you want to turn into a sentence.
- ✔ Decide if any other related ideas should go in the same sentence.
- ✔ Try to express the idea completely and clearly.
- ✔ Move on to the next idea, and repeat the process.
- ✔ Check to see that each of your sentences has a subject and a verb.

▶ *Answers begin on page 128.*

REVISING: CORRECT SENTENCE FRAGMENTS

When we speak to each other, we often use sentence fragments. For instance, a man models a new sweater for a friend. The friend says, "Fantastic!" In everyday speech, this sentence fragment is enough because both people know exactly what is being communicated. There is no need to speak a complete sentence, such as, "That sweater looks fantastic!" However, in writing we must avoid sentence fragments.

A sentence fragment is an incomplete sentence. To recognize sentence fragments, you need to know what a complete sentence is. A *complete sentence* always has a subject and a verb, and always expresses a complete thought. A fragment can be tricky to recognize because it can look a lot like a complete sentence. For instance, a fragment often has a capital letter at the start and a period at the end. But a fragment never expresses a complete thought. This is because it lacks either a subject or a verb. The best way to recognize sentence fragments is to check every sentence for both a subject and a verb.

Notice how the following sentence fragments leave you with unanswered questions:

> Threw the pail over the wall.

Who or what threw the pail? This fragment lacks a subject. You could complete this sentence by adding a subject: *The annoyed goat threw the pail over the wall.*

> The table to the left of the couch.

What about the table? What happened to it? This fragment lacks a verb. You could complete this sentence by adding a verb: *The table to the left of the couch collapsed.*

> Wanda, Franklin, Carlos, and Mercedes.

What about them? What did they do? This fragment lacks a verb. You could complete this sentence by adding a verb: *Wanda, Franklin, Carlos, and Mercedes watched the first snowfall through the window.*

REVISING

As you revise, check for sentence fragments. Revise fragments by adding information so that the sentence expresses a complete thought and contains both a subject and a verb.

► *For more work on Sentence Fragments, see pages 218–219 of Section 3.*

The following passage was written in response to Topic A. Find any sentence fragments in it. Revise each fragment so that it is a complete sentence.

People are very important in my life. I am a very social person and like to be with my friends as much as possible. Have fun and just spend time together. Sometimes, we do nothing at all!

I want to move into working with people. I could do lots of things. Personnel officer, nurse, teacher, or sports instructor.

If I did this, I might be able to help other people. Help them to make their lives better and help them to enjoy themselves. I could earn money and help people at the same time.

What do you notice about the third sentence? This fragment lacks a subject. You could revise it into a sentence such as *We have fun and just spend time together.*

What is missing from the last sentence in the second paragraph? It's just a list of occupations. This sentence fragment needs a subject. You could say: *I could be a personnel officer, nurse, teacher, or sports instructor.*

What is wrong with the second sentence in the last paragraph? It doesn't have a complete thought of its own. You could revise this fragment into a sentence such as *If I did this, I might be able to help other people to make their lives better and to enjoy themselves.*

WORKING Together

Practice your revising skills with a classmate or a friend. Use the sentences that you wrote about Topic A or Topic B. Read your partner's sentences, and let your partner read yours. Follow the Revising Checklist to evaluate the sentences. Give yourselves plenty of time. To share comments, follow these guidelines:

1. Always present your comments in a positive way. Point out the strengths first. Help your partner improve his or her writing.
2. Be as specific as you can. Point out particular sentence fragments, words, and phrases that you think should be revised.

REVISING CHECKLIST

- ✔ Does each of the sentences express a complete thought?
- ✔ Does each of the sentences contain a subject?
- ✔ Does each of the sentences contain a verb?

▶ *Answers begin on page 128.*

EDITING: CHECK END PUNCTUATION

The editing stage of the writing process is the time when you identify and correct errors in your sentences. Using correct end punctuation helps your reader understand the meaning of your sentences.

There are three kinds of end punctuation. They are the period, the question mark, and the exclamation point. The period is used much more often than the question mark or the exclamation point. A comma can *never* be used to end a sentence. You can check to make sure that you have used correct end punctuation by remembering the four types of sentences. The question mark is used for questions—sentences that ask something. The exclamation point is used for sentences that express very strong emotion. The period is used for statements and commands.

Take a look at the end punctuation in the following sentences:

Statement: Noel had chicken for lunch.

Command: Step out into the hallway.

Question: Did anyone remember to feed the dog?

Exclamation: You cut off all your hair!

These sentences show the correct use of end punctuation.

EDITING

Probably the most common end punctuation mistake is putting a period at the end of a question. Try listening to the way sentences "sound" in your head as you write them. Most of the time, a question ends with the voice going up a bit.

Practice editing the end punctuation in the following sentences. As you read each sentence, think about what type it is. Then decide if the writer has used the correct punctuation.

Why do delays at the airport bother you so much.

I was surprised about how much a can of coffee costs?

This song makes me want to tear my hair out at the roots!

In the first sentence, the word *why* gives us a clue that this sentence asks a question. The correct end punctuation is a question mark. The second sentence is a statement. The correct end punctuation is a period. This writer may have been thrown off by the words *how much*. But if you look carefully at the meaning of the sentence, you will find it is a statement. The third sentence is an exclamation. It expresses a strong emotion. The exclamation point is correct.

PRACTICE • 4

■ Edit the end punctuation in the following sentences.

What is the most important issue of the 1990s. In my opinion, it is health care? What could be more important than health care. Finally, politicians are paying attention to this topic, Who knows how long that will last! I do know this country needs better health care. The cost of a night in the hospital is outrageous!

EDITING CHECKLIST

- ✔ Does every sentence have the correct end punctuation?
- ✔ Is the grammar correct?
- ✔ Are words spelled correctly?
- ✔ Is the capitalization correct?

SKILL CHECKUP

Write several sentences about the following topic.

TOPIC C: What are some places in the world you would like to visit? Why would you like to visit them?

Follow these steps in your writing:

1. Think: Brainstorm a list of ideas about the topic.
2. Organize: Cluster the list entries.
3. Draft: Turn your ideas into sentences. Put ideas together in a sentence when appropriate.
4. Revise: Refine your sentences. Pay special attention to correcting sentence fragments.
5. Edit: Check your sentences for errors. Check to see that you have used end punctuation correctly.

▶ *For more work with End Punctuation, see pages 224–225 of Section 3. Answers begin on page 128.*

Journal Writing

Writing in a journal can be like having a relaxed conversation with a good friend. A journal is a place where you can spend time with your thoughts. Here is an example of a journal entry:

No surprise, Phil was on my back again today. He has to show that he's better than everyone else. Well, I can't work this way much longer. But I don't know how to stand up to him. Maybe I should say, "Hey, Phil, you're not my boss, so lay off." Or should I tell him how it makes me feel to be criticized all the time? But I don't want him to think I'm weak. Still, I like my job, except when he's making me miserable. There must be a way to get him to stop.

This writer uses a journal as a safe place to explore private thoughts and feelings about a situation at work. A journal can be completely private or something you share with others.

THINKING: ASK "5 W AND H" QUESTIONS

You can use your journal to practice particular writing skills. For instance, you might want to write about your memories of your grandmother. Since this is a large topic, you might not know where to begin.

In your journal you can ask yourself "5 W and H" questions. The 5 W's are *who?*, *what?*, *where?*, *when?*, and *why?* The H is *how?* Asking questions that begin with these words helps you bring the topic into focus. They also also help you learn what interests you most about a topic.

One writer asked these "what" and "why" questions about her grandmother: *What did Grandma do before the war? What did she think about my grandfather when she first met him? Why did she decide to become a nurse? Why did she move out west in the 1970s?*

You can ask "5 W and H" questions again and again until you have enough ideas and focus to begin writing.

BRAINSTORMING

TIPS

Remember that a journal is a place where you don't have to worry about the rules of writing and other people's expectations. Let your thoughts wander freely as you write.

Practice your brainstorming skills. Think about this topic:

TOPIC A: What is interesting about your community?

In the space below, jot down any ideas you have. If you run out of ideas, ask yourself "5 W and H" questions. Write your questions and the answers to them.

Remember, you don't have to write complete sentences. Instead, list words and phrases until you come upon a set of details or ideas you would like to write about.

____

____

____

____

____

PRACTICE • 1

■ Write three "5 W and H" questions about your grandmother or grandfather.

1. ____

2. ____

3. ____

Journal Writing

Brainstorm a list of foods you enjoy eating. Then choose one of these foods and ask yourself "5 W and H" questions about it. Use the answers to write a paragraph in your journal.

► *Answers begin on page 128.*

ORGANIZING: MAKE A "5 W AND H" CHART

Asking "5 W and H" questions will help you gather a lot of ideas about your topic. After you've gathered the ideas, however, you'll need to put them in some kind of order. Organizing your ideas will give you a focus for writing your first draft. As you already learned in Foundation Skill 2, one way of putting ideas in order is to cluster them together. You also can organize your ideas by making a "5 W and H" chart.

For instance, one writer asked "5 W and H" questions about the topic below:

TOPIC A: What is interesting about your community?

Then he organized his questions and answers into a "5 W and H" chart:

Who lives in my community?	*What kinds of jobs are there here?*	*Where do people go for fun?*
factory workers *shipyard workers* *my family*	*mill work* *shipyard work* *fishing industry* *many people are unemployed*	*The Green Lantern Pub* *Dantonville*
When did my family come here?	*Why do I like it here?*	*How old is the town?*
My grandparents moved here in the 1920s.	*people are friendly* *near the ocean* *near a big city*	*I think it was built in the 1800s.*

This writer used his journal as a place to focus on the topic. Putting his ideas in a "5 W and H" chart helped this writer see which aspect of his community most interested him. He decided to write about a restaurant and lounge called The Green Lantern Pub where many people from the community go to relax after work and on weekends.

The writer's "5 W and H" chart also helped him decide if he needed to add more details before he began writing. He looked at the topic again and thought about what he wanted to say. He decided to add a few details about The Green Lantern Pub. He also decided that he could use some ideas from other parts of the chart, particularly ideas about who lived in the community and where they worked.

ORGANIZING TIPS

Focus on the topic. Look at the ideas and details you have gathered. Put them in order or in clusters, and decide whether or not you're prepared to begin drafting. If not, gather more ideas or details.

TRY IT!

Practice your organizing skills. Take another look at the topic below:

TOPIC A: What is interesting about your community?

Reread your brainstorming notes on page 43. In the space below, create a "5 W and H" chart to help you organize the questions and answers you brainstormed.

Did your chart help you focus on the topic? If so, you did a good job of organizing your ideas!

PRACTICE • 2

■ Think about the writing topic below.

TOPIC B: What does the word *loyalty* mean to you?

In your journal, brainstorm ideas for this topic. Ask "5 W and H" questions to help you come up with ideas. Use the Organizing Checklist to help you organize your ideas.

ORGANIZING CHECKLIST

- ✔ Focus on the writing topic.
- ✔ Make a "5 W and H" chart.
- ✔ Decide what you want to write about.
- ✔ Decide whether you have enough details to begin writing.

► *Answers begin on page 128.*

DRAFTING: WRITE A JOURNAL ENTRY

Your journal is a place where all the pressure is off. You can write about you in whatever way you want. Of course, your journal also can be a place where you try to stretch yourself as a writer. Some people use their journals to challenge themselves. In their journals they try new things, experiment, and work on the parts of writing they find most difficult.

For instance, the writer of the journal entry on page 42 uses his journal to record his reactions to his life and his job. Occasionally, however, he sets himself certain tasks. For instance, he decided to write something about his community. On page 44 you saw the "5 W and H" chart in which he organized his responses to Topic A. Below is the journal entry he wrote in response to that topic. Notice that he has not worried about sentence structure. This will be corrected later.

The people who live in Freeport are mostly fishermen. They are some people who own a ferry. There are a lot of people working at the shipyard. Everything has to do with the water, the ocean. After they have finished working, everybody goes to The Green Lantern Pub. This restaurant has been here since the 1800s. It's comfortable. Everybody mixes together. The windows of The Green Lantern look right out over the water. Relaxing at The Green Lantern, we're not far away from it.

This writer used his "5 W and H" chart to find details about the people who live in his community. His first four sentences are about the towns-people and their work. Then he wrote six sentences about The Green Lantern Pub. He describes the restaurant and why people like to go there.

Turn back to page 44, and look at the writer's "5 W and H" chart. Notice that he did not include all of the details from his chart in his entry. Trying to tell too many facts in one paragraph is a common error in writing. If a fact or idea does not seem to fit in with other facts and ideas in a paragraph, you should not include that "extra" item.

DRAFTING

Try to stay relaxed as you write. A journal is a great place to practice writing without getting nervous. Nobody has to read your words except you. Your journal is also a place for you to experiment. You can write anything that comes into your head, and no one can call it wrong.

Practice your drafting skills. In your journal, write a paragraph based on the "5 W and H" chart you made about your community on page 45. Try to write as naturally as you can. As you write, include all the details that fit your paragraph.

PRACTICE • 3

■ In Practice 2 on page 45, you brainstormed and made a "5 W and H" chart about this topic:

TOPIC B: What does the word *loyalty* mean to you?

Look over your notes. Then draft a journal entry about this topic.

____

____

____

____

____

____

____

____

____

____

____

____

DRAFTING CHECKLIST

- ✔ Focus on the your topic.
- ✔ Look over your "5 W and H" chart.
- ✔ Decide which detail or idea will be a good starting point.
- ✔ Begin turning the words and phrases from your chart into sentences.

► *Answers begin on page 128.*

REVISING: CONNECT IDEAS LOGICALLY

As you read over a first draft, try to "step outside yourself" and read your writing as someone else would. Reading this way will help you recognize places where your meaning is not clear. Perhaps you need to develop an idea more fully, or maybe you need to take out words or whole sentences.

As you revise your work, it is important to think about the way ideas are connected. Sometimes a first draft is weakened by "leaps of logic." The writer moves from Point A to Point C without mentioning Point B at all. The writer may have *thought* about Point B while writing, but forgot to include it on paper. Notice how a "Point B" is left out between these sentences: *My friend's car is great. The park where we had lunch last weekend was quiet and beautiful.* A connection about using the car to go somewhere on the weekend needs to be added.

Another problem to watch out for is when a writer includes Points A, B, and C but does not make the connections clear. Points A, B, and C simply sit side by side. For example: *My work room is large for my house. I like having a lot of guests over. They squeeze into the living room.* This writer needs to show what each sentence has to do with the other sentences. In this case, the writer could show two things: that it is *because* the work room is large for the house that the living room is small, *so* the guests have to squeeze in.

One way to help you see if ideas are connected logically is to ignore all punctuation and sentence structure. Instead, allow yourself to see just a paragraph of ideas. There may be four ideas in your first paragraph, although there are seven or nine sentences. When you see the ideas in your writing this way, you can more easily judge whether they are clearly and logically connected to each other.

Take a look at some revisions the writer made to his journal entry to fix obvious errors and to connect ideas more clearly:

The people who live in Freeport are mostly fishermen. ~~They~~ There are also some people who own a ferry, ~~There are~~ and a lot of people working at the shipyard. ~~Everything~~ All of these people do work that has to do with the water, the ocean. After they have finished working, everybody goes to The Green Lantern Pub. This restaurant has been here since the 1800s. It's a comfortable place for ~~E~~everybody to mix~~es together~~. The windows of The Green Lantern look right out over the water. Even when we're off work and ~~R~~relaxing at The Green Lantern, we're not far away from the ocean ~~it~~.

REVISING

As you revise, imagine that you are a person who knows nothing about your topic. Would you understand each sentence in the writing? Would you understand the connections between ideas? If the answer is *no*, you need to make things clearer.

REVISING **CHECKLIST**

- ✔ Do all of your sentences have to do with the topic?
- ✔ Are the ideas in your writing logically connected?
- ✔ Do you use words such as *also, therefore, however, instead, consequently,* and *but* to connect ideas?

The writer found some places to better connect ideas. First of all, he recognized that the first four sentences were all about people's jobs. But there was no signal that each sentence had to do with the other sentences. By adding the word *also* and by connecting the second and third sentences with the word *and*, the writer made a more logical connection of ideas. He corrected the obvious error, *They*, to *There*.

Second, the writer realized that there was a connection between the idea that The Green Lantern was comfortable and the idea that "everybody mixes together." He revised these two sentences into one clear sentence. Third, the writer saw that he could improve the connection between the ideas of working by the sea and relaxing by the sea. He added a phrase to the last sentence to make this connection clearer.

TRY IT!

Review your journal entries for Topic A and Topic B. Choose one of your drafts to revise. Use the Revising Checklist. Try to make sure that your ideas are clearly and logically connected.

WORKING Together

Practice your revising skills with a classmate or a friend. If you feel comfortable sharing a journal entry, you and a partner can give each other feedback. You might use the draft of the journal entry that you did not revise in the Try It! exercise above.

Read your partner's narrative and let your partner read yours. Follow the Revising Checklist to evaluate the entry. When you are ready to share comments, follow these guidelines:

1. Remember, these are someone's thoughts and feelings entered in a journal. Be extremely respectful of the person who allowed you to read this work. Present any reactions or comments in a positive way.

2. Be specific. Point out certain words or sentences that you think should be revised. Try to offer some suggestions for possible revisions.

► *Answers begin on page 128.*

EDITING: CHECK PRONOUN-ANTECEDENT AGREEMENT

antecedent: the noun or pronoun to which a pronoun refers

gender: the state of being male, female, or neuter (such as pronoun "it")

Often you will write a sentence that contains both a noun and a pronoun that refers to that noun. For example: *As Duane drove off, he listened to the car radio.* In this sentence, the pronoun *he* refers to the name *Duane.* The word a pronoun refers to is called its antecedent. A pronoun and its antecedent must always "agree," or match, in number and in gender. Look at these examples of pronouns and antecedents. (Gender and number are shown in parentheses.)

Henry is reading the magazine he bought last week. (masculine, singular)

The waiter smiled at Maria and then took her order. (feminine, singular)

Austin and Linda moved into their new house. (plural)

The chair looks nice, but it is uncomfortable. (neuter, singular)

In each of the sentences above, the pronouns agree with their antecedents. Notice that plural pronouns such as *their* do not indicate a gender, so you are concerned only with agreement in number. An important part of the editing process is checking pronoun-antecedent agreement. In the following journal entry, some of the pronouns didn't match their antecedents. They have been corrected.

Today, Phil yelled at me in front of everyone. He said it was my fault he couldn't move into ~~their~~ his new office. Tonya is so lucky. Phil likes Tonya. He's always buying ~~his~~ her lunch.

Practice checking for pronoun-antecedent agreement. Correct any pronouns that don't agree with their antecedents:

I saw Jerome yesterday. He said their car broke down. It's a new car; he just bought it last month. Maybe the car has a defect in his engine. I told her to go to Joe's Garage.

You should have changed the pronoun *their* in the second sentence to "his" because it refers to Jerome. *His* in the fourth sentence should be "its" because it refers to the car. *Her* in the fifth sentence should be "him" because it refers to Jerome.

► *For more work with Pronoun-Antecedent Agreement, turn to pages 154–155 of Section 3.*

EDITING TIPS

Whenever possible, set your draft aside for a few hours or a day before you edit it. You'll see things you might have missed if you had edited it right after drafting.

PRACTICE • 4

■ Edit the following journal entry. Use the editing checklist. Pay special attention to pronoun-antecedent agreement.

What I like about living in Greenville is the fact that she is in the mountains. I like to go hiking. and camping. I also enjoy the cool whether in summer. My friend Luis told me she would never think of living anywhere else. I agree. I think I might live in greenville forever.

EDITING CHECKLIST

- ✔ Do the pronouns and antecedents agree?
- ✔ Is the grammar correct?
- ✔ Are words spelled correctly?
- ✔ Is the capitalization correct?

SKILL CHECKUP

Write a journal entry about the following topic.

TOPIC C: What is your favorite season? Why?

Follow these steps in your writing:

1. Think: Ask the "5 W and H" questions.
2. Organize: Make a "5 W and H" Chart.
3. Draft: Write the entry.
4. Revise: Make sure your ideas are connected clearly and logically.
5. Edit: Check to see that your pronouns and antecedents agree.

► *Answers begin on page 129.*

FOUNDATION SKILL 4

Identifying Purpose and Audience

Whenever you write, it is important to know your *purpose* (why you are writing) and your *audience* (the person or people for whom you are writing). You can identify your purpose by answering the question, "Why am I writing?" Maybe you want to tell a story, to explain or inform, to entertain, to describe, or to persuade. Each of these could be a purpose for writing. You can identify your audience by answering the question, "For whom am I writing?" Is it for a teacher, a friend, a relative, or a possible employer?

THINKING: IDENTIFY YOUR PURPOSE AND AUDIENCE

Thinking about your purpose will help you plan and focus your writing. For example, it will be easier to focus the topic "the part of California where I live" if you realize that your purpose is to describe. Thinking about your audience also helps you focus and shape your writing. For instance, if you are writing for an audience that knows a lot about California, you will probably write a description with many details. If, on the other hand, your audience is someone who has never been to California, your decisions about what to describe and how to describe it will be different.

Read the following message and see if you can figure out its purpose and audience:

Orlando,

I forgot to tell you that we can't take my car to the basketball game on Sunday. I got a flat tire last week and haven't been able to get it fixed yet. This is the third flat tire I've gotten this month. I don't know if I've been driving over a lot of nails and broken glass or if my tires are just worn out. Anyway, could you write a note to Tia and see if she can drive? Thanks.

Herb

In this message, Herb is telling Orlando that he has a flat tire and won't be able to drive to the game.

In the message below, Herb is writing to his wife. This message is also about the flat tire. However, the audience and purpose are different.

Honey,

I've been so busy with work all week that I didn't get a chance to fix the flat tire on the car. Will you have time on Sunday to get it fixed? I think we need to replace it since it is our third flat. I'd do it myself but I'm going to the basketball game with Orlando and Tia.

Love,

Herb

PRACTICE • 1

■ Answer the questions below. If necessary, review the message on page 52.

1. What is Herb's purpose in writing the first message? ______________

____

2. Who is his audience? ______________________________

3. What is Herb's purpose in writing the second message? __________

____

4. If Orlando writes the note at Herb's request, what would his purpose be?

____

5. Who would Orlando's audience be? ______________________

Journal Writing

Write a message to a friend inviting him or her to a birthday party. Remember to keep your purpose and audience in mind as you write.

► *Answers begin on page 129.*

ORGANIZING: MAKE A WORD WEB

Identifying your purpose and audience is an important part of prewriting. When you are organizing your ideas, you should check to see that they fit your intended purpose and audience. One good way to organize your ideas is to create purpose and audience word webs.

To make a purpose word web, write your purpose for writing in the middle of a piece of paper and circle it. Then think of words and phrases that relate to your purpose. Write these words down and draw lines connecting them to the purpose. Do the same thing to make an audience word web. Use these webs to make sure you are keeping your purpose and audience in mind when you write.

Take a look at the following topic.

TOPIC A: Write a message to someone explaining how to do something.

Now look at the word webs one writer created for her message. She wanted to explain to her son how to change a flat tire. Notice that the words and phrases in the purpose word web all have to do with changing a tire. The words and phrases in the audience word web have to do with the writer's son rather than the way to change a tire.

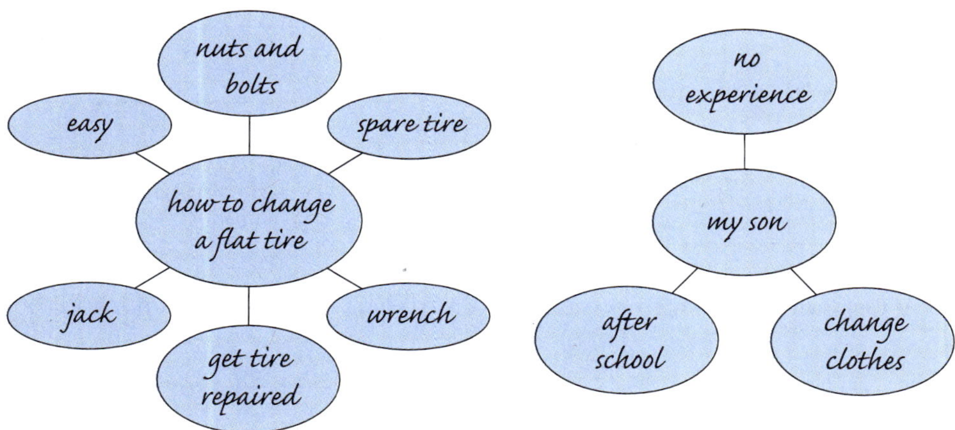

Now she can refer to these word webs when she writes her message. By keeping her purpose and audience in mind, she can be sure she won't forget anything.

TIPS

ORGANIZING WORD WEBS

Be sure to put both the purpose web and the audience web on one piece of paper. This will make it easier to refer to them when you are writing.

Now practice your prewriting skills. Reread Topic A and decide on your purpose and audience. For example, you might tell a child how to sort laundry. After you choose a purpose and an audience, brainstorm words and phrases that relate to your purpose and audience. Fill them in below.

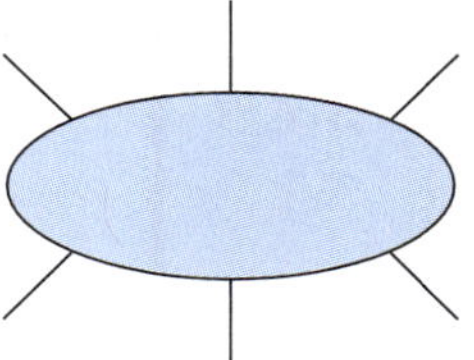

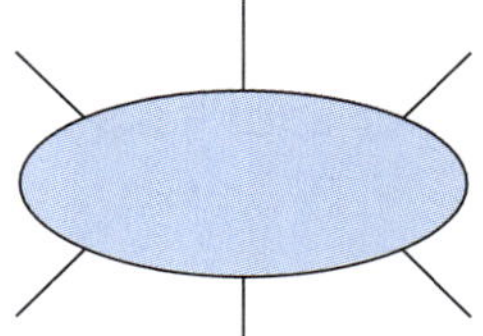

The words you place in your word webs will depend on the purpose and audience you have chosen. For example, a purpose word web for telling someone how to sort laundry might contain words like *bright colors, whites, red, laundry bag,* and *permanent press.* The audience word web may contain phrases such as *never done laundry* or *usually neat.*

ORGANIZING CHECKLIST

- ✔ Focus on your topic.
- ✔ Think about your purpose and audience.
- ✔ Brainstorm words and phrases related to each one.
- ✔ Make purpose and audience word webs.

PRACTICE • 2

■ Now think about the message topic below.

TOPIC B: Write a message to a coworker explaining that you will be late for a meeting.

► **Part A:** IDENTIFY YOUR PURPOSE AND AUDIENCE

1. What is the purpose of your message? ______________________________

____

2. Who is your audience? ______________________________

► **Part B:** MAKE WORD WEBS Make your own word web to organize ideas related to your purpose and audience.

► *Answers begin on page 129.*

DRAFTING: WRITE A SHORT MESSAGE

Once you begin to write, it's important to keep your purpose and audience in mind. Remember, two messages with the same purpose could be different if they are intended for different audiences. By the same token, two messages with the same intended audience will be different if the two purposes differ.

The following model was written about Topic A. The writer identified her purpose as explaining how to change a flat tire. She identified her audience as her son. This is the message she wrote:

James,

When you get home from school, could you please change the tire? It's the right front wheel. The spare is in the trunk with the tools. Change your clothes. This job is messy!

Take the jack and put it in the metal slot underneath the front door. Jack up the car until the tire is just off the ground. Loosen the nuts on the wheel with the wrench. Take off the nuts by turning them counter clockwise. Take off the tire. Put the spare tire on by fitting the holes in the rim right over the bolts in the wheel. Put on the nuts and tighten them with your fingers. Jack down the car all the way. Tighten the nuts with the wrench. Put the jack and the tools away.

You should be able to do this by yourself. Be careful! Put the flat tire in the garage. I'll get it fixed tomorrow.

Love,

Mom

Notice how the writer addressed her message to James, her intended audience. She states her purpose in the first line. She then explains it.

DRAFTING

TIPS

When describing how to do something, explain each step in the order in which it occurs.

Practice your writing skills. Write a message based on the word webs you made for Topic A on page 55. Before you begin, focus on your purpose and your audience.

TRY IT!

Purpose ______________________________

____

Audience ______________________________

____

Now write your message. Be as clear as possible. Keep your purpose and audience in mind.

____

____

____

____

____

DRAFTING CHECKLIST

- ✔ Write a first sentence that states your purpose.
- ✔ Be sure to explain your purpose in the message.
- ✔ Keep your audience in mind.

PRACTICE • 3

■ On page 55, you made a purpose and audience word web for the topic below.

TOPIC B: Write a message to a coworker explaining that you will be late for a meeting.

Study your word web. Then write your message. Keep your purpose and audience in mind as you write.

____

____

____

____

____

____

▶ *Answers begin on page 129.*

REVISING: USE CONNECTING WORDS

Connecting words help your reader follow your train of thought. Connecting words such as *first, before, then, after, later, as long as, as soon as, until, when, whenever, while,* and *finally* show the order of events in time. The connecting word *and* can join two related ideas. The connecting words *but* and *however* can join two contrasting ideas.

Take a look at how the writer improved her message about changing a flat tire by inserting connecting words:

James,

When you get home from school, could you please change the tire? It's the right front wheel. The spare is in the trunk with the tools. ^*First,* *change your clothes. This job is messy!*

Take the jack and put it in the metal slot underneath the front door. ^*Then* *jack up the car until the tire is just off the ground. Loosen the nuts on the wheel with the wrench* ^*and* *take* ^*them* *off* ~~*the nuts*~~ *by turning them counter clockwise.* ^*Then* *take off the tire. Put the spare tire on by fitting the holes in the rim right over the bolts in the wheel. Put on the nuts and tighten them with your fingers.* ^*Then* *jack down the car all the way.* ^*Finally,* *tighten the nuts with the wrench.* ^*After you finish,* *put the jack and the tools away.*

You should be able to do this by yourself. Be careful! Put the flat tire in the garage. I'll get it fixed tomorrow.

Love,

Mom

The writer made her explanation clearer by stressing the order of events. She used connecting words to help her son understand the steps involved in changing a tire.

► *For more work on Connecting Words, see pages 68–69 and pages 212-213.*

REVISING **TIPS**

As you revise, look for opportunities to help your reader by linking ideas with connecting words. Sometimes you can add a connecting word at the beginning of a sentence to show its relation to the previous sentence. Sometimes you can combine two or more sentences by adding a connecting word.

Review Topic A and Topic B, as well as your word webs and messages. Choose one of your two messages to revise. Do your revision on a separate sheet. Follow the Revising Checklist as you work. See if you can improve your writing by using connecting words.

WORKING Together

It is good practice to work on your revising skills with another person. You and a partner—a classmate or a friend—can give each other feedback on your messages.

Use the message you did not revise in the Try It! exercise above. Read your partner's message as he or she reads yours. Keep in mind the purpose and audience of your partner's message as you read. Follow the Revising Checklist to evaluate the paragraph. If you are reading a message that explains how to do something, you might wish to try doing it by following your partner's message. When you are ready to share comments, follow these guidelines:

1. Always present your comments positively. Point out the strengths of the message first.

2. In your suggestions, be as specific as possible. For instance, point out certain places where ideas could be better expressed or connected and make suggestions for corrections.

REVISING CHECKLIST

- ✔ Is your purpose clear?
- ✔ Is your audience clear?
- ✔ Have you explained your ideas clearly?
- ✔ Have you used connecting words to link ideas?
- ✔ Is the time order clear?

► *Answers begin on page 129.*

EDITING: CORRECT SENTENCE FRAGMENTS

In writing, connecting words are used to link ideas. They can be especially useful in correcting sentence fragments. You have already learned that a sentence fragment is an incomplete sentence that is missing either a subject or a verb. Because a fragment does not express a complete thought, it leaves a reader with unanswered questions. Sometimes the best way to correct a sentence fragment is to add the missing subject or verb. At other times, however, it makes sense to connect a fragment to a nearby related sentence. Then connecting words (such as *and, because, since, so that, when, before,* and *while*) come in handy. Take a look at the following underlined fragments and the ways they were corrected:

The car was parked on the lawn. <u>Have no idea how it got there.</u>

Possible corrections: The car was parked on the lawn. Marie and I have no idea how it got there. *OR* The car was parked on the lawn, but Marie and I have no idea how it got there.

I will meet you at noon. <u>Talk about my project.</u>

Possible correction: I will meet you at noon and talk about my project.

EDITING

As you edit, check to make sure you have corrected all sentence fragments. Turn fragments into complete sentences by adding information (either a verb or a subject) or by connecting the fragment to a nearby related sentence. Your revised sentence should express a complete thought.

Read the paragraph below. It contains many "sentences" that do not express a complete thought and do not contain both a verb and a subject.

Household pets. I have always had them, ever since I was a child. Especially dogs, my favorites. The best pet I ever had was a mongrel named Toddy. Lived to be fourteen years old. Had a smooth, pretty coat. The color of cream. He was a very devoted animal.

The following "sentences" are really fragments. *Household pets* contains no verb and doesn't express a complete thought. *Especially dogs, my favorites* contains no verb. *Lived to be fourteen years old* is missing a subject. *Had a smooth, pretty coat* is missing a subject. *The color of cream* is missing a subject.

Parts of the paragraph on page 60 appear below. Edit the fragments.

TRY IT!

Household pets. I have always had them, ever since I was a child.

Had a smooth, pretty coat. The color of cream.

Your sentences may vary. Here are some possible corrections. *I have always had household pets, ever since I was a child. Toddy had a smooth, pretty coat the color of cream.*

PRACTICE • 4

■ Edit the following paragraph. Use the Editing Checklist to help you.

In all the years I've worked there. Never been late for work without a good reason. The reason each times was that my son was home sick from school. On the other hand, my friends and coworkers Bobbie, Eduardo, and Quinn. At least a dozen times, maybe a few more. They drive as a group. If one is late then they all is late.

EDITING CHECKLIST

- ✔ Have sentence fragments been corrected?
- ✔ Is the grammar correct?
- ✔ Is the punctuation correct?
- ✔ Is the capitalization correct?
- ✔ Are words spelled correctly?

SKILL CHECKUP

Write a short message about the following topic.

TOPIC C: Write a message to a friend giving directions to your home.

Follow these steps in your writing:

1. **Think:** Identify your purpose and audience.
2. **Organize:** Make purpose and audience word webs.
3. **Draft:** Write your message.
4. **Revise:** Link ideas with connecting words.
5. **Edit:** Check for sentence fragments.

► *For more work with correcting sentence fragments, see pages 38–39 and pages 218–219. Answers begin on page 129.*

Writing a Paragraph

Just as you group words together to create sentences when you write, you group sentences together to create paragraphs. A *paragraph* is made up of several sentences that all focus on a *single* idea. Each sentence in the paragraph helps explain this idea to the reader. Paragraphs divide a large piece of writing into a series of smaller ideas.

THINKING: NARROW THE TOPIC

You can improve your writing even before you begin to write by deciding whether or not your topic needs to be narrowed. It is difficult to write a good paragraph about a topic that is too large. For instance, the topic "Argentina" is too large for a paragraph. This topic would require a writer to cover Argentinean history, climate, government, and so on.

In thinking about these different parts of the topic "Argentina," we begin to see how we can narrow the topic. Begin by picking just one of the parts. "The climate of Argentina" seems more manageable, but it's still too large for a single paragraph. Keep going, though. You can narrow the topic even further. Think of more specific things about Argentina's climate. Possible topics might be "summer in Buenos Aires" or "the wet weather of northeast Argentina." As you can see, a general topic has become much more manageable.

Take a look at the following paragraph:

> My job at the Littleton Parks Department showed that I am responsible. I did not miss a single day of work for a year and a half. I ran a swimming program for kids. I got promoted to manager, and I was in charge of youth volunteers. I held the keys to all the public park buildings. My bosses trusted me completely.

In the paragraph above, the writer discusses a single idea: the level of responsibility she held in a previous job. Each sentence in the paragraph adds details and other information to explain this idea.

Before the writer drafted this paragraph, she needed to narrow her topic. She was asked to write about "why you are a good candidate" for a job at a local factory. She brainstormed a list of words and phrases that answered this question. Then she realized that she couldn't write about all the ideas she had listed.

As the writer organized her list and crossed out items, she began to see ways to narrow the topic. Eventually she decided to write two paragraphs—the one printed above and another one that described how she is a fast learner. The two paragraphs together provided a detailed description of why she was a good candidate for the job.

Now practice your skill at narrowing a topic. Take a look at the writer's brainstorming list below. Circle the ideas that relate to the topic she chose, *the level of responsibility she held in a previous job.* Don't circle ideas that are too broad or too general to talk about in one paragraph.

a. ran swimming program **b.** am a friendly person **c.** fast learner

d. in charge of volunteers **e.** held keys to all buildings **f.** like people

If you circled *a*, *d*, and *e*, you did a good job of narrowing the topic. Choices *b, c,* and *f* don't directly relate to the topic she chose, the level of responsibility the writer held in her previous job.

PRACTICE • 1

■ Use the paragraph on page 62 to answer the questions below.

1. What idea does the writer address in her paragraph?

____

2. What do all of the sentences in the paragraph have in common?

____

3. What details or examples does the writer use to support her idea?

____

4. How are the first and the last sentence in the paragraph related?

____

Journal Writing

What is the best job you've ever had? In your journal, write a paragraph about it and why it was good. Or, if you prefer, write a paragraph about a friend's or relative's job.

► *Answers begin on page 130.*

ORGANIZING: MAKE AN IDEA MAP

Organizing your ideas can help you narrow your topic. By organizing, you can easily see which ideas are related and which are unrelated. This will help you decide which ideas to put aside and which ones to keep.

Making an idea map is one good way to organize your ideas. Begin by writing your general topic. Then list your ideas about that topic. Jot down your first idea, circle it and draw a line connecting it to the general topic. You might connect your next idea to the first idea, or you might start another branch from the general topic. Continue listing your ideas and connecting them. You may end up with several branches. As you make your map, let your ideas flow naturally. You don't have to "finish" one branch before jumping over to another branch.

Take a look at the topic below.

TOPIC A: What makes you a good candidate for employment with this company?

Now see how one writer organized his ideas so that he could narrow this general topic.

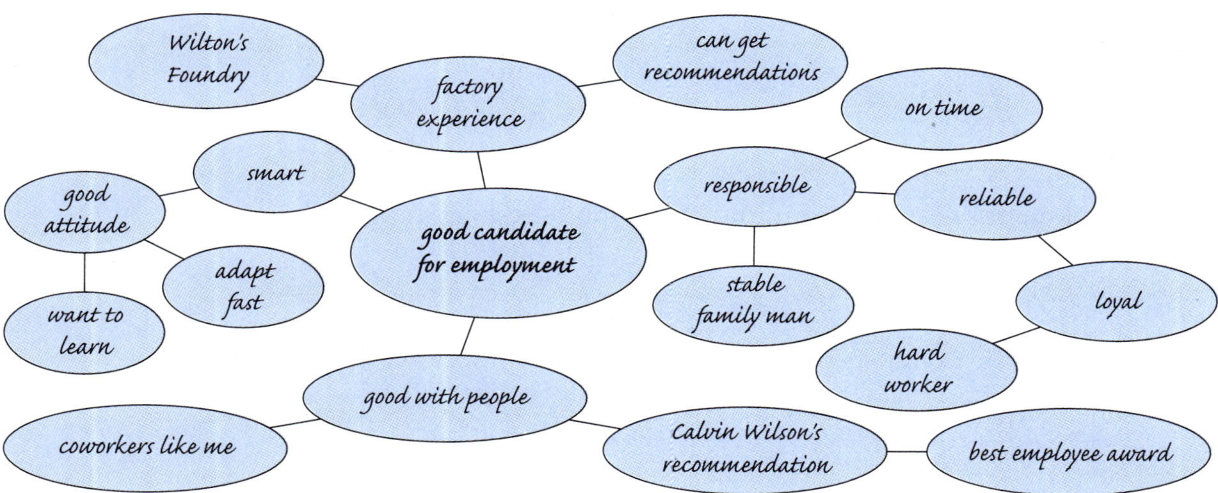

The first idea the writer listed was "factory experience." This led him to the related details of possible recommendations and "Wilton's Foundry." Then he started a separate branch, "good with people." He continued to list ideas and group them as he proceeded.

ORGANIZING TIPS

One kind of idea map looks like a tree. The general topic is the trunk. Each branch contains related ideas and details. You could write a separate paragraph from each branch. After you finish your map, choose one branch to concentrate on for your paragraph.

Now practice your prewriting skills. Reread Topic A. On a separate piece of paper, make your own idea map for it. Remember that there are no right or wrong answers. If you are having problems mapping your ideas, take another look at the completed idea map on page 64.

Thinking about your purpose and audience can help you choose which branch of your idea map to use. Look back at the idea map on page 64. The writer's purpose here is to explain why he is a good candidate for a job. His audience is the company to which he is applying. However, depending on what type of job he wants, he might choose different branches from his idea map. Look at the following examples:

Purpose: to explain why he is a good candidate for a waiter position in a restaurant

Audience: a restaurant manager

Since restaurant employees must interact with customers, the writer might choose the branch of his map that explains how he is good with people.

Purpose: to explain why he is a good candidate for a bicycle delivery job

Audience: a delivery company manager

In this case, the writer might choose the branch of his map which emphasizes that he is a hard worker, physically fit, and always on time.

ORGANIZING CHECKLIST

- ✔ Focus on the topic.
- ✔ Make an idea map.
- ✔ Choose a branch from your map to use for your paragraph.

PRACTICE • 2

■ Now think about the topic given below for another paragraph.

TOPIC B: Why are you interested in this particular job?

Decide for what job you would be applying, then follow the steps below.

1. Identify the purpose and audience for your paragraph.
2. Make an idea map about the topic.
3. Choose one branch from your map for your paragraph.

▶ *For more work with Purpose and Audience, turn to pages 52–61 of Section 2. Answers begin on page 130.*

DRAFTING: WRITE A PARAGRAPH ON A JOB APPLICATION

Nearly all job applications ask the applicant to provide a variety of factual information, such as addresses, names of former employers, schools attended, and so on. Many applications also ask you to write a paragraph on a particular topic. Usually the topic is directly related to the job or your qualifications. Being asked to write a paragraph may seem frightening. However, if you understand the structure of a paragraph, you will have an easier time writing a good one.

A good paragraph contains a *topic sentence*, which states the main idea of the paragraph. The topic sentence does not usually contain any examples or details. It should be general enough to include all the information that follows it.

The topic sentence is followed by a series of supporting sentences. Supporting sentences include details, examples, reasons, and facts that back up or explain the main idea. Finally, a good paragraph contains a concluding sentence that ties together all the information already given.

Read this first draft of a paragraph written in response to Topic A on page 64. The writer was applying for a sales job in a store:

> I am a good candidate because I am very good with people. In other jobs, my coworkers have always liked me. I won the employee of the month award three times at Goodall Fabrics. My boss, Calvin Wilson, said that I was the leader of the guys on my shift. I look forward to contact with the public. I am a people person who is very sociable and good with the give and take of business.

In the paragraph above, the writer began with a topic sentence that expressed his main idea: he is good with people. Then he wrote sentences that give examples ("coworkers have always liked me"), facts ("employee of the month"), and details (Calvin Wilson's opinion) that support his main idea. This writer also included a reason that doesn't show up on his idea map (his eagerness to work with the public). The writer concluded his paragraph with a sentence that summed up the details: he is a "people person."

DRAFTING

It is a good idea to write two or three different topic sentences for a paragraph. Then you can decide which topic sentence makes the best general statement about the information that you will cover in the paragraph.

Now look at another paragraph based on the idea map shown on page 64. This time the writer is applying for a job at a factory.

> My experience with this type of work makes me a good candidate for this job. I have worked in factories for over four years. I am very familiar with this type of work. My boss at Wilton's Foundry thought I was an excellent worker. He gave me a good recommendation. When I worked for Goodall Fabrics, I was the employee of the month three times. I am a skilled and experienced factory worker.

Because he has a different purpose and audience for this paragraph, this time the writer emphasizes his factory experience and references. Experience is more important than customer contact for this type of job. However, he did choose one idea, that he was "employee of the month," from another branch of the idea map. It is a related positive fact about his work experience.

Practice your drafting skills. Write a paragraph for a job application based on the idea map you made for Topic A on page 64. Before you begin, think about your purpose and your audience.

Topic: ______________________________

Purpose: ______________________________

Audience: ______________________________

Now draft your paragraph. Use your idea map to help you stay focused on your main idea. Write your main idea in a good topic sentence. Then, write sentences that support your main idea. Finally, write a concluding sentence that ties up the paragraph.

DRAFTING CHECKLIST

- ✔ Decide on the main idea for your paragraph.
- ✔ Write your main idea in a good topic sentence.
- ✔ Support your main idea with sentences containing details, examples, reasons, and facts.
- ✔ Write a concluding sentence that ties up the paragraph.

PRACTICE • 3

■ On page 65, you brainstormed and organized an idea map on this topic:

TOPIC B: Why are you interested in this particular job?

Look over your idea map. Choose one idea. On a separate sheet, write a paragraph using the idea you chose. As you write, refer to the Drafting Checklist.

► *Answers begin on page 130.*

REVISING: USE CONNECTING WORDS

All the sentences in a paragraph should be related to one another since they all have to do with a single idea. When two sentences are closely related, a writer can use a connecting word to show how the thoughts are linked. This helps the reader follow the writer's thought progress. In a longer essay, connecting words can be used to make transitions from one paragraph (and one idea) to the next paragraph (and the next idea).

Connecting words such as *also, in addition, furthermore,* and *finally* can be used to show how two thoughts are related. *Finally* is used to show the last related thought. Look at the following examples:

> The Chin family has lived in this neighborhood for over 20 years. Furthermore, they are active in community affairs.
>
> Mark and his daughter sat in the waiting room for over two hours. Finally, the doctor was able to see them.

Connecting words such as *but, however, on the other hand,* and *nevertheless* can be used to show how two thoughts are different from one another. Look at the following examples:

> LaToya decided to stay home Saturday night. However, she had plenty of excitement planned.
>
> Chad was looking forward to visiting his grandmother. Nevertheless, he was not looking forward to the 12-hour bus ride to Tucson.

The connecting word *therefore* can be used to show how one thought results from another thought.

> Julia learned how to write a good resume. Therefore, she impressed the woman who interviewed her for the job.

REVISING

As you revise, see if you can make your writing clearer by adding connecting words to join related ideas. A connecting word can be used at the beginning of a sentence to link it with a previous sentence. Or, sometimes a connecting word can be used after a comma or a semicolon to link two thoughts in the same sentence.

► *For more work on Connecting Words, see pages 58–59 and pages 212–213.*

Look at the paragraph below to see how the writer revised his paragraph from page 67, using connecting words to link ideas. The connecting words help show how the sentences in the paragraph are related.

> My experience with this type of work makes me a good candidate for this job. I have worked in factories for over four years. *Therefore,* I am very familiar with this type of work. My boss at Wilton's Foundry thought I was an excellent worker *and* gave me a good recommendation. *In addition*, when I worked for Goodall Fabrics, I was employee of the month three times. *Overall*, I believe I am a skilled and experienced factory worker.

Review Topic A on page 64 and Topic B on page 65, as well as your idea maps and first drafts. Choose one of your two first drafts to revise now. Follow the Revising Checklist as you work. See if you can use connecting words to make your writing clearer for your reader.

____

____

____

____

____

WORKING Together

It can be helpful to practice your revising skills with another person. Choose a partner—a classmate or a friend—and give each other feedback on your paragraphs for a job application. Use the first draft of the paragraph you did not revise in the Try It! exercise above.

Read your partner's paragraph, and allow him or her to read yours. Keep in mind both the original topic and your partner's main idea as you read. Follow the Revising Checklist to evaluate the paragraph. You and your partner also could role play how an employer might react to the paragraph on a job application. When you are ready to share comments, follow these guidelines:

1. Always present your comments positively. Point out the strengths of the paragraph first.
2. In your suggestions, be as specific as possible. For instance, point out certain places where ideas could be better expressed or connected.

REVISING CHECKLIST

- ✔ Is there a clear topic sentence?
- ✔ Do the supporting sentences contain details, facts, reasons, and examples that clarify or explain the main idea?
- ✔ Have you used connecting words to link ideas?
- ✔ Does the concluding sentence sum up the paragraph?

▶ *Answers begin on page 130.*

EDITING: CORRECT RUN-ON SENTENCES

At the editing stage of the writing process, you check your writing for mistakes. One error to look for is *run-on sentences*. Run-on sentences are one of the most common errors found in first drafts. A run-on sentence incorrectly joins two complete thoughts. You can correct a run-on sentence by making the two thoughts into two sentences. Sometimes you also can correct it by using a comma and a connecting word or a semicolon to join the two thoughts in a single sentence.

Run-on sentence: I took the rotten lumber to the dump, the dump was closed.

Correction: I took the rotten lumber to the dump. The dump was closed.

Correction: I took the rotten lumber to the dump, but the dump was closed.

Run-on sentence: My hands get cold easily I don't have any gloves.

Correction: My hands get cold easily. I don't have any gloves.

Correction: My hands get cold easily, and I don't have any gloves.

Practice editing the run-on sentences in the paragraph below. As you read the paragraph, see if you find any "sentences" that express more than one complete thought or that are difficult to understand.

A survey shows that one of six violent crimes in the United States happens at work, the workplace is the scene of almost one milion violent crimes each year. Most people find this surprising. About ten percent are committed by people with handguns. The survey does not include information on homicides another study shows that four percent of homicides occur in the workplace.

The first "sentence" is a run-on sentence. Here is one way you can make the correction: *A survey shows that one of six violent crimes in the United States happens at work. The workplace is the scene of almost one milion violent crimes each year.*

The last "sentence" also needs to be corrected. You could correct this run-on sentence this way: *The survey does not include information on homicides. Another study shows that four percent of homicides occur in the workplace.*

EDITING TIPS

As you edit, check to make sure you have corrected all run-on sentences. Turn a run-on sentence into two complete sentences by adding end punctuation. Or turn a run-on sentence into one complete sentence by adding a connecting word after a comma or by adding a semicolon. Your edited work should contain two closely related, complete thoughts.

PRACTICE • 4

■ Edit the following paragraph. Use the Editing Checklist to help you. Pay special attention to errors involving run-on sentences.

My friend Maria goes hiking this summer she is going to northern Maine, there are fantastic wilderness areas north of Moosehead lake. Maria is preety excited, she wanted to go canoeing on the Silver river in Arkansaw, however that river dries up in the summer.

EDITING CHECKLIST

- ✔ Is the grammar correct?
- ✔ Are sentences punctuated correctly?
- ✔ Are words spelled correctly?
- ✔ Is the capitalization correct?
- ✔ Are all the sentences complete?

SKILL CHECKUP

Write a paragraph about the topic below.

TOPIC C: What is your ideal job? Why?

Follow these steps in your writing:

1. **Think:** Narrow the topic.
2. **Organize:** Make an idea map.
3. **Draft: Write** a topic sentence and supporting sentences about a single idea.
4. **Revise:** Use connecting words to link ideas.
5. **Edit:** Check for run-on sentences.

▶ *For more work with Run-On Sentences, see pages 218–219 of Section 3. Answers begin on page 130.*

Writing to Narrate

Writing that tells a story is called *narrative writing*. People all over the world tell stories. In fact, most of us tell stories every day about ourselves or about other people. Every time you relate an incident to a friend or describe a news event you are telling a story.

THINKING: UNDERSTAND NARRATIVE WRITING

Narrative writing allows you to tell a story on paper. A narrative can be about an experience that happened to someone else. Or, it can be a personal narrative, a story that relates an experience from your own life. Take a look at the following personal narrative.

Dear Sylvia,

You'll never believe what happened today. I made it into the movies!

I was walking to the train station after work. Near State Street I noticed a lot of trucks and huge trailers parked along the sidewalk. The police had blocked off all the traffic. When I saw people setting up cameras, I knew they were shooting a movie.

I had time to kill before my train so I stopped to watch. While I was standing there, someone tapped me on the shoulder and asked me if I wanted to be in the movie. Of course, I said YES right away!

I had to carry shopping bags and pretend I was window-shopping. They told me to drop the bags when they gave a signal. So they gave the signal, and I dropped them, and guess who walked up to me? Harrison Ford! He helped me pick up the bags!

They filmed the same scene three times from three different angles. I can't wait to see it on the big screen. As I always say, it pays to be curious!

Rosario

Rosario bases her personal narrative on an interesting experience she had—being an extra in a movie. She describes the story's events simply and clearly. A reader can tell *what* happened, *when* it happened, and *how* Rosario felt. She uses details to help you "see" the story.

Everyday life contains many stories that are rich in detail and full of surprises. Each story we tell others about our lives is a narrative, and written narratives can be about these same everyday events. Narratives often have one of these main ideas, or themes:

the unexpectedness of life: a surprising, interesting, or amusing experience;
learning a lesson: what a person learns from an experience;
surviving a conflict: how a person deals with a decision or problem.

PRACTICE • 1

■ Answer the following items about the narrative on page 72.

1. What is the main idea of the narrative? Check one.

______ **a.** an amusing, surprising, or interesting experience
______ **b.** a lesson the writer learned about life
______ **c.** a conflict the writer overcame

2. Number the events in the order in which they occurred:

______ **a.** The writer drops her shopping bags.
______ **b.** The writer is asked to be in a movie.
______ **c.** Harrison Ford helps the writer pick up the bags.
______ **d.** The writer is walking to the train station after work.

3. List the details that help you "see" the story.

____

____

Journal Writing

A common narrative theme is surviving a conflict. Have you recently experienced a conflict? You may have had an argument with someone. Perhaps you were faced with a hard decision. Or maybe you were challenged by an illness or a natural disaster, such as a storm or a tornado. In your journal, write a personal narrative describing the conflict. If you can't think of a conflict in your own life, write a narrative describing a situation in which you helped a friend deal with a problem.

► *Answers begin on page 131.*

ORGANIZING: MAKE A TIMELINE

chronological order: order according to time

When you tell a story, you usually tell what happened first, what happened next, and finally what happened at the end. Stories told this way are organized in chronological order. To write a narrative in chronological order, you must arrange the details according to what happened when. A timeline can be a good way to do this. Read the following topic, and think for a few moments about how you would answer it.

TOPIC A: Have you ever had a day when everything seemed to go wrong? What happened?

First, you focus on the story you plan to tell. Your topic will be *a day when everything went wrong*. This topic is an example of the narrative theme of *surviving a conflict*. In this case, the conflict is with the problems that make your day go so badly. Then, think about exactly what happened on that day, and list the things you remember. Here is a model that shows one writer's brainstorming list:

cut my hand, burned chicken, car repair cost $280, overslept, walked to work, late for work, car wouldn't start, Knicks lost, forgot my lunch

BRAINSTORMING TIPS

Ask yourself the questions *who?, what?, where?, when?, why?,* and *how?* Answering these questions can often help you remember important details for your narrative. As you brainstorm, don't worry about the order in which things happened. Just write down everything that comes to your mind that added to your bad day.

After you brainstorm a list, arrange the details you listed along a timeline. Timelines can cover hours, days, months, years—even centuries. Once you have completed your timeline, you can refer to it as you write your narrative to make sure you describe events in chronological order.

Now look at the model of one writer's timeline.

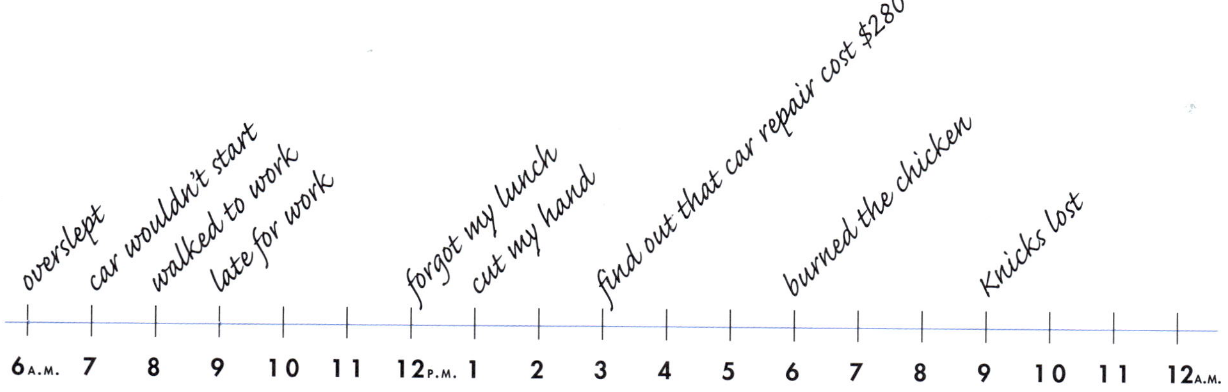

Now practice your brainstorming and organizing skills. Reread Topic A and think about your own response. On a separate sheet, list the details you remember. Then organize the details along the timeline below.

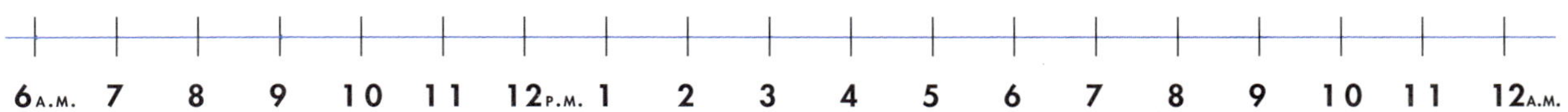

6 A.M. 7 8 9 10 11 12 P.M. 1 2 3 4 5 6 7 8 9 10 11 12 A.M.

Check your work. Are the details in chronological order? ■

PRACTICE • 2

ORGANIZING CHECKLIST

- ✔ Focus on the topic of the story you plan to tell. Identify the main idea.
- ✔ List details. Ask *who?, what?, where?, when?, why?,* and *how?*
- ✔ Arrange the details in chronological order along a timeline.

■ The topic below is an example of the theme *learning a lesson*. Read and reflect on Topic B.

TOPIC B: Think of and describe an experience that illustrates this idea: jumping to conclusions can get you in trouble.

▶ **Part A:** LIST IDEAS Answer the questions that follow.

1. What is the main idea of the story you will tell?

____

2. Focus on the details of the story you will tell. Ask yourself *who?, what?, where?, when?, why?,* and *how?* List some details of the story.

____

____

▶ **Part B:** MAKE A TIMELINE Make a timeline to organize the events and details of your story.

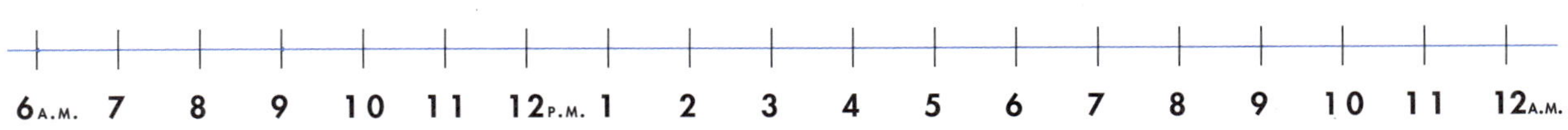

6 A.M. 7 8 9 10 11 12 P.M. 1 2 3 4 5 6 7 8 9 10 11 12 A.M.

▶ *Answers begin on page 131.*

DRAFTING: WRITE A NARRATIVE

Once your ideas are organized, you can write the first draft of your narrative. Begin by writing a topic sentence that states the main idea in an interesting way. Then, using your list of details and timeline, describe the first event or detail of your narrative. Develop the topic by describing the rest of the events in chronological order. Use as many details as you can. Finally, wrap up your story with a concluding sentence. Remember, this is your first draft. It does not have to be perfect.

The following is an example of a first draft written in response to Topic A on page 74. The writer began by writing the topic sentence. Notice how the topic sentence states the theme, or main idea, of the narrative in an interesting way. The writer then used this topic sentence to begin the narrative: Last Friday, it seemed as if everything that could go wrong did go wrong.

Last Friday, it seemed as if everything that could go wrong did go wrong. First, I overslept. Then my car wouldn't start, so I had to walk to work, and I was an hour late. To make matters worse, at lunch time I discovered that I had left my lunch at home. My friend offered me an apple, and I was slicing off a piece when I cut my hand with my jackknife. Later I called to see if my wife could pick me up, and she said that the car's starter was gone. It would cost $280. Then, at dinnertime, I burned the chicken. So I ate a peanut butter sandwich and watched the Knicks lose by thirty points. It was a fitting ending to a bad day.

In the first draft above, the writer began with a topic sentence. The details then follow the order of the timeline on page 74. Notice how words such as *first, later,* and *then* signal the chronological order of the details. This writer also connected related ideas. For example, the sentence *Then my car wouldn't start, so I had to walk to work, and I was an hour late* contains three items from the list of details. The writer finished up the narrative with a clear concluding sentence.

DRAFTING

When drafting a narrative, use words that show the chronological order of events.

finally	meanwhile	then	about (noon)	by (Friday)
first	next	until	after (today)	during (lunch)
later	soon	when	before (five o'clock)	last (night)

Practice your drafting skills. Write a first draft based on the timeline you made for Topic A on the top of page 75 . Before you begin, focus on your main idea and write a topic sentence.

Topic: *a day when everything went wrong*

Topic Sentence:

____

____

Now, on a separate piece of paper, draft your narrative. Include as many details as you can. Write the events in chronological order. When possible, use words that show the order of events. Also, connect ideas whenever you can. Remember that first drafts are not final, so don't worry about being perfect.

PRACTICE • 3

■ For Practice 2 on page 75, you made a timeline for a narrative about the topic below. Study your timeline. Then answer the items below.

TOPIC B: Think of and describe an experience that illustrates this idea: jumping to conclusions can get you in trouble.

1. What is the main idea of your narrative?

____

____

____

2. Write a topic sentence for your narrative.

____

____

____

■ Now, on a separate sheet, write a first draft of your narrative. Make sure to follow each step of the Drafting Checklist.

▶ *Answers begin on page 131.*

DRAFTING CHECKLIST

- ✔ Write a topic sentence that expresses the main idea.
- ✔ Follow your timeline to keep the events in chronological order.
- ✔ Use words that signal when events took place.
- ✔ Connect related ideas.
- ✔ Write a concluding sentence.

REVISING: USE THE ACTIVE VOICE

Revising will improve your first draft. Ask yourself these questions as you study your narrative: *Have you stated the main idea in a clear and interesting topic sentence? Did you present the details in chronological order? Could you add any details to make the story clearer? Have you varied your choice of words and sentence structure?*

The following is a personal narrative written in response to Topic A, about a day when everything went wrong. Notice the revisions the writer made to improve the first draft.

One of the worst days of my life was my 30th birthday. I ~~was woken up by~~ [woke up with] an itchy rash all over my body. [My new sheets caused] ~~An~~ [an] allergic reaction ~~was caused by my new sheets~~. [I called in sick to work and then called the doctor.] I sat in the doctor's office for hours. [I had to cancel my lunch date with my best friend.] That night, [my family threw] ~~a surprise party was thrown~~ [a surprise party] for me at my mother's house. I didn't know about the party. When my sister tried to get me out of my apartment, I would not go. Instead of going to the party, I sat on the couch with ointment on my skin. ~~I had to cancel my lunch date with my best friend.~~

The writer made these revisions: The last sentence is out of chronological order. It has been moved. The writer added a sentence containing additional information about how she spent the afternoon.

This narrative had another problem. Many of the verbs were not in the active voice. When a verb is in the passive voice, the subject *receives* the action of the verb. When a verb is in the active voice, the subject of the verb *performs* the action. Verbs in the active voice are stronger. They make your narrative more interesting. Notice how the writer changed three verbs from the passive voice to the active voice.

► *For more work with Active and Passive Voice, see pages 190–195 of Section 3.*

As you revise your writing, it's a good idea to check for varied sentence structure. If all the sentences are very short, or if the subject is the same in every sentence, a paragraph can read more like a list than an interesting narrative. Look at the example below.

> I left my apartment. I went to the employment agency. I picked up an application. I saw that it was short. I finished it rapidly.

To make the paragraph more interesting, vary the sentence structure by using different subjects and adding connecting words to combine related sentences. Read the revised example below.

> I left my apartment and went to the employment agency. There, I picked up an application. The application was short so I finished it rapidly.

Review your drafts for Topics A and B.

TOPIC A: Have you ever had a day when everything seemed to go wrong? What happened?

TOPIC B: Think of and describe an experience that illustrates this idea: jumping to conclusions can get you in trouble.

Choose one of them to revise. Follow the Revising Checklist as you revise. Be sure that your verbs are in the active voice.

REVISING CHECKLIST

- ✔ Is the main idea of the story stated in the topic sentence?
- ✔ Do all other sentences in the narrative support the main idea?
- ✔ Are the details in the story in chronological order?
- ✔ Are there enough descriptive details?
- ✔ Is there a variety of sentence types?
- ✔ Are sentences connected by linking words or words showing time order?

WORKING Together

Practice your revising skills with a classmate or a friend. You and your partner will give each other comments on your narratives. Use the first draft of the essay that you did not revise in the Try It! exercise above.

Read your partner's narrative and have your partner read yours. Give yourselves plenty of time to read the narratives. Follow the Revising Checklist to evaluate the narratives. When you are ready to share comments, follow these guidelines:

1. Try to present your comments in a positive way. Point out the strengths of the narrative first. Your job is to help your partner improve his or her writing.

2. Be as specific as you can. Point out certain words or sentences that you think should be revised. If possible, try to offer your partner some revision suggestions.

► *For more work with varying sentence structure, see pages 204–205 of Section 3. Answers begin on page 131.*

EDITING: CHECK VERB TENSE

When you edit, you check your writing for mistakes. In narrative writing, it is important to check verb tenses. A verb's *tense* tells when the action takes place: the present, the past, or the future. Notice the verb tenses in the following sentences:

Present tense: I play the lottery almost every week.

Past tense: Last Friday I played the lottery.

Future tense: Next Friday I will play the lottery.

Read the following paragraph. The verbs are underlined.

When I brought the baby home from the hospital, my older children were thrilled. When Dee ~~asks~~ asked to hold him, I showed her how. She held him very carefully. Sharise ~~will want~~ wanted to feed him. I showed her how to hold the bottle. I was very happy that the girls loved the baby so much.

This story is in the past tense. However, some of the verbs were in the wrong tense. They have been corrected to be in the past tense.

Practice editing the verb tense of a narrative paragraph. Correct any verbs that are not in the past tense but should be.

Last week my brother let me go with him to the pool hall for the first time. I watch him and his friends play. I will beg them to let me play. Finally, they gave in. Maybe it was beginner's luck, but I win the game. I've never shocked my brother as much as I do that day.

The main verb tense of the story is *past.* The verb ***watch*** is in the present tense. Edit it to its past tense form, ***watched***. The verb ***will beg*** is in the future tense, but the action already occurred. The past tense form is *begged*. The past tense of the verb ***win*** is ***won***. The past tense of the verb *do* is *did*.

▶ *For more work with verb tenses, see pages 160–171 of Section 3.*

PRACTICE • 4

■ Edit the following narrative paragraph. Check for errors using the Editing Checklist. Pay special attention to possible errors in verb tense.

Every time I call my mother on the phone, we have the same conversation. First, we discussed my job. Then she told me what's going on in her life. Next, we discuss general things like the whether and the news. But there comes a time in every conversation. When my mother asked if I'm dating anyone special. I roll my eyes make a joke and quickly ended the conversation.

EDITING CHECKLIST

✔ Is the grammar correct?

✔ Are the sentences punctuated correctly?

✔ Are words spelled correctly?

✔ Is the capitalization correct?

SKILL CHECKUP

Write a personal narrative based on the following topic.

TOPIC C: What event or experience in your life has made you feel proud? Why?

Follow these steps in your writing:

1. **Think:** What is the main idea of the narrative?
2. **Organize:** List any details and arrange them on a timeline.
3. **Draft:** Write a topic sentence. Then write a first draft.
4. **Revise:** Revise the first draft.
5. **Edit:** Check the narrative for grammar, spelling, and punctuation.

► *Answers begin on page 131.*

Writing to Explain

Explanatory writing is writing that explains or informs. It is the most practical type of writing. When you write a recipe, a phone message, or a note for a child to take to school, you are writing to explain.

THINKING: UNDERSTAND EXPLANATIONS

In explanatory writing, facts, details, and examples help the reader understand the subject. Read the following example:

December 4, 1992

Dear NYC Parking Violations Bureau:

I was issued summons #62601-3 on 12/1/92 for illegally parking in front of 223 Congress Street in Brooklyn. This summons was issued unfairly.

I admit that on December 1, 1992, my car was illegally parked. However, when I went out to my car at 8:35 that morning, I found two tickets on the windshield. Summons #60765-1 was written at 8:12 a.m., and Summons #62601-3 was written at 8:14 a.m. Clearly, the parking officer did not see the first ticket when he or she gave me the second ticket.

I have paid the $25 fine for the first summons because that was rightly issued to me. Please cancel Summons #62601-3, which was wrongly issued.

Thank you.

Now practice your skills at understanding explanations. Review the letter above. Then answer the following questions:

Identify the purpose and audience for this letter.

____

What facts and details does the writer use to support his main idea?

____

In the letter, the writer's purpose is to explain that he was wrongly issued a ticket. His audience is the Parking Violations Bureau. He supports his main idea with summons numbers, dates, and times.

It is important to use language that is appropriate for your audience. It is also important to arrange your ideas so the reader can easily follow your thinking.

appropriate: fitting or proper

Some common and useful examples of explanatory writing are: *letters of complaint*, *recipes*, *appliance instruction manuals*, *explanations on insurance claims*, and *detailed telephone messages*.

Read the following example of a letter of complaint:

Dear Jeffries Bus Company,

I am writing to complain that your buses sometimes leave ahead of schedule.

Yesterday, I arrived at the 7th Avenue bus stop at 2:55 P.M. I wanted to catch the 3:00 bus downtown. When I got there, a person standing at the stop told me that the downtown bus had just left. She had missed it as well. I know we weren't late. We had to wait one hour for the 4:00 bus. When your buses leave early, it can be a big inconvenience for your passengers.

Thank you.

PRACTICE • 1

■ Answer the following questions about the letter of complaint. Look back at the Try It! exercise on page 82 to help you.

1. Identify the purpose and audience for this letter.

____

2. What is the main idea of this letter?

____

Journal Writing

Have you ever bought a defective product at a store? In your journal, write a letter of complaint to the company that manufactures the product. If you have not had this experience, imagine it happening with a product you have purchased.

▶ *Answers begin on page 132.*

ORGANIZING: MAKE A CAUSE-AND-EFFECT CHAIN

When you explain an event or a situation, your goal is to be as clear as possible. Putting your thoughts in logical order will help your reader clearly understand your meaning. One way to do this is to create a cause-and-effect chain.

A cause-and-effect chain can be a useful way to organize. It shows how a number of events are related. One event causes another event. That second event (the "effect" of the first event) then causes another event and so on. This is known as a cause-and-effect chain.

Take a look at the topic below.

TOPIC A: Write a letter of complaint to a landlord about a problem in your home.

Now look at how one writer created a cause-and-effect chain for this topic. Here are her brainstorming notes:

plaster falling, afraid of cave-in, large pieces of plaster, water drips in, rug and floor damage, pots all over—I cannot empty them, hole in roof, stained ceiling will need repainting, can't stay home from work, rained four days in a row, I called you last month but "wait and see what happens next time"

After brainstorming, she looked through her notes to find the first event. This was *hole in roof*. She put this in the first bubble of her cause-and-effect chain. Then she looked to see if any specific event was caused by that first event and so on. Here is the way her chain shaped up:

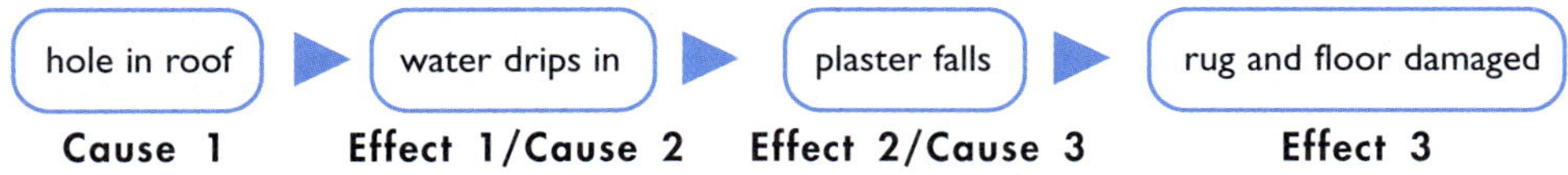

As you can see from the chain, many effects go on to cause other effects.

TIPS

To find events for your cause-and-effect chain, ask yourself *why?* and *how?* questions about your situation.

Now practice your prewriting skills. Reread Topic A and brainstorm ideas about it. Then organize your notes into a cause-and-effect chain. What is the first event or fact? What effects did that event cause? Figure out your cause-and-effect chain. Check your work by asking yourself if you have been accurate and thorough with the facts.

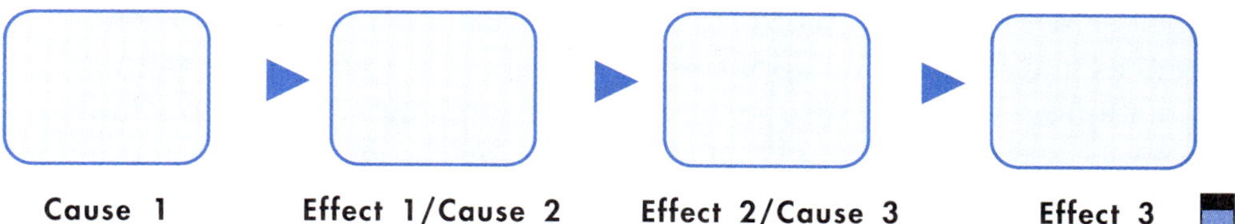

Cause 1 | Effect 1/Cause 2 | Effect 2/Cause 3 | Effect 3

PRACTICE • 2

■ Now think about the explanatory writing topic below.

TOPIC B: Write a letter of complaint about poor service or rude treatment that you received from some person or organization.

▶ **Part A:** THINK Answer the items below.

1. What is your purpose? Who is your audience?

____

2. List the details of the event below.

____

____

____

____

____

▶ **Part B:** MAKE A CAUSE-AND-EFFECT CHAIN Make a cause-and-effect chain to organize your events in order.

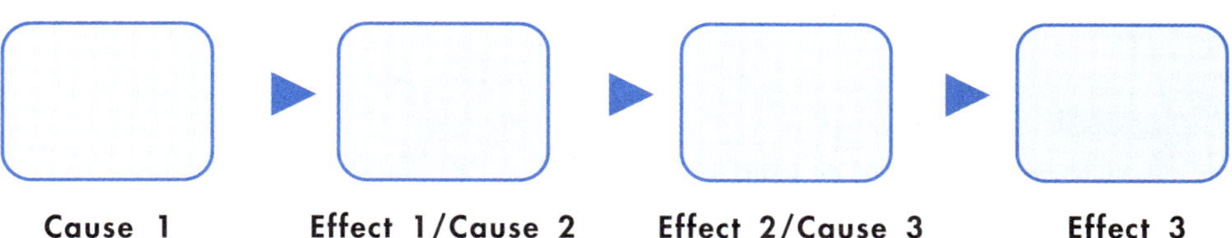

Cause 1 | Effect 1/Cause 2 | Effect 2/Cause 3 | Effect 3

▶ *Answers begin on page 132.*

ORGANIZING CHECKLIST

- ✔ Focus on the topic.
- ✔ Ask yourself *why?* and *how?* questions to help discover events for your chain.
- ✔ Fill in your cause-and-effect chain.

DRAFTING: WRITE A LETTER OF COMPLAINT

Once you have organized your facts in a cause-and-effect chain, you can write the first draft of your letter. Begin by writing an opening sentence that clearly states the main idea. Then, using your cause-and-effect chain, explain in order the events or reasons that support your main idea. Use connecting words to show the relationship between sentences and ideas when appropriate. Finally, finish your letter with a concluding sentence that sums up your complaint. In your concluding sentence, you also might wish to indicate the response you expect to get from the landlord.

Below is the first draft of a letter of complaint. It was written in response to Topic A on page 84.

Dear Mr. Jellerson,

In the past few days, water has come through my ceiling and caused a lot of damage.

Four weeks ago water came through the ceiling and I noticed a hole in the roof. I called you, but you said "wait and see what happens." These past few days were rainy. Today (Wednesday) water began to drip on the floor. The ceiling became badly stained and soggy. I have pots under the leaks to catch water, but I can't stay home from work to keep emptying them.

Because of the water, huge pieces of plaster fell to the floor. Two rugs and the floor were damaged. I also am afraid the ceiling is going to cave in.

This situation has been very disruptive. Please call me to arrange when the roof and floor will be fixed. I also would like to talk to you about reimbursing me for the cost of repairing my rugs. Thank you.

In the first draft above, the writer began with an opening sentence that stated clearly the main idea of the complaint. Then she wrote sentences using the facts from her cause-and-effect chain on page 84. She also added details from her original notes that she thought were important. She concluded her letter by summing up the situation and stating the response she expected to receive.

DRAFTING

When you are explaining a series of events or a situation, write about each event or fact in the order it appears on the cause-and-effect chain.

Practice your drafting skills. Write a first draft based on the cause-and-effect chain you made for the Try It! exercise on page 85. Before you begin, jot down your main idea. Then rewrite it in an opening sentence.

Main Idea: ____________________

Opening Sentence: ____________________

____

Now draft your letter of complaint. Describe the events in the order they appear in your cause-and-effect chain. Include as many details as you can. Use connecting words to show how thoughts are related. ■

DRAFTING CHECKLIST

- ✔ Write an opening sentence that expresses the main idea.
- ✔ Follow your cause-and-effect chain to keep facts and events in order.
- ✔ Use connecting words when necessary.
- ✔ Write a concluding sentence.

PRACTICE • 3

■ For Practice 2 on page 85, you made a cause-and-effect chain for a letter on the topic below.

TOPIC B: Write a letter of complaint about poor service or rude treatment that you received from some person or organization.

Study your chain. Write the main idea in an opening sentence on the lines below. Then write a first draft of your letter. Follow each step of the Drafting Checklist.

____

____

____

____

____

____

____

____

____

____

▶ *Answers begin on page 132.*

REVISING: GIVE EXAMPLES

Giving examples makes an explanation stronger and easier to understand. By using examples, you can turn a general and unfocused explanation into a specific and powerful one. A reader can more easily grasp your meaning if you provide examples. In fact, backing up general statements of fact with examples is a good way to improve any type of writing. Take a look at the following two paragraphs:

PARAGRAPH A

My wife and I need to have our rent reduced. The apartment is not kept up very well. It doesn't seem worth the money we pay. Please consider making the rent $200 less. If not, we will have to move out.

PARAGRAPH B

My wife and I need to have our rent reduced. When we moved into this apartment, the rent seemed fair. But in three years a lot has changed. Now the apartment is not kept up very well. For instance, the heat is not reliable. The plumbing needs work every month or so. Three burners on the kitchen stove are broken. The lock on the front door also is broken. Please consider making the rent $200 less. If not, my wife and I will have to move out.

Paragraph A communicates only basic information. Without examples, it is hard to understand what the writer means by "the apartment is not kept up very well." In Paragraph B, the writer uses four examples to help explain what he means by "the apartment is not kept up very well." The reader of Paragraph B has a much clearer idea of the situation the writer describes.

REVISING

As you revise, look for opportunities to use examples to back up general statements.

Review Topic A on page 84 and Topic B on page 85 as well as your cause-and-effect chains and the drafts you wrote. Choose one of your first drafts to revise now. Follow the Revising Checklist as you work. Be sure that you have backed up the facts in your letter with examples.

TRY IT!

REVISING CHECKLIST

- ✔ Did you start your letter with a sentence that expresses the main idea?
- ✔ Do the other sentences in your letter support the main idea?
- ✔ Do you explain the cause-and-effect chain of events that led to your complaint?
- ✔ Do you use examples to support your facts?
- ✔ Have you used connecting words to link related ideas?

____

____

____

____

____

____

____

____

____

____

____

WORKING Together

Practice your revising skills with a partner. You and a classmate or friend can give each other feedback on your letters of complaint. Use the first draft of the letter that you did not revise in the Try It! exercise above.

Read your partner's letter as your partner reads yours. Keep your partner's purpose and audience in mind as you read. It might be helpful to read the letter and react as you think the intended reader might react. Follow the Revising Checklist to evaluate the letter. When you are ready to share comments, follow these guidelines:

1. Always present your comments positively. Point out the strengths of the letter first.

2. In your suggestions, be as specific as possible. For instance, point out certain places where ideas could be better expressed or examples could be added.

► *Answers begin on page 132.*

EDITING: USE ACTION VERBS

When you edit, you can strengthen your writing by making sure you have used action verbs. Action verbs are exact about their meanings in a way that non-action verbs are not. For instance, compare these two sentences:

The baby squirmed in the crib.

The baby was in the crib.

The first sentence contains an action verb that describes the baby's movement. The verb is specific in its meaning, and it makes the sentence interesting. The second sentence contains a passive verb. It doesn't tell you anything about what the baby is doing. The second sentence is less interesting and less informative than the first.

The writer of the letter on page 86 changed some of the verbs in the second paragraph of her first draft. She replaced them with action verbs. Here is the portion of the draft that she changed:

Four weeks ago water ~~came~~ poured through the ceiling and I noticed a hole in the roof. I called you, but you said "wait and see what happens." These past few days ~~were rainy.~~ it poured hard. Today (Wednesday) water began to drip on the floor. The ceiling became badly stained and soggy. I ~~have~~ spread out pots under the leaks to catch water, but I can't stay home from work to keep emptying them.

By using the verbs *poured* and *spread*, the writer provides a clearer and more vivid description of the actions she took and events that occurred.

EDITING

Look for places in your letters where you have used the verb *to be* or have used verbs in the passive voice. Replace these with action verbs if possible.

PRACTICE • 4

■ Edit the following paragraph. Use the Editing Checklist to help you. Look for opportunities to use active verbs.

A customer of your for several years. I am not happy to be treated rudely. Yet, this was what happened yesterday when I got my car, from the repair shop. My wife was insulted, by the shop manager. And I was told to watch my attitude when I asked him to apologize to her. I would like a response from you, or I'll go somewhere else for repairs.

EDITING CHECKLIST

- ✔ Is the grammar correct?
- ✔ Are the sentences punctuated correctly?
- ✔ Is the capitalization correct?
- ✔ Are words spelled correctly?
- ✔ Have you replaced passive verbs with action verbs?

SKILL CHECKUP

Write a letter of complaint about the following topic.

TOPIC C: Have you ever been kept waiting an unreasonable length of time, perhaps in a restaurant, by a repairperson, or by an automated telephone system? Describe the problems you experienced.

Follow these steps in your writing:

1. Think: Decide on your main idea.
2. Organize: Make a cause-and-effect chain.
3. Draft: Write an opening sentence that clearly states your main idea. Then write your first draft.
4. Revise: Give examples to strengthen your explanation.
5. Edit: Check to see that you have used active verbs.

▶ *For more work with Action Verbs, see pages 78–79 of Section 2 and pages191–193 of Section 3. Answers begin on page 132.*

Writing to Describe

When you tell friends about a great purchase you have made or an exciting gift you have received, you use details to describe the item and explain why it is so fantastic. This description allows your friends to picture in their minds the item you are describing. Writing that uses details to help the reader get a clear picture is called *descriptive writing*.

THINKING: UNDERSTAND DESCRIPTIONS

When we are interested in something, we are eager to hear details about what it is like. Describing the details of a subject (whether the subject is Aunt Sheila or the Lincoln Elementary School) is a way to help your reader picture and understand that subject. Saying that the Lincoln Elementary School is "old" is too general and not especially interesting. On the other hand, saying that "the wooden stairs are worn smooth from seven generations of small shoes" gives the reader a vivid picture of a particular school. Providing details that help a reader picture what you are describing is what descriptive writing is all about.

Learning how to write descriptively is useful not only for the GED but for other kinds of writing as well. For instance, you can improve a narrative with a good description of a person or place. Or, you can use description to help explain a topic in a piece of explanatory writing.

Take a look at the following example of descriptive writing:

Mr. Johnson is a little bit strange but extremely likeable. He is a short, heavy-set man about sixty years old with smooth jowls and the energy of a young puppy. He has a big, booming voice that carries a strong Boston accent. He works in the bakery and always smells like freshly baked bread. Every day you can hear his ancient pick-up truck rumbling off to work as he greets each neighbor, "Howdy there chief." He calls everybody chief. He is a true "people person" who loves to break rules. He does so with such charm that people simply smile at him and shake their heads. For instance, if he likes the food in a restaurant, he might jump up from the table, run into the kitchen, and compliment the cook. When he gives you a handshake with his strong, ***callused*** *hands, you feel like you've got a friend.*

callused: roughened by work

This writer began by introducing the person she was describing: "Mr. Johnson is a little bit strange but extremely likeable." Then the writer went on to provide many details and examples that help describe him. She chose words and phrases that would help readers picture Mr. Johnson in their minds. She did this by including lots of adjectives, such as booming and ancient. She also tried to make her details as specific as possible.

You can improve your ability to write good descriptions if you think of your five senses. Try to *see* interesting details, to *hear* sounds that you might normally block out, and to become more sensitive to details you can *smell, touch,* and *taste* in the world around you.

PRACTICE • 1

■ Look back at the example of descriptive writing on page 92. Then answer the items below.

1. Identify the purpose of this paragraph.

____

2. Identify the audience for this paragraph.

____

3. What details does the writer use to create a picture of Mr. Johnson?

____

____

4. What details does the writer use that relate to the five senses?

____

____

Journal Writing

Think of someone in your life who has had a great influence on you. What is this person like? How would you describe this person to someone who has never met him or her? In your journal, write a few paragraphs describing this important person.

► *Answers begin on page 132.*

ORGANIZING: MAKE A FIVE-SENSES CHART

One of the best ways to describe something is to use sensory details. *Sensory details* are details relating to the five senses. Our senses help us understand the world. They help us describe the people, places, animals, and objects around us. You may be most comfortable describing things in terms of the sense of sight. But the other senses—hearing, touch, taste, and smell—also can provide valuable details that will make a description vivid.

Read the following topic, and think about how you would respond to it.

TOPIC A: Think about an individual who is an important part of your daily life. Perhaps it is a family member or someone you know at work.

If you were preparing to write on this topic, what details would you include in your description? Some of them might have to do with the person's occupation, background, and home. Other details, however, might be about what you see, hear, taste, smell, and touch when you are around this person. A good way to organize these sensory details is to make a five-senses chart. In a five-senses chart, details are arranged according to the sense you used to observe them.

Look at how one writer created a five-senses chart for Topic A:

SIGHT	5'7", short curly brown hair, great smile, green eyes, a little heavy
HEARING	laughs a lot, loud voice, likes salsa music, great singer
TOUCH	great with kids, hugs everyone, soft skin
TASTE	her rice and beans, carne asada
SMELL	smells like "baby," perfume mixed with food smells from the restaurant

carne asada: grilled meat

ORGANIZING

Try asking yourself *who?, what?, when?, where?, why?,* and *how?* questions about your subject. Although the answers may not contain sensory details, they can help you find new ways of thinking about your subject.

To come up with details for a five-senses chart, think of adjectives related to a particular sense. Then use these adjectives to ask questions about your subject. For instance, the sense of hearing might make you think of the adjective *loud*. You could ask yourself, "Does this person have a loud voice?" If the answer is no, try to think of other adjectives that describe the person's voice.

Now practice your prewriting skills. Reread Topic A on page 94. Then, on a separate piece of paper, make a five-senses chart about an important person in your life. Think of adjectives and phrases that describe the person you choose. Fill in your chart. Try to use details that create an interesting, accurate, and vivid description of your subject.

Finally, think about how you will arrange the details in your description. Will you describe the person's appearance first? Will you describe his or her personality first? Will you present groups of details together? ■

PRACTICE • 2

■ Now think about the topic below for another piece of descriptive writing. Read and reflect on this topic. Then follow the steps listed.

TOPIC B: Think about someone you admire a good deal. Describe this person and what you admire about him or her.

1. Decide on your subject.

2. Make a five-senses chart about your person.

SIGHT	
HEARING	
TOUCH	
TASTE	
SMELL	

3. List the details you will use to begin your description.

____

____

ORGANIZING CHECKLIST

- ✔ Focus on the subject you are planning to describe.
- ✔ Make a five-senses chart about your subject.
- ✔ Decide how to arrange the details in your description.

▶ *Answers begin on page 133.*

DRAFTING: DESCRIBE AN IMPORTANT PERSON

Once your details are organized, you can write the first draft of your description in response to Topic A on page 94. Begin by writing an opening sentence that introduces the character you are going to describe. This sentence can include the most important qualities of the person, or explain why you are describing the person. Then, write the rest of your first draft. Include important facts such as the person's occupation. Use your five-senses chart to describe details about the person. As you write, try to help readers picture the person you are describing. Finally, wrap up your description with a concluding sentence. In this sentence, you can state your total impression of the person.

Below is an example of the first draft of a description written in response to Topic A on page 94.

My sister Rosa is a friendly and easygoing person. She has a perky personality. This helps her in her job as the night-shift waitress in a Mexican restaurant. Rosa's smile radiates in a room. It is infectious. She is not like my other sister, who is very serious. She has a great sense of humor. Her laughter rings out in her home and in the restaurant. She has soft skin, short curly brown hair, and beautiful green eyes. She is just a little heavy. Rosa loves salsa music and goes to Latin clubs on her nights off. She will often dance all night. I go over to her apartment for dinner every Sunday. She usually makes delicious rice and beans and carne asada. When she sees me, she always gives me a big hug. I don't know anyone as warm, friendly, and lively as my sister.

In the first draft above, the writer began with an opening sentence that introduces the person he is describing: his sister Rosa. Then he wrote sentences using the details from the five-senses chart on page 94 and included important facts about her—where she works and what she likes to do when she is not working. He concluded his description with a sentence that conveyed an overall impression of his subject. Note how the writer included sensory details about sight, hearing, and touch. This technique creates a vivid, detailed picture of Rosa for the reader.

DRAFTING TIPS

When writing a description, look for precise adjectives and phrases that will help "paint a word portrait" of your subject.

Practice your drafting skills. Write the first draft of a description of the person you selected who is important to your daily life. Use the five-senses chart that you created for the Try It! exercise on page 95. First, write an opening sentence to introduce the person you are describing. Now draft your description. Include all the important or revealing details you listed in your chart. Write about these ideas and use the details in the order you chose. ■

PRACTICE • 3

■ For Practice 2 on page 95, you made a five-senses chart for the topic below.

TOPIC B: Think about someone you admire a good deal. Describe this person and what you admire about him or her.

Study your chart. Then write a description of the person you chose. Think about the details you should include to create a vivid portrait of the person.

____

____

____

____

____

____

____

____

____

____

____

____

____

DRAFTING CHECKLIST

- ✔ Write an opening sentence that introduces the person you are describing.
- ✔ Follow your five-senses chart in order to include sensory details in your description.
- ✔ Connect related ideas with connecting words when necessary.
- ✔ Write a strong concluding sentence.

▶ *Answers begin on page 133.*

REVISING: USE DESCRIPTIVE WORDS

The revising stage of the writing process gives you a chance to improve your writing by using more descriptive words and phrases. In your first draft there may be places where you used words that are general or vague. Sometimes it is possible to make a description more vivid by adding a word or phrase. Or, you can replace a weak word or phrase with one that is more precise.

Remember, too, that the best description is not necessarily the one with the most adjectives. Vivid adjectives are important, but they should be well chosen and used clearly and precisely. Bland nouns and verbs also can be replaced with more descriptive ones. Many nouns and verbs are too general and can be replaced by more specific ones.

Below is the first draft from page 96, written in response to Topic A. Take a look at the revisions the writer made to improve the description.

My sister Rosa is a friendly and easygoing person. She ~~has a~~ uses her perky personality~~.~~ ~~This helps her~~ in her job as the night-shift waitress in a Mexican restaurant. Rosa's infectious smile radiates in a room. ~~It is infectious. She is not like my other sister, who is very serious.~~ She has a great sense of humor. Her laughter rings out in her home and in the restaurant. She has soft skin, short curly brown hair, and beautiful green eyes. She ~~is just a little heavy.~~ struggles a bit with her weight. Rosa loves salsa music and goes to Latin clubs on her nights off. She will often dance all night. I go over to her apartment for dinner every Sunday. She usually makes delicious garlicky rice and beans and succulent carne asada. When she sees me, she always gives me a ~~big~~ bone-crushing hug. I don't know anyone as warm, friendly, and lively as my sister.

▶ *For more work on Descriptive Words, see pages 196–197 of Section 3.*

In the second sentence, the writer changed the verb *has* to the more precise verb *uses* and joined two related thoughts. He added an adjective to the fourth sentence that allowed him to delete the fifth sentence. He took out the sixth sentence because it didn't belong in the description. He replaced the general verb *is* with the specific verb *struggles* in the tenth sentence and added more specific adjectives to make the description more vivid.

REVISING TIPS

As you revise, look for opportunities to replace weak or vague words with precise nouns, verbs, and adjectives. For example, the phrase "he is handsome" can be revised to read "he has a handsome face: a strong jaw, a playful grin, and deep-set brown eyes." The revision is an improvement because it shows how the man is handsome instead of just stating that he is handsome.

Review Topic A and Topic B as well as your five-senses charts and first drafts. Choose one of your two first drafts to revise now. Follow the Revising Checklist on this page as you work. See if you can improve your writing by using descriptive words. Look for places in your writing where you can add vivid adjectives or strong verbs and nouns that make the description more specific.

WORKING Together

It is a good idea to practice revising skills with another person. You and a partner—a classmate or a friend—can give each other feedback on your writing. Try this now using the first draft that you did not revise in the Try It! exercise above.

Read your partner's work as your partner reads yours. Keep in mind the purpose of your partner's writing as you read. See if you can picture the person being described. Follow the Revising Checklist to evaluate the description. When you are ready to share comments, follow these guidelines:

1. Always present your comments positively. Point out the strengths of the description first.

2. Be as specific as possible. For instance, point out places where vivid adjectives or strong verbs and nouns could be included.

REVISING CHECKLIST

- ✔ Did you write an opening sentence that introduces the person you are describing?
- ✔ Are there any ideas or descriptions that do not belong?
- ✔ Did you include sensory details to help describe the topic?
- ✔ Are the details arranged in a clear and effective way?
- ✔ Is there a concluding sentence that gives an overall impression of the person?

► *Answers begin on page 133.*

EDITING: USE MODIFIERS CORRECTLY

You will probably find a lot of adjectives and adverbs, known as *modifiers*, in descriptive writing. When you edit a piece of descriptive writing, you need to make certain you have used these modifiers correctly. Take a look at the following sentences:

Jerry's facial expressions can change quick.

My boss speaks loud and rudely sometimes.

The wonderfulest gift was when she complimented me on my good work.

Each of the sentences above contains a modifier used incorrectly. In the first sentence, the subject is *expressions* and the verb phrase is *can change*. The word *quick* is an adjective. However, in this sentence, it modifies the verb, so it should be the adverb *quickly*. In the second sentence, the verb *speaks* is modified by two words that should be adverbs. *Rudely* is correct, but *loud* is an adjective. It should be the adverb *loudly*. In the third sentence, the writer uses an incorrect adjective form to modify the word *gift*. The phrase should be edited to read *most wonderful*.

EDITING TIPS

As you edit, check to make sure you have used adverbs and adjectives correctly. Remember that adjectives modify nouns and pronouns and answer the questions *what kind?, which one?,* and *how many?* Adverbs modify verbs, adjectives, and other adverbs and answer the questions *how?, when?, where?,* and *to what extent?*

As you read the paragraph below, see if you find any errors in the use of modifiers. Correct any misused modifiers.

Radio stations in our area are the worse I've ever heard. I thought careful about this before I came to the conclusion. You would think a big city would have decent radio stations. But I could run a station good. Or at least I could make a better music show for four hours in the afternoon. I would not repeated play about fifteen or twenty songs.

In the first sentence, the adjective *worse* should be *worst*. The word *worse* is used to compare two things, but this writer is comparing more than two radio stations. The adverb *carefully* should be used in the second sentence to modify the verb *thought*. The adjective *decent* is correct in the third sentence because it modifies the noun *stations*. In the next sentence, the adjective *good* should be replaced by the adverb *well*; it modifies the verb *run*. In the last sentence, the adverb *repeatedly* should be used to modify the verb *play*. ■

PRACTICE • 4

■ Edit the following paragraph. Use the Editing Checklist on this page to help you. Pay special attention to errors involving the use of modifiers.

My great uncle started a successfully business in our town. He ran it good, it grew fast for the first ten years. He was a stubbornly and harsh man. Who always treated people fair. He also could be hardly to get a long with. He had a loud voice and he used it in mightily arguments with my father. He was a short man who drove his cars fast. My father always respected him.

EDITING CHECKLIST

- ✔ Is the grammar correct?
- ✔ Are the sentences punctuated correctly?
- ✔ Is the capitalization correct?
- ✔ Are words spelled correctly?
- ✔ Are modifiers used correctly?

SKILL CHECKUP

Write a description about the following topic.

TOPIC C: Describe a good friend you have now or had when you were younger.

Follow these steps in your writing:

1. **Think:** Decide on the main idea of your description.
2. **Organize:** Make a five-senses chart.
3. **Draft:** Describe your friend.
4. **Revise:** Use descriptive words.
5. **Edit:** Check for the correct use of modifiers.

► *For more information on using modifiers correctly, see pages 196–197 of Section 3. Answers begin on page 133.*

Writing to Persuade

If you are like most people, you have strong opinions about certain issues. *Persuasive writing* tries to convince a reader to agree with an opinion or to take an action. Letters to the editor, political speeches, editorials (in newspapers, magazines, and on television), and advertisements are good examples of persuasive writing.

THINKING: UNDERSTAND PERSUASION

There are two ways to persuade a reader to agree with an opinion or to take a particular action. The first way is to appeal to the reader's reason. By using logic, good examples, and facts, you show the reader why your opinion is right. The second way is to appeal to the reader's emotions. By using examples or facts that make the reader feel something strongly, you convince the reader that your opinion is correct.

Read the following example of persuasive writing:

To the Editor:

Once again, hardworking citizens of this city are being asked to swallow a rate increase for cable television service. The reason is simple. We have no choice about where to get cable TV service because only one cable company serves the entire area. This allows the cable company to raise rates because customers can't look elsewhere for cheaper service.

The rate increases are outrageous. This is the fourth increase in a little over 18 months. The difference between the basic rate for this month and next month is "only" two dollars. But if you look at what we were paying a year ago—and three years ago—you will be outraged.

Isn't there some law on the books concerning business ***monopolies****? If not, one should be written. An entire city is being ripped off by a small group of greedy business people. Let's not take it any more.*

monopolies: groups or businesses that have exclusive control of a product or services

Sincerely,

Harold King

As you can see, the purpose of this letter is to persuade the reader to agree with an opinion. It is important for the author to know who will be his or her audience. When writing to persuade, you might use different arguments to convince different people of something. Or, you might choose different combinations of appeals to reason and to emotion.

The writer of the letter on page 102 knew his audience paid monthly bills to the same company he did. This helped him decide which arguments, facts, and tone to use in his letter. He used a combination of two approaches. Most of the letter uses facts and examples that appeal to reason. The last two sentences, however, are an emotional appeal to persuade readers to take action.

PRACTICE • 1

■ Look back to the letter on page 102. Then answer the items below.

1. Identify the purpose and audience for this letter.

____

2. What opinion is the writer expressing?

____

3. What facts and examples does the writer use to support his opinion?

____

____

4. How did the writer organize his letter in order to persuade his audience?

____

Journal Writing

Think of something you would like someone to do on your behalf. It might be something that would benefit you or your family in some way, such as granting a loan. It could be something as simple as getting a friend to do you a favor. In your journal, write a letter in which you try to persuade someone to do something for you.

► *Answers begin on page 133.*

ORGANIZING: MAKE A COMPARISON/CONTRAST CHART

When you try to persuade someone to agree with you, you need to be as clear and convincing as possible. Understanding the different sides of an issue can help you present your opinion in an informed and persuasive manner. A comparison/contrast chart can help you organize the different sides of an issue.

Take a look at the topic below.

TOPIC A: Drunk driving has become an issue of national concern. Two different penalties for people found guilty of drunk driving are a one-year driver's license suspension or a $1,000 fine. Which do you think is a better penalty? Write a letter to the editor of your local newspaper arguing for your choice.

Now look at how one writer made a comparison/contrast chart in response to Topic A. The chart shows the similarities and differences between the two penalties.

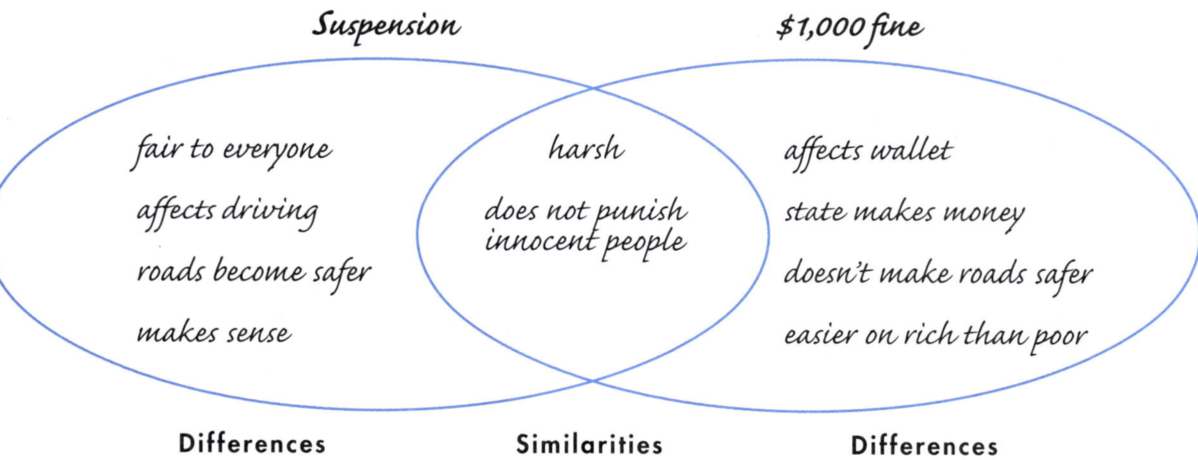

As the writer listed her facts and examples, she realized that there were far more differences than similarities. She can now use her understanding of the different sides to express her opinion clearly and find persuasive reasons from the chart to support her opinion.

ORGANIZING TIPS

As you list a fact or example on one side of the chart, think about whether there is a contrasting fact or example for the other side. If there is, list it on the other side. Don't be afraid to list similarities between your opinion and another opinion. It can help your argument to show that it agrees in some ways with other opinions.

Now practice your organizing skills. Read the topic below.

TOPIC B: How do you feel about violence on television today? Is there too much of it? Should it be censored or not?

Fill in the comparison/contrast chart below. List facts and examples about the two sides.

TV violence should be censored | *TV violence shouldn't be censored*

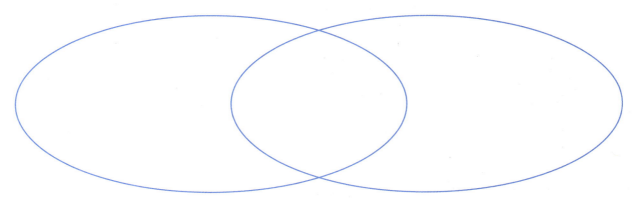

Write your opinion in a single sentence below. Then list several reasons from your chart that will help you make a persuasive argument.

Opinion: ______________________________________

____

Reasons: ______________________________________

____

PRACTICE • 2

Now think about the topic below for another piece of persuasive writing. Then follow the steps listed.

TOPIC C: Write a letter to the editor about some controversial issue in your community or state. In your letter, try to persuade readers to agree with your opinion.

1. Identify the purpose and audience for your piece of writing.
2. Make a comparison/contrast chart.
3. Make sure that you have included enough information to clearly explain an opinion.

ORGANIZING CHECKLIST

- ✔ Read the topic and think about both sides of it.
- ✔ List details in a comparison/ contrast chart.
- ✔ List similarities in the overlapping space in the middle of the chart.
- ✔ Look at the finished chart and think about how it can help you present a strong case for one side of the issue.

▶ *Answers begin on page 134.*

DRAFTING: WRITE A LETTER TO THE EDITOR

Once your ideas are organized, you can write the first draft of your letter to the editor. If you have not already done so, begin by writing an opening sentence that states your opinion in a clear and convincing way.

Then, using your comparison/contrast chart, present facts, reasons, and examples that support your opinion. Present your details in order according to their importance. As you explain your opinion, use connecting words to link related ideas. Finally, end your letter with a concluding sentence that sums up your opinion in a concise, powerful way.

Below is an example of the first draft of a persuasive letter to the editor. It was written in response to Topic A on page 104.

To the Editor:

I believe that license suspensions are the fairest and most effective punishment for drunk driving.

Drivers convicted of operating a motor vehicle while drunk should have their driver's licenses suspended for a period of one year. I know that this is a harsh punishment. However, I believe it fits the crime perfectly. A suspension punishes everybody equally, no matter how rich or poor they are. A fine (even a heavy fine like the $1,000 being proposed) sounds like a punishment that would make people think twice before driving drunk. However, if you look at the statistics from states that use fines, you'll see that fines do not work. Also, wealthy people should not get off easier than poor people, but that's the way it is if the punishment is focused on people's wallets.

I think the attention should be on getting drunk drivers off the road. Somebody who has an entire year to think about why he or she cannot drive will probably not drive drunk again.

In the first draft of the letter, the writer began with a sentence that clearly presented her opinion—that suspension is the best punishment for drunk driving. She presented two solid reasons why a suspension is a good punishment. Then, she presented two solid reasons why a fine is not a good punishment. She concluded the letter with a sentence that summed up her ideas in a fresh way.

DRAFTING TIPS

In a piece of persuasive writing, it is best to arrange your supporting examples and facts in order according to their importance. You can begin with the most important fact and end with the least important fact. Sometimes, however, it is more effective to begin with the least important fact and build toward your most important fact at the end.

Practice your drafting skills. On a separate sheet, write a first draft based on the comparison/contrast chart you made for the Try It! exercise on page 105. Before you begin, focus on your main idea and write an opening sentence that clearly presents your opinion.

Opening Sentence: ______________________________

____

Now draft a letter to the editor. Present your argument clearly. Use details that support your argument. Feel free to note both the similarities and the differences between the two sides of the argument. Use connecting words to show how your ideas are related. ■

PRACTICE • 3

■ For Practice 2 on page 105, you made prewriting notes and a comparison/contrast chart for a letter about the topic below.

TOPIC C: Write a letter to the editor about some controversial issue in your community or state. In your letter, try to persuade readers to agree with your opinion.

Study your chart. Write an opening sentence that clearly expresses your opinion. Then, on a separate sheet, write a first draft of your letter. Follow each step of the Drafting Checklist on this page.

Opening Sentence: ______________________________

____

▶ *Answers begin on page 134.*

DRAFTING CHECKLIST

- ✔ Write an opening sentence that expresses your opinion.
- ✔ Follow your comparison/contrast chart to keep your facts and reasons organized.
- ✔ Use connecting words to help your reader understand how ideas are related.
- ✔ Write a concluding sentence that sums up your position.

REVISING: USE EXPLANATIONS

The revising stage of the writing process is a good time for you to check to see whether you have supported your ideas clearly.

Take a look at how the writer revised the first draft of her letter to the editor about punishment for drunk drivers:

To the Editor:

I believe that license suspensions are the fairest and most effective punishment for drunk driving.

Drivers convicted of operating a motor vehicle while drunk should have their driver's licenses suspended for a period of one year. I know that this is a harsh punishment. However, I believe it fits the crime perfectly.

The crime of drunken driving puts innocent people on the road in great danger. So we need a punishment that makes the road safer. The only punishment that would do this is suspension. Also, ~~A~~ a suspension punishes everybody equally, no matter how rich or poor they are.

A fine (even a heavy fine like the $1,000 being proposed) sounds like a punishment that would make people think twice before driving drunk. However, if you look at the statistics from states that use fines, you'll see that fines do not work. Many people pay the fine and drive drunk again. I know two people who have several convictions for DUI, but they continue to drive drunk. Also, wealthy people should not get off easier than poor people, but that's the way it is if the punishment is focused on people's wallets.

I think the attention should be on getting drunk drivers off the road. Somebody who has an entire year to think about why he or she cannot drive will probably not drive drunk again.

The writer made her argument stronger by adding explanations of why suspensions would be effective. She added three sentences to her second paragraph. In these sentences, she explains why suspension "fits the crime perfectly." In her third paragraph, she added one sentence that explains why fines don't work, as well as another sentence showing real-life examples.

REVISING TIPS

As you revise, try to think like a reader who knows nothing about your opinion. Look for places in your writing where a particular idea is not explained clearly enough. See if you can find opportunities to add helpful facts or reasons to support your opinion.

Review Topic B and Topic C on page 105 as well as your comparison/contrast charts and first drafts. Choose one of your two first drafts to revise now. Follow the Revising Checklist on this page as you work. See if you can improve your draft by using clear explanations.

WORKING Together

It is always good practice to work on your revising skills with another person. You and a partner—a classmate or a friend—can share feedback on your writing with one another. Use the first draft of the letter you did not revise in the Try It! exercise above for this activity.

Read your partner's letter as he or she reads yours. Keep in mind the purpose and audience for your partner's writing as you read. Follow the Revising Checklist to evaluate the letter. You might try to react to your partner's letter from the point of view of someone who disagrees with his or her opinion. When you are ready to share comments, follow these guidelines:

1. Always present your comments positively. Share the strengths of the letter first.
2. In your suggestions for improvement, be as specific as possible. For instance, point out certain places where ideas could be explained more clearly.

REVISING CHECKLIST

- ✔ Is your opinion clearly stated in the opening sentence of your letter?
- ✔ Do all the sentences in the letter support the main idea?
- ✔ Do you use examples, facts, and reasons to explain your opinion?
- ✔ Have you arranged your supporting details according to their order of importance?
- ✔ Does your letter conclude with a sentence that sums up your opinion?

▶ *Answers begin on page 134.*

EDITING: MAKE SUBJECTS AND VERBS AGREE

In persuasive writing (as in all other types of writing), you have to avoid errors in subject-verb agreement. Subjects and verbs must agree, or match each other, in number. For example, a singular subject (*one* person, place, or thing) must have a singular verb. To avoid or correct mistakes in subject-verb agreement, you must be able to identify the subject and verb of a sentence. Look at the following sentences:

> Fifteen brand-new automobiles was delivered to the local Ford dealer this week.
>
> The German Shepherd are one of the gentlest dogs with children.
>
> They is due for a promotion and a pay raise.

In each sentence above, the subject and verb are not in agreement. In the first sentence, the plural subject *automobiles* must take a plural verb. The verb should be changed to *were delivered*. In the second sentence, the singular subject is *German Shepherd*, so the verb should be changed to *is*. In the third sentence, the singular verb *is* does not agree with the plural subject *they*. The verb should be changed to *are*.

EDITING TIPS

As you edit, check to make sure that subjects and verbs agree in number. A compound subject connected by the word *and* takes a plural verb. A compound subject connected by the words *or* or *nor* takes a verb that agrees with the subject nearest to it.

Look for errors in subject-verb agreement in the following paragraph. Correct any errors that you find.

> We is in need of more money for youth athletic facilities. By playing sports, young people stays healthy and out of trouble. Sometimes I passes by a basketball court with no baskets or a garbage-filled lot that used to be a baseball field. These facilities must be fixed up.

In the first sentence, did you replace the verb *is* with *are* to agree with the plural subject *we*? The verb *stays* in the second sentence should be replaced by the verb *stay* to agree with the subject *young people*. In the third sentence, the singular verb *pass* replaces *passes* to agree with the singular subject *I*.

► *For more work with Subject-Verb Agreement, see pages 172–183 of Section 3.*

PRACTICE • 4

Edit the following sentences, which contain a variety of errors. Use the Editing Checklist on this page to help you. Pay special attention to possible errors in subject-verb agreement.

1. Small towns in this country has to struggle to keep its downtowns alive.

2. According to some people, many southern cities is growing almost too quick.

3. Interesting to live in sevral different places during your life.

4. However, experts says that moveing is one of the five most stressful events in a persons' life.

5. Do you knows any person who have lived in the same place his or her whole life?

EDITING CHECKLIST

- ✔ Is the grammar correct?
- ✔ Do all subjects and verbs agree?
- ✔ Is the capitalization correct?
- ✔ Are sentences punctuated correctly?
- ✔ Are words spelled correctly?

SKILL CHECKUP

Write a letter to the editor in which you express your opinion about the following topic.

TOPIC D: Do you think there should be health-care coverage for each person in the United States? Why or why not?

Follow these steps in your writing:

1. Think: What do you want to persuade people of in your letter?
2. Organize: Make a comparison/contrast chart.
3. Draft: Write a letter to the editor.
4. Revise: Use explanations to strengthen your argument.
5. Edit: Check for correct subject-verb agreement.

▶ *Answers begin on page 134.*

Writing an Essay

An *essay* is a clear and detailed discussion of a particular topic. There are several different types of essays, including descriptive, explanatory, and persuasive. An essay should always say something about a topic in an organized and effective way.

THINKING: NARROW THE TOPIC

To write a good essay, begin by thinking carefully about your writing topic. Make sure that you understand what the topic requires you to do. Do you need to write a descriptive, explanatory, persuasive, or narrative essay? After you decide which type of essay you need to write, you can begin to explore your thoughts and ideas.

Brainstorming about a topic helps you explore your thoughts and gather information. You can make important discoveries about what you want to say. After you have generated a lot of ideas and details, stop and see how they are related. If many of your ideas are unrelated, you probably need to narrow your topic. You can do this by choosing several related ideas and details and eliminating the others. Then when you draft your essay, you will present each related idea in a separate paragraph.

Take a look at the following short essay:

> In the last few years there has been a big movement to restrict smoking in this country. I think that laws restricting smoking are a bad idea.
>
> I don't think the government has any right to tell me what I can and can't do to my own body. If I want to smoke, that's my business. I know that smoke can be dangerous to other people, and I respect that. But an individual smoking on a city street doesn't harm anybody but himself. An individual shouldn't have his rights taken away, whether he's smoking or not.
>
> Restricting or banning smoking will only make it more appealing to young people. Young people are in danger of getting addicted to smoking for life. They are impressionable, and they love breaking the rules. I think that making smoking illegal will actually encourage a whole new generation to smoke.
>
> Although there seems to be a lot of support for restricting smoking, I think the government should be told that it will not work.

In this essay, the writer began with an *introductory paragraph* that contained his main idea. Then he wrote two more paragraphs. In each paragraph, he presented one idea that supported his main idea. These paragraphs are known as the *body*. He ended his short essay with a *concluding paragraph* that restated and summed up his main idea. The first and last paragraphs contain general statements, whereas the second and third paragraphs contain specific information and details.

PRACTICE • 1

■ Answer the questions below. Look back to the essay on page 112 to help you.

1. Identify the purpose and audience of the essay.

____

2. What main idea is the writer expressing?

____

____

3. What facts, examples, and reasons does the writer use to support his main idea?

____

____

4. How did the writer structure his essay?

____

____

Journal Writing

Do you think the individual is valued in America? Do you think the rights of individual citizens should be protected more or less strongly than they are now? Use your journal to brainstorm ideas for this topic. Then, narrow your topic by selecting related ideas and eliminating others. Write the main idea for an essay on this topic.

▶ *Answers begin on page 134.*

ORGANIZING: MAKE AN OUTLINE

After brainstorming ideas and narrowing your topic, you need to focus on two or three points you will use to support your main idea. Then, you can make an outline of information. An outline will save you time and help you stick to the subject. It also will help you present information in clear, logical order.

Your goal is to make an organized and complete outline. Your outline will have a section for the introductory paragraph, a section for each of the supporting paragraphs in the body of the essay, and a section for the concluding paragraph. The outline will briefly note the information that you want to appear in each of these paragraphs.

Take a look at the following writing topic. Then look at the outline that one writer created in response to it.

TOPIC A: Describe the home of your dreams.

1. Introduction
   a. Main idea: year-round oceanside home
2. Body
   a. House
      i. large, old, wooden house with many rooms
      ii. windows, light, see and hear the waves
      iii. clean, simple decorations and furniture
   b. Location
      i. in Maine or Massachusetts
      ii. right at edge of rocks, beach, and water
      iii. land enough around it for privacy
3. Conclusion
   a. Restate main idea: every day of the year by the ocean

Notice how the writer chose to organize her ideas. The three main parts of the essay—the introduction, body, and conclusion—are numbered. Paragraphs within these three parts are lettered. Details within the paragraphs are shown with lowercase Roman numerals.

Don't worry too much about precise numbers and letters in your own outline. Be sure, however, that you create separate sections for the introduction, each supporting paragraph, and the conclusion.

ORGANIZING

As you look over your brainstorming notes, think about in which order each detail should be presented. Then think about the best way to arrange the details within each paragraph. Incorporate these organizing ideas into your outline.

Practice your organizing skills. Reread Topic A, and think about your own response. Write your main idea below.

TRY IT!

Main Idea: ____

____

____

On a separate sheet of paper, make a detailed outline of your response to the topic. State your main idea in the section for the introductory paragraph. Restate it in the section for the concluding paragraph. These are the places for general statements about the topic. Use the body of your essay for specific information and ideas that support your main idea. Use the Organizing Checklist on this page to help you.

PRACTICE • 2

Now think about the topic below for another short essay. Read the topic and think about your response to it. Then follow the steps.

TOPIC B: Explain why you believe it is important to get your GED.

1. Identify the purpose and audience for your essay.
2. Brainstorm ideas about your topic.
3. Focus on two or three points that support your main idea.
4. Create an outline that organizes your ideas.

____

____

____

____

____

____

____

____

____

ORGANIZING CHECKLIST

- ✔ Narrow your topic.
- ✔ Create an outline that has a separate section for the introduction, body, and conclusion.
- ✔ Place details in the outline in the order in which you will use them in a paragraph.

▶ *Answers begin on page 134.*

DRAFTING: WRITE A SHORT ESSAY

Once your ideas and details are organized in an outline, you can write the first draft of your short essay. Begin by writing an introductory paragraph that expresses your main idea in an interesting way. You should have two goals as you write the introductory paragraph of the essay. You need to express your main idea clearly, and you need to grab the reader's interest.

Then, using your outline, begin to write the body of your essay. The second paragraph should be about the first group of details in your outline. The third paragraph should be about the second group of details in your outline. Finally, write a concluding paragraph that sums up your thoughts and restates your main idea.

Below is the first draft of a short essay. It was written in response to Topic A on page 114.

People dream about things they want someday. I dream about a house. I've never seen the home I dream about, but I know it is a beautiful house right next to the water.

The house is special. It is a large (probably two- or two-and-a-half stories), old, wooden house. It was probably built in the 1800s, and it has many rooms. Since the house is filled with windows, it has plenty of light and air. I can see and hear the sea all the time. The house is filled with simple furniture and decorations, so it feels clean and open.

My dream house is located in a very special place. It is in a small village in Maine or Massachusetts. It sits right on the edge of large rocks that go down to the water. Below the rocks is a soft sandy beach. The house sits on nice land—enough so that I can have all the privacy I need.

If I could, I would live in my dream house right next to the water every day of the year. Right now it's really just a dream. Maybe someday I'll find a way to make my dream come true.

In the first draft above, the writer began with an introductory paragraph that contained her main idea: her dream house is a beautiful waterside home. Notice that this introductory paragraph is quite general. Then she introduced two supporting ideas in the body—the second and third paragraphs—of the essay. The second paragraph describes the house itself. The third paragraph describes the location of the house. She included the details from her outline in these paragraphs. She ended her essay with a concluding paragraph that restated her main idea.

DRAFTING TIPS

In a short essay, use your outline to help you stick to the subject and to remind you of what to say next. If you think of a new detail that is closely related to the paragraph you are writing, include it in your first draft. You can always take it out later when you revise.

Practice your drafting skills. On a separate sheet, write a first draft based on the outline you made for the Try It! exercise on page 115. Before you begin, reread your main idea. Then, write an introductory paragraph that expresses it clearly and in a way that grabs the reader's interest. Next, continue your first draft. Write two or three paragraphs for your body that present the supporting details you listed in your outline. Write a concluding paragraph that restates your main idea. Write your details in the order you put them on your outline.

PRACTICE • 3

■ For Practice 2 on page 115, you created an outline for a short essay on the topic below.

TOPIC B: Explain why you believe it is important to get your GED.

Study your notes and your outline. Then, write an introductory paragraph that expresses your main idea. Now, continue writing a first draft of your short essay. Follow each step of the Drafting Checklist.

____

____

____

____

____

____

____

____

____

DRAFTING CHECKLIST

- ✔ Express your main idea in a clear and interesting way in your introductory paragraph.
- ✔ Follow your outline to present your ideas in order.
- ✔ Use connecting words to help your reader understand how ideas are related.
- ✔ In the body of your essay, write about a single idea in each paragraph.
- ✔ Conclude with a paragraph in which you restate your main idea.

► *Answers begin on page 134.*

REVISING: REVISE THE INTRODUCTION AND CONCLUSION

The revising stage is when you make changes in the first draft of your essay. First, read through your essay to make sure that you have addressed the topic. Then, take a closer look at your introductory paragraph. Can a reader tell what the topic is and what you are going to say about that topic? You may need to rewrite a sentence or change a word or phrase to improve the way you state your main idea. Next, read the body of your essay to see if you develop the main idea. Finally, compare your concluding paragraph to your revised introductory paragraph. If necessary, change the restatement of your main idea to make it stronger, clearer, and more interesting.

Take a look at how the writer improved the first draft of her short essay about her dream house.

People dream about things they want someday. I dream about a house. I've never seen the home I dream about, but I ~~know~~ imagine it is a beautiful house right next to the ~~water~~ ocean.

The house is special. It is a large (probably two- or two-and-a-half stories), old, wooden house. It was probably built in the 1800s, and it has many rooms. Since the house is filled with windows, it has plenty of light and air. I can see and hear the sea all the time. The house is filled with simple furniture and decorations, so it feels clean and open.

The location of ~~My~~ my dream house is ~~located in a very special place~~ also important. It is in a small village in Maine or Massachusetts. It sits right on the edge of large rocks that go down to the water. Below the rocks is a soft sandy beach. The house sits on nice land—enough so that I can have all the privacy I need.

If I could, I would live in my dream house right next to the water every day of the year. Right now it's really just a dream. ~~Maybe~~ However, someday ~~I'll~~ I hope to find a way to make my dream ~~come true~~ house real.

The writer made her essay stronger by revising her introductory paragraph. She replaced the word *water* with the word *ocean*. Perhaps most importantly, she realized there might be confusion about whether this was a real house she had seen in a photograph or whether it was a house she imagined. The writer made her main idea much clearer by simply changing the verb *know* to the verb *imagine*. She made similar changes in the concluding paragraph. Then, she made a few changes in wording and sentence structure in the body of the essay.

REVISING TIPS

As you revise, try to be as objective as possible. In other words, try to read the essay not as the person who wrote it but as a stranger might read it. This will help you discover places where there are confusing or incomplete ideas.

TRY IT!

Review Topic A from page 114 and Topic B from page 115 as well as your outlines and first drafts. Choose one of your first drafts to revise now. Follow the Revising Checklist on this page as you work. Be sure that you have stated your main idea clearly and simply in the introductory paragraph. Also make sure that you have summed up your main idea in an interesting way in the concluding paragraph.

WORKING Together

Practice your revising skills with another person. You and a partner can share feedback about each other's writings. Use the first draft of the short essay that you did not revise in the Try It! exercise above for this activity.

Read your partner's essay as he or she reads yours. As you read, keep in mind the purpose and audience for the writing. Follow the Revising Checklist to help you evaluate the essay. You might try reading your partner's essay as if you were completely unfamiliar with the topic. When you are ready to share comments, follow these guidelines:

1. Always present your comments positively. Share the strengths of the writing first.

2. In your suggestions, be as specific as possible. For example, suggest how you think the introduction or conclusion could be revised to make the main idea of the essay clearer or more interesting.

REVISING CHECKLIST

- ✔ Does your introductory paragraph state your main idea in a way that will interest the reader?
- ✔ Did you present one idea in each paragraph of the body of the essay?
- ✔ Does your concluding paragraph restate your main idea?
- ✔ Do your paragraphs appear in an order that will make sense to the reader?

► *Answers begin on page 134.*

EDITING: PROOFREAD AN ESSAY

Proofreading an essay is a little bit like checking your home before you leave for a vacation. You probably make sure that the windows are closed, certain appliances are unplugged, the stove and oven have been turned off, and the doors are locked. However, you don't check to see if the ceilings are sagging or if the walls need a new coat of paint.

It's the same way with proofreading. When you proofread your essay, you check to see that words are spelled correctly and that you have made no errors in punctuation or grammar. However, proofreading does not mean rewriting or restructuring your essay.

Take a look at how one writer caught several careless errors as he proofread a paragraph:

Pets can be terrific companions, (e)specially for people who live alone. For two years, I lived alone. However, I ~~weren't~~ wasn't really alone because I had a dog named Jack. I got this large brown mongrel from the animal shelter. I named him Jack after my grandfather. ~~he~~ Jack was quiet, friendly, and devoted, and he loved to go place(s) in the car with me. Jack helped me get ~~thru~~ through a ~~lonley~~ lonely period in my life after my divorce.

PROOFREADING

Read each sentence in your essay carefully. It sometimes helps to read out loud. Begin at the capital letter, and don't stop reading until you come to punctuation or a connecting word. This is a good way to help you locate run-on sentences. If you have run two sentences together incorrectly, you probably will run out of breath before you get to the end punctuation or connecting word.

PRACTICE • 4

EDITING **CHECKLIST**

- ✔ Have you used correct punctuation?
- ✔ Are there any errors in capitalization?
- ✔ Have you spelled words correctly?
- ✔ Are there any errors in grammar?

■ Edit the following paragraph. Use the Editing Checklist on this page to help you. Be especially alert to errors in spelling, punctuation, and grammar.

My freind and myself, spend about two hours yesterday changing a tire on his car. The tire was not flat but it were bald and cracked—in other words, dangerous. However, they're was put a brand, new tire in his trunk. That was fine but could we get the nuts off those rusty bolts. No we could not. Finally I found some oil that losened it up. Then we changed her quick.

SKILL CHECKUP

Write a short essay about the following topic.

TOPIC C: Describe an important day in your life. You can write about a day you started a new job, met your best friend, were visited by somebody famous, or any other day that was important to you.

Follow these steps in your writing:

1. **Think:** Brainstorm ideas. Then narrow the writing topic.
2. **Organize:** Make an outline.
3. **Draft:** Write a short essay.
4. **Revise:** Revise your introductory and concluding paragraphs. Make sure the body of your essay supports the main idea.
5. **Edit:** Proofread your essay.

► *For more work with Punctuation, Capitalization, and Spelling, see pages 224–253 of Section 3. Answers begin on page 134.*

REVIEW: Foundation Skills

Part I

Choose the one best answer for each item. Items 1 to 6 refer to the following paragraph.

(1)An atlas is a useful and enjoyable reference book. (2)With it you can go on hundreds of journeys right in your own home. (3)In one evening, you could spend time in Calcutta, Micronesia, *and* Siberia! (4)The structure of Earth's interior is shown with beautiful maps. (5)Charts and diagrams show how weather develops and moves around the globe. (6)Other maps provide information on Earth's population, natural resources, and languages. (7)An atlas is a book that lets a person learn and have fun at the same time.

1. What is the main idea of this paragraph?
(1) An atlas contains charts and diagrams.
(2) An atlas is full of maps.
(3) An atlas is both useful and enjoyable.
(4) A person can take "journeys" at home.
(5) Many languages are spoken around the world.

2. How does the writer support the main idea of the paragraph?
(1) by giving examples
(2) by comparing and contrasting
(3) by using sensory details
(4) by narrowing the topic
(5) by identifying the audience

3. What is the purpose of this paragraph?
(1) to explain or inform
(2) to persuade
(3) to entertain
(4) to describe a person, place, or event
(5) to relate a story

4. The writer originally wanted to write about a variety of reference books: atlases, encyclopedias, dictionaries, thesauruses, and indexes. However, the paragraph the writer finally wrote concerns only atlases. What did the writer do before writing the first draft?
(1) brainstormed ideas
(2) proofread
(3) used connecting words
(4) narrowed the topic
(5) chose a new topic

5. What is the paragraph's topic sentence?
(1) An atlas is a useful and enjoyable reference book.
(2) With it you can go on hundreds of journeys right in your own home.
(3) In one evening, you could spend time in Calcutta, Micronesia, *and* Siberia!
(4) The structure of Earth's interior is shown with beautiful maps.
(5) Charts and diagrams show how weather develops and moves around the globe.

6. Sentence 4 is in the passive voice: *The structure of Earth's interior is shown with beautiful maps.* Which of the following choices best rewrites the sentence in the active voice?
(1) Earth and its interior are shown with beautiful maps.
(2) Beautiful maps show the structure of Earth's interior.
(3) The surface of Earth is shown with maps.
(4) Maps show Earth.
(5) The interior of Earth is shown.

Items 7 to 11 *refer to the following letter.*

Damon,

(1)Get yourself to our house this weekend. (2)Do you read me? (3)I will not take no for an answer. (4)Honestly, I can't believe that you haven't set foot in your friends' house for nearly a year!

(5)Don't even *think* about suggesting some weekend next month. (6)Next month won't work because I plan to be busy all month—every day and every night, all the time. (7)Next month doesn't exist, so there's nothing to talk about on that score.

(8)However, I have made plans for this weekend. (9)Caroline, Herbie, you, and I will be having a barbecue, spending an afternoon watching Shawn play shortstop under the lights, and taking a swim in Long Pond. (10)Plus there will be lots of other good times that I haven't pre-arranged. (11)I trust this is an offer you won't refuse.

(12)We hope you can make it. (13)We can't wait to see your blue car pulling around the corner.

Wanda

7. What is the main idea of this message?
(1) The writer has made exciting plans for the weekend.
(2) It has been almost a year since the reader has visited the writer's home.
(3) There can be no visits during weekends the following month.
(4) The reader should visit the writer this weekend.
(5) The reader should visit the writer next weekend.

8. What is the purpose of this message?
(1) to explain or inform
(2) to persuade
(3) to entertain
(4) to describe a person, place, or event
(5) to relate a story

9. Who is the intended audience for this message?
(1) Wanda
(2) Herbie
(3) Caroline
(4) Shawn
(5) Damon

10. What type of sentence is Sentence 1?
(1) a command
(2) a question
(3) an exclamation
(4) an opinion
(5) a statement

11. Which sentence begins with a connecting word that links ideas from two separate paragraphs?
(1) Sentence 4
(2) Sentence 5
(3) Sentence 7
(4) Sentence 8
(5) Sentence 12

***Items 12 to 18** refer to the following essay.*

(1)One of my favorite places in the world is the Goodall Public Library. (2)The building stands just outside of the small town of Goodall. (3)It is a modest two-story building. (4)It seems clean and trim because of its white clapboards.

(5)Inside, the small library offers a magical world away from the real world. (6)On the first floor, there are narrow stacks of books on tall, oak bookcases. (7)A few people work or read silently at desks and in armchairs. (8)There is a quiet that seems peaceful and full of goodness. (9)The smell of old leather, yellowing paper, and dusty woolen rugs mix in the cool air. (10)There are little dark corners and nooks by the windows where a person can get comfortable and flip through a book.

(11)In the upstairs part of the library, a children's room has small furniture and hundreds of books for kids. (12)While my child turns the pages of a picture book, I love to sit and listen to the sound of rain tap against the window and glance at a newspaper or magazine.

(13)The library in Goodall is where I go when I want to read, relax, and dream.

12. What is the main idea of this essay?
(1) The building is handsome physically.
(2) Goodall Public Library is a favorite place of the writer's.
(3) The writer appreciates the quiet in the library.
(4) The library has an impressive stock of books.
(5) The variety of smells pleases the writer.

13. What is the purpose of this essay?
(1) to explain the Goodall Library's borrowing system
(2) to persuade readers to read books
(3) to tell a story about the Goodall Library
(4) to describe the Goodall Library
(5) to persuade the audience to take advantage of public libraries

14. How does the writer organize the essay?
(1) by comparing and contrasting two environments
(2) by describing the cause-and-effect relationship of events
(3) by describing sensory reactions, beginning with sight
(4) by listing details in their order of importance
(5) by describing the outside, the first floor, and the second floor of the library

15. How does the writer support the main idea?
(1) by using facts, reasons, and examples
(2) with sensory details
(3) by brainstorming
(4) by asking "5 W and H" questions
(5) by including the topic sentence in an introductory paragraph

16. Which of the following sentences does *not* contain any sensory details?
(1) It seems clean and trim because of its white clapboards.
(2) On the first floor, there are narrow stacks of books on tall, oak bookcases.
(3) One of my favorite places in the world is the Goodall Public Library.
(4) A few people work or read silently at desks and in armchairs.
(5) The smell of old leather, yellowing paper, and dusty woolen rugs mix in the cool air.

17. Sentence 12: While my child turns the pages of a picture book, I love to sit and listen to the sound of rain tap against the window and glance at a newspaper or magazine.

Which sense or senses does the writer use to describe the details in this sentence?
(1) sight and hearing
(2) sight and touch
(3) touch and hearing
(4) hearing
(5) sight, hearing, and touch

18. Which paragraph or paragraphs make up the body of the essay?
(1) paragraphs one and two
(2) paragraph two
(3) paragraphs two and three
(4) paragraphs two, three, and four
(5) paragraphs one, two, three, and four

Items 19 to 20 *refer to the following paragraph.*

(1)The Lugo family took a long, winding path to Philadelphia. (2)Until 1987, they lived in San Juan, Puerto Rico. (3)However, neither Vincente nor Iris Lugo was able to find and keep a good job. (4)So, they emigrated to Florida and lived in several small cities during 1987 and 1988. (5)Then they moved to the Bushwick neighborhood in Brooklyn, New York. (6)Finally, in 1994, Iris Lugo was offered a job in Philadelphia. (7)The pay was good, and the company offered health insurance. (8)The Lugos have become some of Philadelphia's newest residents.

19. What is the purpose of this paragraph?
(1) to persuade the reader to take some action
(2) to describe a person, place, or thing
(3) to relate a narrative
(4) to explain an idea
(5) to amuse the reader

20. Which of the following sentences does *not* contain a word that connects two sentences or ideas?
(1) Sentence 3
(2) Sentence 4
(3) Sentence 5
(4) Sentence 7
(5) Sentence 8

► *Answers begin on page 135.*

Part II

Read the following essay topic. Take some time to plan what you want to say. Then draft, revise, and edit your essay.

TOPIC: If you could plan your future, what would it be like? Do you have any hopes and dreams for the future? Describe where you would like your life to go from here.

► *Answers begin on page 135.*

FOUNDATION SKILL 1

Practice 1, page 23

1. Brainstorming is thinking intensely about a topic and then jotting down ideas.
2. It is useful because it helps you to be creative and to think of ideas without worrying about things like spelling, punctuation, and grammar.

Practice 2, page 25

Brainstorming lists will vary. Here is a sample list:

<u>My Friend Danita</u>

<u>PERSONALITY</u>:

friendly, warm, smart, funny, sometimes too quiet

<u>APPEARANCE</u>:

short, a little overweight, light skin, smiles a lot, green eyes

<u>MEMORIES</u>:

the time we went to the beach together, our graduation, her awful haircut in 4th grade

Practice 3, page 27

Sentences will vary. Here is a sample sentence: My friend Danita is a friendly, smart, and funny person.

Working Together, page 29

Revisions will vary. Be sure you use the Revising Checklist.

Practice 4, page 31

Antonio and Rolanda wanted to hear music at a club last night. They tried the West End Lounge, but ~~the West End Lounge~~ *it* was closed ~~.~~ *for renovations* ~~For Renovations~~. ~~rolanda~~ *Rolanda* suggested the Harborside Club. She said that ~~hers~~ *her* friend Herb loves the atmosphere there. So, Rolanda and Antonio went there and ~~listen~~ *listened* to a salsa band. They ~~did~~ danced until 4:00 A.M.

Skill Checkup, page 31

Sentences will vary. Here are some sample sentences:

I take my responsibility to study very seriously.

It's important to learn.

The only way to learn is by studying and doing my work.

FOUNDATION SKILL 2

Practice 1, page 33

1. She is brainstorming a list of ideas for the topic: *Describe the things in life that are important to you.*
2. her cat

Practice 2, page 35

Clustered lists will vary. Here is a sample list:

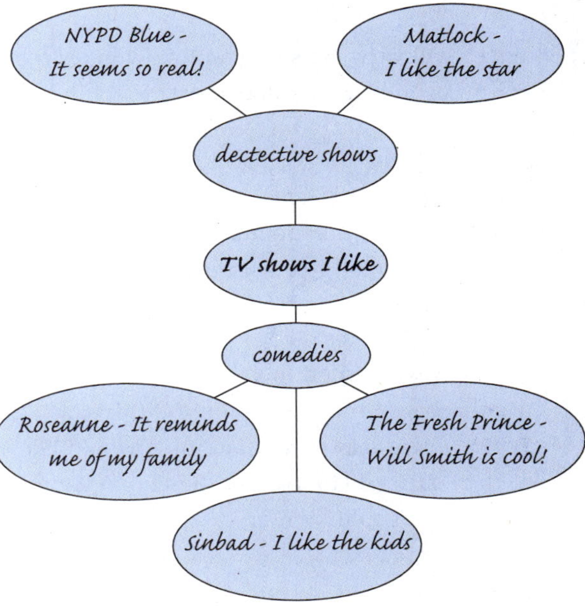

Practice 3, page 37

Sentences will vary. Here are some sample sentences:

> I like many different kinds of TV shows. I like the detective shows *NYPD Blue* and *Matlock*. Sitcoms are my favorite, however. *Roseanne* is great. *The Fresh Prince* and *Sinbad* are hysterical.

Working Together, page 39

Revisions will vary. Be sure you correct any sentence fragments.

Practice 4, page 41

> What is the most important issue of the 1990s? In my opinion, it is health care. What could be more important than health care? Finally, politicians are paying attention to this topic. Who knows how long that will last? I do know this country needs better health care. The cost of a night in the hospital is outrageous!

Skill Checkup, page 41

Sentences will vary. Be sure you followed each of the five steps in your writing. Here are two samples:

> I would like to visit Jamaica. I would like to go there because my grandmother came from Kingston. She still has a sister there. I would like to meet her someday.

> I have always wanted to visit New York City. I always see it in movies and on TV. It looks exciting! It is also very beautiful. I would like to see the Statue of Liberty and the Empire State Building. It would be fun!

FOUNDATION SKILL 3

Practice 1, page 43

Questions will vary. Here are some sample questions:

1. What did my grandmother do?
2. Where did she grow up?
3. When was she born?

Practice 2, page 45

Ideas, questions, and answers will vary. Here are some sample questions and answers:

> What does *loyalty* mean to me? always sticking by a friend
>
> When has my loyalty been questioned?
> when Nina was going through a hard time
>
> How can you show loyalty?
> by always being there to listen
>
> Why is loyalty important?
> friends can feel secure

Practice 3, page 47

Journal entries will vary. Here is a sample:

> Loyalty is important to me. It means sticking by friends, even when you think they are doing wrong. I learned this last year when Nina was arrested for robbery. I hurt her by not being loyal, and when she was acquitted she was angry with me. Now I know that loyalty means standing by your friends no matter what happens.

Working Together, page 49

Revisions will vary. Be sure you use the Revising Checklist.

Practice 4, page 51

What I like about living in Greenville is the fact that ~~she~~ *it* is in the mountains. I like to go hiking. and camping. I also enjoy the cool ~~whether~~ *weather* in summer. My friend Luis told me ~~she~~ *he* would never think of living anywhere else. I agree. I think I might live in ~~greenville~~ *Greenville* forever.

Skill Checkup, page 51

Journal entries will vary. Be sure you followed each of the five steps in your writing. Here is a sample:

Fall is my favorite season. It is my favorite season because I really like to watch the leaves on the trees change color. I also like the cooler weather after the hot summer. I take long walks in the park with Rashad. This is why fall is my favorite season.

FOUNDATION SKILL 4

Practice 1, page 53

1. Herb's purpose is to tell Orlando that he can't drive to the game on Sunday because his car has a flat tire.
2. Orlando is his audience.
3. Herb's purpose is to ask his wife if she can get the flat tire fixed.
4. Orlando's purpose would be to ask Tia if she can drive to the game.
5. Tia would be Orlando's audience.

Practice 2, page 55

Part A

1. The purpose is to explain that you will be late.
2. Your audience is your coworker.

Part B

Word webs will vary. Here is a sample word web:

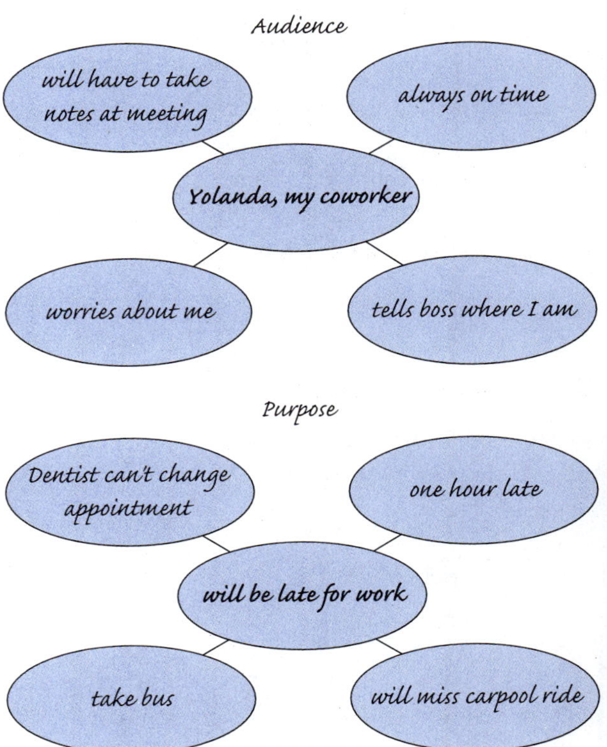

Practice 3, page 57

Messages will vary. Here is an example:

Yolanda,

I have a dentist appointment at 1:00 P.M. today, so I will be late for the 2:00 meeting. I called my dentist's office, but they couldn't reschedule me. I will come as soon as I am finished.

Barry

Working Together, page 59

Revisions will vary. Be sure the purpose and audience are clear.

Practice 4, page 61

In all the years I've worked there, I have never ~~Never~~ been late for work without a good reason. The reason each time ~~times~~ was that my son was home sick from school. On the other hand, my friends and coworkers Bobbie, Eduardo, and Quinn have been late at ~~At~~ least a dozen times, maybe a few more. They drive as a group. So if ~~If~~ one of them is late then of them are ~~they~~ all ~~is~~ late.

Skill Checkup, page 61

Messages will vary. Be sure you followed each of the five steps in your writing. Here is a sample message:

Dear Gabriel,

I'm glad you can finally see my new apartment. You'll probably take your car straight from work. Here is how to drive to my place from your shop. First, get on the parkway and stay in the right lane. Then, take the 4th St. exit and make a left onto Marvis Boulevard. Continue for two blocks until you see number 457, a red brick building. That's where I live. Ring buzzer 4-E, and I'll come down.

See you soon,

Otis

FOUNDATION SKILL 5

Practice 1, page 63

1. She writes about her previous job in order to prove that she is responsible.
2. All the sentences have to do with the idea that the writer is a responsible employee.
3. She uses details about attendance, a swimming program, a promotion, holding the keys to buildings, and how her bosses treated her.
4. The sentences express the same idea, although the last sentence is more detailed about how responsible the writer is.

Practice 2, page 65

Idea maps will vary. Here is a sample map:

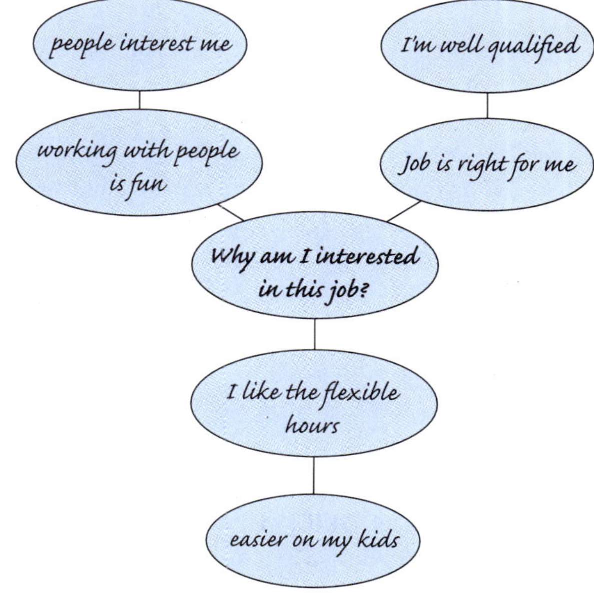

Practice 3, page 67

Paragraphs will vary. Here is a sample paragraph:

I am interested in this job because it really suits my needs. I need a job with flexible working hours, which this one has. I also like jobs where I get to work with people, and this job will give me that opportunity. Finally, I think I am well qualified for this job, so I am interested in it because it seems like the perfect match.

Working Together, page 69

Revisions will vary. Be sure you use the Revising Checklist.

Practice 4, page 71

> My friend Maria goes hiking *. This* ~~this~~ summer she is going to northern Maine*.* ~~there~~ *There* are fantastic wilderness areas north of Moosehead ~~lake~~ *Lake*. Maria is ~~preety~~ *pretty* excited*.* ~~she~~ *She* wanted to go canoeing on the Silver ~~river~~ *River* in ~~Arkansaw,~~ *Arkansas.* ~~however~~ *However,* that river dries up in the summer.

Skill Checkup, page 71

Paragraphs will vary. Be sure you followed each of the five steps in your writing. Here is a sample paragraph:

> My ideal job would be to manage the pet store where I work. I would like to be manager because I want the responsibility. I am very good with the customers, and I like the animals. I know exactly what people want for their pets. My boss thinks I am ready, too.

FOUNDATION SKILL 6

Practice 1, page 73

1. a
2. d, b, a, c
3. You may have listed any of the following details: walking to train station after work; near State Street; a lot of trucks and huge trailers parked along the sidewalk; police blocked traffic; people setting up cameras; shooting a movie; someone tapped me on the shoulder; carry bags, pretend I was window-shopping, drop bags; Harrison Ford

Practice 2, page 75

Part A

1. Main ideas will vary around the theme of *learning a lesson.*
2. Details will vary.

Part B

Timelines will vary.

Practice 3, page 77

1. Main ideas will vary around the theme of *learning a lesson.*
2. Topic sentences will vary. Here is a sample:

   When I accused my best friend of lying, I learned that jumping to conclusions can get you in trouble.

Working Together, page 79

Revisions will vary. Be sure you use the Revising Checklist.

Practice 4, page 81

> Every time I call my mother on the phone, we have the same conversation. First, we ~~discussed~~ *discuss* my job. Then she ~~told~~ *tells* me what's going on in her life. Next, we discuss general things like the ~~whether~~ *weather* and the news. But there comes a time in every conversation ~~When~~ *when* my mother ~~asked~~ *asks* if I'm dating anyone special. I roll my eyes*,* make a joke*,* and quickly ~~ended~~ *end* the conversation.

Skill Checkup, page 81

Personal narratives will vary. Be sure you followed each of the five steps in your writing.

FOUNDATION SKILL 7

Practice 1, page 83

1. The purpose is to complain because Jeffries buses sometimes leave ahead of schedule. The audience is an employee of the Jeffries Bus Company.
2. The main idea is that Jeffries buses leave ahead of schedule and inconvenience passengers.

Practice 2, page 85

Part A

1. Purpose and audience will vary. The purpose could be to complain about some kind of defective merchandise. The audience is someone at the company that manufactures the merchandise.
2. Details will vary. Here is a sample list:

   bought vacuum cleaner for $109.95

   upright

   rug attachment

   plugged it in—it made a burning smell

   doesn't pick up dirt

   handle doesn't lock

   want a new one

Part B

Charts will vary. Here is a sample chart:

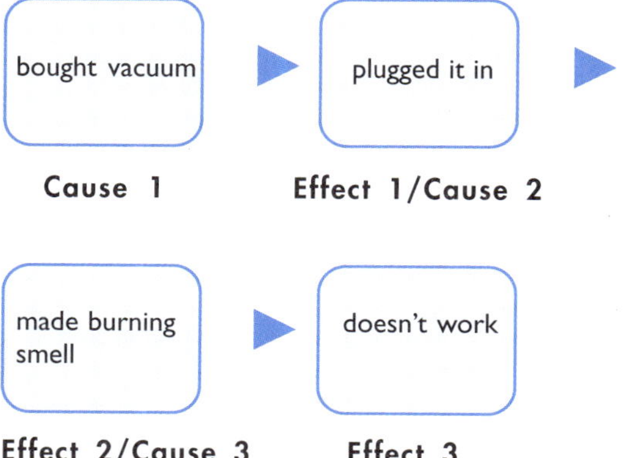

Practice 3, page 87

Letters will vary. Here is a sample letter:

Dear Clean-O-Vac,

I recently bought one of your upright vacuum cleaners for $109.95. When I brought it home and plugged it in, it made a horrible burning smell. It doesn't pick up any dirt, and the handle doesn't lock, too.

I am writing to you to ask for a new vacuum cleaner or a full refund.

Working Together, page 89

Revisions will vary. Be sure the purpose and audience are clear.

Practice 4, page 91

I have been a ~~A~~ customer of yours for several years*, and* I am not happy to be treated rudely. Yet, this is what happened yesterday when I got my car from the repair shop. *The shop manager* ~~My wife was~~ insulted *my wife* ~~by the shop manager. And~~ *and* I was told to watch my attitude when I asked him *for an apology* ~~to apologize to her~~. I would like a response from you, or I'll go somewhere else for repairs.

Skill Checkup, page 91

Letters will vary. Be sure you followed each of the five steps in your writing.

FOUNDATION SKILL 8

Practice 1, page 93

1. The purpose is to describe a person.
2. The audience is people who have never met Mr. Johnson.

3. Details include the following: short, heavy-set man about sixty years old with smooth jowls and the energy of a young puppy, a big, booming voice that carries a tangy Boston accent, smells like fresh-baked bread, hear his ancient pick-up truck rumbling, he greets each neighbor, "Howdy there chief," jump up from the table like a rabbit, run into the kitchen, and compliment the cook, and strong, callused hands.

4. Sensory details include the following: firm handshake with his strong, callused hands (touch), truck rumbling and booming voice (hearing), fresh-baked bread (smell), and smooth jowls (sight).

Practice 2, page 95

1. Subject: my cousin Andrea, a fire fighter

2. Charts will vary. Here is a sample chart:

SIGHT	5'5", short black hair, big eyes, carries firefighter equipment
HEARING	polite, soft voice, sounds confident, calm
TOUCH	strong, when she lifts me off the ground I feel like a feather
TASTE	I always drink orange soda with her at the firehouse
SMELL	smoky, like dust and coal sometimes

3. 5'5" but strong, with a confident voice

Practice 3, page 97

Descriptions will vary. Here is a sample description:

> The person I admire most is my cousin Andrea, a firefighter. Although her job is dangerous, she's never scared or upset. She speaks in a quiet but confident voice all the time. The other fire-fighters say she's this way even inside a burning house. She's only 5'5" with short black hair and looks slight even with her hat, boots, and big gray firefighting suit. However, she's strong enough to lift me off the ground like a feather when she greets me. After returning from an alarm, she relaxes in the firehouse and drinks a lot of orange soda. I get scared just smelling the smoke on her uniform from the last fire. I admire her because she's always calm and brave.

Working Together, page 99

Revisions will vary. Be sure you use the Revising Checklist.

Practice 4, page 101

> My great uncle started a ~~successfully~~ *successful* business in our town. He ran it ~~good~~ *well*, *and* it grew ~~fast~~ *quickly* for the first ten years. He was a ~~stubbornly~~ *stubborn* and harsh man, ~~Who~~ *who* always treated people ~~fair~~ *fairly*. He also could be ~~hardly~~ *hard* to get ~~a long~~ *along* with. He had a loud voice, and he used it in ~~mightily~~ *mighty* arguments with my father. He was a short man who drove his cars fast. My father always respected him.

Skill Checkup, page 101

Descriptions will vary. Be sure you followed each of the five steps in your writing.

FOUNDATION SKILL 9

Practice 1, page 103

1. The purpose is to persuade the reader to agree with the writer's opinion. The audience is the residents of a particular city who subscribe to cable television.

2. A recent rate increase in cable television service is unfair.

3. The writer discusses a series of rate increases and the cable television company's monopoly.

4. He saved his strongest argument (about a series of rate increases) for last.

Practice 2, page 105

Comparison/contrast charts will vary. Be sure that the similarities and differences are clear.

Practice 3, page 107

Letters will vary. Be sure you have a strong opening sentence.

Working Together, page 109

Revisions will vary. Be sure you use the Revising Checklist.

Practice 4, page 111

1. Small towns in this country ~~has~~ *have* to struggle to keep ~~its~~ *their* downtowns alive.
2. According to some people, many southern cities ~~is~~ *are* growing almost too ~~quick~~ *quickly*.
3. ~~Interesting~~ *It is interesting* to live in ~~sevral~~ *several* different places during your life.
4. However, experts ~~says~~ *say* that ~~moveing~~ *moving* is one of the five most stressful events in a ~~persons'~~ *person's* life.
5. Do you ~~knows~~ *know* any person who ~~have~~ *has* lived in the same place his or her whole life?

Skill Checkup, page 111

Letters will vary. Be sure you followed each of the five steps in your writing.

FOUNDATION SKILL 10

Practice 1, page 113

1. The purpose of the essay is to persuade readers to agree with the view that laws restricting smoking are bad. The audience is other people—both smokers and nonsmokers.
2. The main idea is that legislation restricting smoking is a bad idea.
3. The writer's reasons include a strong belief in personal liberty and privacy, as well as the belief that a banned substance is more desirable to young people.
4. The writer began with an introductory paragraph. Then he supported his main idea with two reasons, which he presented in two separate paragraphs. He ended his essay with a concluding paragraph.

Practice 2, page 115

Outlines will vary. However, they should have clear, separate sections for introduction, supporting paragraphs (body), and conclusion.

Practice 3, page 117

Essays will vary. Check your draft using the Drafting Checklist.

Working Together, page 119

Revisions will vary. Be sure you use the Revising Checklist.

Practice 4, page 121

My ~~freind~~ *friend* and ~~myself~~ *I* ~~spend~~ *spent* about two hours yesterday changing a tire on his car. The tire was not flat*,* but it ~~were~~ *was* bald and cracked—in other words, dangerous. However, ~~they're~~ *there* was ~~put~~ a brand new tire in his trunk. That was fine*,* but could we get the nuts off those rusty bolts*?* No*,* we could not. Finally I found some oil that ~~losened~~ *loosened* it up. Then we changed ~~her~~ *the tire* ~~quick~~ *quickly*.

Skill Checkup, page 121

Essays will vary. Be sure you follow each of the five steps in your writing.

REVIEW: FOUNDATION SKILLS

Part I, pages 122–125

1. (3) (Comprehension) The ideas in Choices (1), (2), and (4) are supporting ideas. Choice (5) doesn't have anything to do with the paragraph.

2. (1) (Analysis) Choices (2), (3), (4), and (5) are techniques that this writer did not use.

3. (1) (Comprehension) Since the writer uses no techniques to persuade the reader to take any action, Choice (2) is not correct. Although some readers might be interested in the paragraph, it is not the purpose of the writer to entertain, as indicated by Choice (3). Choices (4) and (5) don't apply to this paragraph at all.

4. (4) (Analysis) Choice (1) is not an activity that limits a topic. Choice (2) is a task performed after a draft has been written. Choice (3) is incorrect because a writer uses connecting words as he or she drafts, not beforehand. Choice (5) is incorrect because the topic of atlases was not brand new.

5. (5) (Analysis) Choices (1), (3), and (4) contain examples that support the main idea. Choice (2) expresses the main idea, but the sentence doesn't appear in the paragraph.

6. (2) (Application) Choices (1), (3), and (5) remain in the passive voice. Although Choice (4) is in the active voice, it contains only part of the information listed in the sentence.

7. (4) (Comprehension) The ideas in Choices (1), (2), and (3) are supporting ideas. Choice (5) is inaccurate.

8. (2) (Comprehension) Choices (1), (4), and (5) are not included in the letter. Choice (3) is not the main purpose of the letter.

9. (5) (Comprehension) Choices (1), (2), (3), and (4) are mentioned in the message but do not make up its audience.

10. (1) (Analysis) Choices (2), (3), and (5) are incorrect. Choice (4) is not a type of sentence.

11. (4) (Analysis) Choice (1), *Honestly*, Choice (2), *Don't*, and Choice (5), *We*, are not connecting words. Choice (3), *Next*, is not used as a connecting word in this sentence.

12. (2) (Comprehension) Choices (1), (3), and (5) contain supporting ideas. Choice (4) is never mentioned by the writer.

13. (4) (Comprehension) Choice (1) is not mentioned in the essay. Choices (2) and (5) are incorrect because this is not a persuasive essay. Choice (3) is incorrect because no story is included in the essay.

14. (5) (Analysis) The essay does not include comparisons or contrasts, as suggested by Choice (1), or cause-and-effect statements, as offered by Choice (2). Choice (3) is incorrect because references to senses are scattered throughout the essay. Choice (4) is incorrect because the importance of details is not discussed.

15. (2) (Analysis) The essay does not contain facts and reasons, Choice (1), as much as it does impressions of a place. Choice (3) may have been used during prewriting, but it does not support the main idea. Choices (4) and (5) are not methods for supporting a main idea.

16. (3) (Analysis) Choices (1) and (2) contain sight details. Choice (4) contains sound and sight details. Choice (5) contains smell, sight, and touch details.

17. (5) (Analysis) Choices (1), (2), (3), and (4) do not include all the forms of details found in the sentence.

18. (3) (Analysis) Choices (1), (4), and (5) include the introductory and concluding paragraphs; Choice (2) does not include the entire body of the essay.

19. (3) (Comprehension) Choices (1), (2), and (4) are never attempted by the writer. There is no evidence to support Choice (5).

20. (5) (Analysis) In Choice (1), However connects Sentences 2 and 3. In Choice (2), So connects Sentences 3 and 4. In Choice (3), Then connects Sentences 4 and 5. In Choice (4), and connects the two ideas in Sentences 6 and 7.

Part II, page 126

Essays will vary. Make sure you follow the five steps for good writing: think, organize, draft, revise, and edit.

FOUNDATION SKILLS REVIEW REFERRAL CHART

When you have completed the Foundation Skills Review, check your answers against the Answers and Explanations beginning on page 135. On the chart below, circle the items you answered correctly. Then, in the last column on the chart, list the total number of items you answered correctly.

SECTION 2: FOUNDATION SKILLS		PART I ITEMS	NUMBER OF ITEMS CORRECT
Foundation Skill 1:	Beginning to Write (pp. 22–31)	14	
Foundation Skill 2:	Writing Sentences (pp. 32–41)	10, 20	
Foundation Skill 3:	Journal Writing (pp. 42–51)		
Foundation Skill 4:	Identifying Purpose and Audience (pp. 52–61)	3, 9, 11, 13	
Foundation Skill 5:	Writing a Paragraph (pp. 62–71)	1, 2, 5, 7, 12	
Foundation Skill 6:	Writing to Narrate (pp. 72–81)	19	
Foundation Skill 7:	Writing to Explain (pp. 82–91)	6, 15	
Foundation Skill 8:	Writing to Describe (pp. 92–101)	16, 17	
Foundation Skill 9:	Writing to Persuade (pp. 102–111)	8	
Foundation Skill 10:	Writing an Essay (pp. 112–121)	4, 18	

TOTAL: ____ of 20

Each item in Part I of the Review is related to a specific skill. The essay you write in Part II uses many of these skills. Do you notice any patterns in the items you did not circle? Try to identify areas where you need more practice. Then review those Foundation Skills before moving on to Section 3 of this book.

Writing Skills Lessons

The three units of Writing Skills lessons in Section 3 cover the same content areas as Part I of the GED Writing Skills Test. Part I of the test is almost evenly divided among items on usage, sentence structure, and mechanics. In Part II, you will use your skills to write an essay.

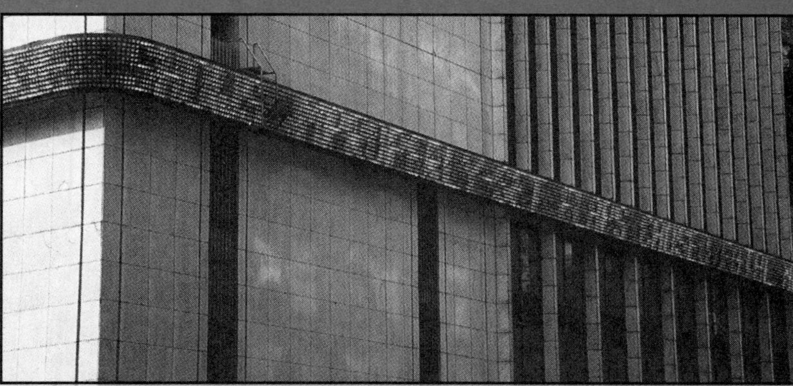

UNIT 1: Learning proper usage helps you communicate clearly.

UNIT 2: Good sentences, like buildings, are constructed with precision.

UNIT 3: The rules of mechanics are like gears that work together to make a machine run smoothly.

UNIT 1

Usage

LESSON 1

Nouns

Nouns are words that name people, places, things, and ideas. You probably think of nouns as words that name real objects you can see, hear, touch, smell, and taste. Many nouns fit this description perfectly. They are called *concrete nouns.* However, other nouns, called *abstract nouns,* are used to name things that can't be recognized by the senses. Here are some examples of concrete nouns and abstract nouns:

concrete nouns: skirt, leaf, salt, smoke, corner, scream

abstract nouns: politeness, time, life, joy, volume, beauty

SINGULAR AND PLURAL NOUNS

Most nouns can be *singular* or *plural,* depending on whether they represent *one* person, place, or thing, or *more than one.* Here are some basic rules to help you form plural nouns from singular ones.

RULES FOR FORMING PLURAL NOUNS

For most nouns, you form the plural by adding the letter *-s* to the singular form.

dog	dogs
flavor	flavors

When a noun ends in a consonant followed by a *y*, you form the plural by changing the *y* to an *i* and adding *-es*.

copy	copies
democracy	democracies

When a noun ends in a vowel followed by a *y*, you form the plural by adding the letter *-s*.

relay	relays
toy	toys

For nouns that end in the letters *ch, sh, s,* or *x*, you form the plural by adding the letters *-es* to the singular form.

beach	beaches
bush	bushes
gas	gases
process	processes
tax	taxes

For many nouns that end in the letters *f* or *fe*, you form the plural by changing the *f* to a *v* and adding *-es*.

loaf	loaves
wife	wives

Since there are exceptions to these rules, you should check a dictionary if you are not certain about how to spell a plural noun. Here are some commonly used nouns that don't follow the rules listed above:

singular:	woman	foot	child	tooth
plural:	women	feet	children	teeth

Sentences often contain both singular and plural nouns. Look at these examples:

Three cars were parked behind the house.

The old couch on the sidewalk was pelted by raindrops.

There was a feeling of hope in the cities.

The first sentence contains the plural noun *cars* and the singular noun *house*. In the second sentence, *couch* and *sidewalk* are both singular. The noun *raindrops* is plural. In the third sentence, *feeling* and *hope* are singular abstract nouns. The concrete noun, *cities*, is plural.

PRACTICE • 1

► **Part A** For each of the singular nouns listed below, write the plural form in the space provided.

1. idea ________________ **5.** leaf ________________

2. wish ________________ **6.** bottom ________________

3. city ________________ **7.** box ________________

4. pencil ________________ **8.** boy ________________

► **Part B** The following paragraph contains both singular and plural nouns. Underline all the nouns. Then, on a separate sheet of paper, write the plural forms of the singular nouns and the singular forms of the plural nouns. Use a dictionary if necessary.

The room was full of furniture. There were chairs, bookcases, a table, a bench, a bureau, and a couch that had a bed inside. In the middle of the floor, there were two wooden boxes and an old guitar. This dark room was filled with an atmosphere of gloom and mystery.

► *Answers begin on page 259.*

POSSESSIVE NOUNS

Nouns are often used to show ownership. To do this, you use the possessive form of a noun. To form the *possessive of a singular noun*, add an apostrophe and an *s* to the singular form. To form the *possessive of a plural noun*, add an apostrophe to the plural form. Take a look at the following examples of possessive nouns:

singular possessive: the dentist's office
plural possessive: many dentists' offices

singular possessive: the dog's bone
plural possessive: the dogs' bones

singular possessive: a cat's tail
plural possessive: three cats' tails

Nouns with *irregular plural forms* that do not end in *s*, such as *feet* or *children*, don't follow the above rule for forming the plural possessive. You form the plural possessive of these nouns in the same way you do the singular possessive. Add an apostrophe and an *s*. Here are possessives of some common irregular nouns:

singular possessive: this woman's tools
plural possessive: these women's tools

singular possessive: my child's bicycle
plural possessive: these children's bicycles

singular possessive: a man's hat
plural possessive: the men's hats

All the nouns discussed so far have been *common nouns*. However, you also will use many *proper nouns*. Common nouns are general words. Proper nouns specify a particular person, place, thing, or idea. *Country*, for example, is a common noun. *Mexico*, however, is a proper noun because it specifies a particular country. Below are some more examples that show the difference between common and proper nouns:

common noun: woman
proper noun: Alma

common noun: war
proper noun: Vietnam War

common noun: town
proper noun: Salem

common noun: religion
proper noun: Islam

Proper nouns are often used in their possessive form. For instance, you would use the possessive form of *Rhonda* (a singular proper noun) in the sentence *I forgot to ask if I could borrow Rhonda's hip-hop tape.* Here are other examples of the possessive forms of proper nouns:

proper noun: Detroit
possessive proper noun: Detroit's skyline

proper noun: President Clinton
possessive proper noun: President Clinton's policy

proper noun: the Maine Turnpike
possessive proper noun: the Maine Turnpike's pavement

proper noun: the Joneses
possessive proper noun: the Joneses' backyard

PRACTICE • 2

► **Part A** For each of the nouns listed below, write the possessive form in the space provided.

1. windows ______________

2. goose ______________

3. witch ______________

4. stories ______________

5. Thomas ______________

6. mouse ______________

7. senator ______________

8. Zaire ______________

► **Part B** The following paragraph contains several errors in the form of possessive nouns. First, underline all the nouns. Next, correct any errors. Write your correction in the space just above the noun.

Reading newspapers is one of the best methods I know to become familiar with a cities "personality." A good newspapers readers can detect the community's mood and atmosphere in the stories' and photographs'. With any luck, the paper keeps the citys' good side and its bad side in some kind of balance.

► *Answers begin on page 259.*

FOCUS CAPITALIZATION: PROPER NOUNS

A proper noun—one that specifies a *particular* person, place, thing, or idea—requires capitalization. Some proper nouns contain more than one word. In these cases, all the important words must be capitalized. Small words like *the, and, of,* and *for* do not need capitalization. Here are examples of several types of proper nouns:

Names of People and the Titles of Individuals: David Robinson, Crazy Horse, President Mitterand, Justice Ruth Bader Ginsberg

Names of Places: Mexico, Cape Ann, the Grand Canyon

Names of Ethnic Groups, Nationalities, Languages, and Religions: Native Americans, Koreans, Zulu, Irish, Hebrew, Muslim, Catholics

Names of Organizations, Institutions, and Products: the United Nations, Harvard University, Yamaha, Cool Whip™

Names of Historical Events, Holidays, Dates, and Days of the Week: the Gulf War, Memorial Day, August 12, Monday

EDITING PRACTICE

■ The paragraph below contains errors in the use of nouns. Edit the paragraph by crossing out the incorrect nouns and rewriting them correctly. The first one is done for you.

Josie enrolled in a ~~Community~~ *community* College in Toledo and started school in september. She is taking three courses' and is doing well in all of them. One of Josies' best qualitys is her eagerness. She says her education will be like an insurance's policy for her familys future.

CONNECTIONS

Historical documents often contain specific dates, places, and official titles. The Cultures theme in **CONNECTIONS**, pages C6–C7, includes an excerpt from the Emancipation Proclamation. Read the excerpt, and look for the capitalized proper nouns. List the proper nouns, and identify what each proper noun specifies—person, place, thing, or idea. For example, *Chicago*: place.

▶ *Answers begin on page 259.*

PRE-GED PRACTICE

*Choose the **one best answer** for each item.*
***Items 1 to 5** refer to the following passage.*

(1)Athletes bodies work like finely tuned machines. (2)Most Basketball Players have long, lean bodies with strong muscles and very little fat. (3)Gymnast's have small, muscular frames with very little fat as well. (4)Mens who play football are often beefier than other athletes. (5)However, not many peoples would get up the nerve to say a word like *beefy* to football players.

1. Sentence 1: Athletes bodies work like finely tuned machines.

Which is the best way to rewrite the underlined portion of this sentence? If you think the original is the best way, choose (1).

(1) Athletes bodies work
(2) Athletes' bodys work
(3) Athlete's bodies work
(4) Athletes' bodies work
(5) Athletes' body's work

2. Sentence 2: Most Basketball Players have long, lean bodies with strong muscles and very little fat.

Which is the best way to rewrite the underlined portion of this sentence? If you think the original is the best way, choose (1).

(1) Basketball Players have long, lean bodies
(2) Basketball Players' have long, lean bodies
(3) basketball players have long, lean bodies
(4) basketball Players have long, lean bodys
(5) basketball Players' have long, lean bodies

3. Sentence 3: Gymnast's have small, muscular frames with very little fat as well.

What correction should be made to this sentence?

(1) change *Gymnast's* to *Gymnasts'*
(2) change *Gymnast's* to *Gymnasts*
(3) change *frames* to *frame*
(4) change *frames to frame's*
(5) change *fat to fats*

4. Sentence 4: Mens who play football are often beefier than other athletes.

What correction should be made to this sentence?

(1) change *Mens* to *Men*
(2) change *Mens* to *Mens'*
(3) change *Mens* to *Men's*
(4) change *athletes* to *athlete*
(5) change *athletes* to *athlete's*

5. Sentence 5: However, not many peoples would get up the nerve to say a word like *beefy* to football players.

What correction should be made to this sentence?

(1) change *peoples* to *people's*
(2) change *peoples* to *peoples'*
(3) change *peoples* to *people*
(4) change *players* to *player*
(5) change *players* to *player's*

► *Answers begin on page 259.*

LESSON 2

Pronouns

Anytime we say *her* or *him,* we are using a *pronoun*. A pronoun is a word that takes the place of or refers to a noun. We use pronouns to make our language clearer and less repetitious.

SUBJECT AND OBJECT PRONOUNS

antecedent: the word to which a pronoun refers

Pronouns can be used as subjects. They also can be used to show possession. Every pronoun has an antecedent. Here are two sentences with the pronouns and antecedents underlined.

The <u>drivers</u> walked toward <u>their</u> cars.

Since <u>he</u> was born, my <u>son</u> has been healthy and alert.

Notice that sometimes the pronoun comes before the antecedent, as in the second sentence. The antecedent does not always appear in the same sentence as its pronoun, either. When you write, it is especially important to avoid any confusion about a pronoun's antecedent.

SUBJECT PRONOUNS

A pronoun that performs the action in an action sentence is the *subject*. The sentences below contain subject pronouns:

<u>They</u> lost their directions to the party.

<u>He</u> and <u>I</u> made plans to go together in one car.

In the first sentence, the action verb is *lost*. The subject pronoun *they* performs this action. In the second sentence, the action verb is *made*. The subject pronouns *he* and *I* perform this action. The pronouns *he* and *I* form a *compound subject*, which is two or more subjects put together.

OBJECT PRONOUNS

A pronoun that receives the action of a verb is the object. The sentences below contain object pronouns.

The dog bit <u>her</u> on the foot.

When Cena and Eddie arrived, Uncle Kenny gave <u>them</u> a big hug.

In the first sentence, the action verb is *bit*. The noun *dog* performs the action, and the object pronoun *her* receives it. In the second sentence, the action verb is *gave*, the noun *Uncle Kenny* performs that action, and the object pronoun *them* receives it.

Object pronouns are often used after prepositions. Look at the sentences below:

prepositions: words like *for*, *after*, *above*, or *with* that show a relationship

Jackie always feels comfortable with us.

Carlos sits between you and me.

In the first sentence, the object pronoun *us* follows the preposition *with*. In the second sentence, the object pronouns *you* and *me* follow the preposition *between*.

Here is a chart that shows subject pronouns and object pronouns. If a pronoun is performing an action, it is a subject. If it's receiving an action or used after a preposition, the pronoun is an object.

SUBJECT PRONOUNS		OBJECT PRONOUNS	
I	we	me	us
you	you	you	you
he, she, it	they	him, her, it	them

PRACTICE • 1

▶ **Part A** In the sentences below, underline the pronouns and circle their antecedents. Then draw an arrow from each pronoun to its antecedent.

1. Kathy was shocked because she didn't expect to win the award.
2. Will folded the flag until it fit into the small box.
3. Though the tomcat finds mice, he never manages to kill them.

▶ **Part B** In the following sentences, you will find subject pronouns and object pronouns in parentheses. For each set of parentheses, choose the correct pronoun and circle it.

1. Ron was tense about something Donna had told (he/him).
2. My friend and (I/me) exchanged a look, and then (I/me) drove away.
3. The waiter brought (they/them) a menu.

▶ *Answers begin on page 259.*

POSSESSIVE PRONOUNS

In Lesson 1, page 142, you learned that possessive nouns show ownership. You usually form the possessive of a noun by adding an apostrophe and the letter *s*. For instance:

Angela's hair color was not a color found in nature.

Pronouns also can show ownership or possession. Instead of repeating the word *Angela's* over and over in a paragraph, you could use a possessive pronoun. For example:

Her eyes were full of mischief.

Take a look at the following sentences containing possessive pronouns.

Let me remind you that the shirt on your back is <u>mine</u>.

The boys yawned and disappeared into <u>their</u> bedroom.

As you can see in the sentences above, some possessive pronouns can stand alone (such as *mine*). Others appear before nouns (such as *their*). The chart below lists all the possessive pronouns and shows them in sentences. It may be helpful to compare this chart with the one on page 149 showing subject and object pronouns.

Possessive pronouns	**used before nouns:**
my	*My* bike is the one with the flat tire.
your (singular)	I hope to wear *your* jacket.
his, her, its	Gregory put *his* cassette on the stereo. Nina hastily grabbed *her* jacket. The puppy closed *its* eyes.
our	We took a look at *our* new jade plant.
your (plural)	You all have the right to withhold *your* rent.
their	The students laid *their* books on the table.
Possessive pronouns	**used alone:**
mine	The bike with the flat tire is *mine*.
yours (singular)	The jacket I hope to wear is *yours*.
his, hers, its	The cassette on the stereo is *his*. The jacket Nina grabbed is *hers*. When I closed my eyes, the puppy closed *its*.
ours	That new jade plant is *ours*.
yours (plural)	The right to withhold rent is *yours*.
theirs	All the books on the table were *theirs*.

When using possessive pronouns in your writing, make sure that the antecedent is clear. Look at the two examples below:

> Tanya and Jennifer each have a bike. One bike is painted red. I like hers the best.
>
> Tanya and Jennifer each have a bike. Tanya's bike is painted red. I like hers the best.

In the first example, it is unclear whether *Tanya* or *Jennifer* is the antecedent of the possessive pronoun *hers*. In the second example, the pronoun's antecedent is clearly *Tanya*.

PRACTICE • 2

▶ **Part A** In each sentence below, underline all the pronouns. Then, add a circle to the possessive pronouns you find.

1. Please let me know what your decision is.
2. Her ambition is upsetting to him for some reason.
3. They took their chances when they adopted that grumpy dog.
4. Martha did her share of the driving, but I didn't do mine.
5. There is something strange in your salad, and you probably shouldn't look too closely at it.
6. The officer gave them his word, but they didn't trust him.

▶ **Part B** In the following paragraph, underline all the pronouns. Then label them *S* for subject, *O* for object, or *P* for possessive pronoun. The first sentence is done for you.

> The day I (S) took my (P) driver's test was the worst day of my (P) life. My wife was very supportive, but I was nervous. I wouldn't let her come with me to the test. My friend Jerry loaned me his car, and we went together. Of course, he didn't tell me that his car was on its last legs. Halfway to the test center, it stalled. We finally got it started, but we were late, and my appointment was rescheduled for next month.

▶ *Answers begin on page 259.*

FOCUS PUNCTUATION: POSSESSIVE PRONOUNS

Nouns need apostrophes in order to show ownership or possession. Possessive pronouns, however, *do not*. Look at these possessive pronouns:

my cupboard, your key chain, his doughnut

the coffee is hers, the anniversary is ours, the groceries are theirs

Spellings such as *her's, hers', his', your's, yours', their's,* or *theirs'* are always incorrect. There are no exceptions to this rule.

Another common pronoun punctuation error is confusing the possessive pronoun *its* with the contraction *it's*. The contraction is made from two words: the subject pronoun *it* and the verb *is*. A contraction does not show possession. Look at these examples.

Contraction: It's a beautiful day.

Possessive pronoun: The town had its annual Spring parade.

EDITING PRACTICE

■ In the paragraph below, some of the pronouns are used incorrectly. Edit the paragraph by crossing out the incorrect pronouns and rewriting them correctly. The first one is done for you.

The other day Reiko decided ~~her~~ *she* would like to go to a baseball game. She called her friend Fujio because she knew that him enjoyed baseball. He said him would love to go. Their wondered if they should take her's car or his car. Finally, it was decided by the two of they to take the subway.

CONNECTIONS

Read about word games in the Entertainment theme in **CONNECTIONS**, pages C10–C11. Then play the Pronoun Game with a friend. Each of you should write three sentences about a different famous person. Use subject, object, and possessive pronouns instead of the famous person's name. Finally, try to guess each other's famous person. Here's an example: 1. *He* was our first president. 2. The English tried to defeat *him*. 3. The face on the one dollar bill is *his*. Answer: George Washington.

► *Answers begin on page 260.*

PRE-GED PRACTICE

Choose the ***one best answer*** *for each item.* ***Items 1 to 5*** *refer to the following passage.*

(1)You're birthday always surprises me, since it comes so soon after the new year. (2)But I never forget to buy your a present. (3)I gave your sister a peek at this gift, and she was amazed at its' dazzling charm. (4)I did not allow your brothers' near the package because they have been known to treat a secret without much care. (5)I only have one request: you and me should be alone when you open it.

1. Sentence 1: You're birthday always surprises me, since it comes so soon after the new year.

What correction should be made to this sentence?
(1) change *You're* to *Your*
(2) change *You're* to *Yours*
(3) change *me* to *mine*
(4) change *me* to *I*
(5) change *it* to *its*

2. Sentence 2: But I never forget to buy your a present.

What correction should be made to this sentence?
(1) change *I* to *I's*
(2) change *I* to *me*
(3) change *your* to *you're*
(4) change *your* to *you*
(5) change *you* to *yours*

3. Sentence 3: I gave your sister a peek at this gift, and she was amazed at its' dazzling charm.

What correction should be made to this sentence?
(1) change *your* to *you*
(2) change *your* to *yours*
(3) change *she* to *her*
(4) change *its'* to *it's*
(5) change *its'* to *its*

4. Sentence 4: I did not allow your brothers' near the package because they have been known to treat a secret without much care.

What correction should be made to this sentence?
(1) change *your* to *you*
(2) change *your* to *yours*
(3) change *brothers'* to *brothers*
(4) change *they* to *theys*
(5) change *they* to *their*

5. Sentence 5: I only have one request: you and me should be alone when you open it.

What correction should be made to this sentence?
(1) change *I* to *My*
(2) change *me* to *I*
(3) change *me* to *my*
(4) change the second *you* to *your*
(5) change *it* to *its*

► *Answers begin on page 260.*

LESSON 3

Pronoun Agreement

Have you ever been told a story where it was difficult to keep track of the people or items described? Maybe you couldn't figure out who *he*, *she*, or *it* was. Careless pronoun use can often be a source of confusion.

AGREEMENT WITH ANTECEDENTS AND OTHER PRONOUNS

Recall that the antecedent is the word a pronoun refers to or replaces. A pronoun and its antecedent must match, or agree, in two ways: they must express the same *number* and *person*.

Number is simply another way of saying singular or plural. A singular pronoun is used if its antecedent refers to one object. A plural pronoun is used if its antecedent refers to more than one object. *Person* refers to first person (the person speaking), second person (the person being spoken to), and third person (any person, thing, or idea spoken about, other than me or you). Suppose a writer refers to Dr. Martin Luther King, Jr. and then wishes to use a pronoun to replace the name. The writer would be correct in choosing a singular third person pronoun such as *he, him,* or *his*. (Note that the pronoun is masculine in *gender*. Third person singular pronouns also must agree in gender. They may be masculine, feminine, or neuter [without gender].)

Take a look at the following sentences:

> Earline gave her car keys to Paul.
>
> The girls ran into their classroom.
>
> I gave away many of my records years ago.

In the first sentence, the antecedent of the pronoun *her* is *Earline*. Notice how both words are singular and third person feminine. In the second sentence, both the pronoun *their* and its antecedent *girls* are plural and third person. As you can see from the third sentence, some pronouns have antecedents that are not nouns but other pronouns. In this case, the antecedent of the pronoun *my* is another pronoun, *I*. They are both singular and first person.

Here is a chart showing pronouns according to person:

PERSON	SINGULAR	PLURAL
First person pronouns (speaker)	I, me, my, mine, myself	we, us, our, ours, ourselves
Second person pronouns (person spoken to)	you, your, yours, yourself	you, your, yours, yourselves
Third person pronouns (person, place, or thing spoken about)	he, she, it, him, her, his, hers, its, herself, himself, itself	they, them, theirs, themselves,

When pronoun agreement is incorrect, it can be difficult to understand what the writer means. For example:

The three men leaped into his shoes.

It is unclear to whom *his* refers.

PRACTICE • 1

▶ **Part A** In each sentence below, underline the pronouns and circle the antecedents. Then draw arrows connecting the antecedents to their pronouns.

1. Since Lawrence doesn't mind, Walt is going to use his lawn mower.
2. He looks like Jack Benny, except that his hair is long and curly.
3. Ginnie and Patty knew they were going to the game on Friday night.

▶ **Part B** In the following paragraph, you will find a choice of pronouns in parentheses. Circle the correct pronoun for each sentence.

Sharon and Scott were walking along Kilby Street in Sanford. (Your/Their) favorite place to walk was that particular neighborhood. It was a neighborhood that had seen (its/his) ups and downs. (It/Its) sat on a hill above a steel bridge.

▶ *Answers begin on page 260.*

AVOIDING PRONOUN SHIFTS AND VAGUE REFERENCES

Pronoun shifts occur when a writer uses one pronoun in one part of a sentence. Then in another part of the sentence, the writer shifts to a different pronoun to refer to the first pronoun. Take a look at the following sentence:

We ate ice cream because it cools you off.

Did you notice that the pronoun *you* and its antecedent, the pronoun *we,* are not in the same person? *We* is a first person pronoun, and *you* is a second person pronoun. This writer has made the error of shifting pronouns from the first person to the second person in a sentence. Misusing the pronoun *you* is the most common form of this error.

It's simple to check for pronoun shifts if the antecedent is easy to recognize. But what happens if you're not sure of the antecedent? Take a look at the following example of an unclear antecedent:

When the men approached the lion cubs, <u>they</u> became very nervous.

Who became nervous—the men or the cubs? This vague reference is called an *indefinite antecedent*. The meaning would be clear if the sentence were rewritten. For example:

As they approached the lion cubs, the men became nervous.

The lion cubs became very nervous as the men approached.

Another type of problem occurs when a pronoun has *no antecedent*. Look at the following sentence:

I held the fishing pole tightly and reeled in, but finally <u>it</u> got away.

There is no antecedent here for the pronoun *it*. The word *fish* is implied, but this word doesn't appear in the sentence. The sentence should be revised, replacing *it* with *the fish*.

CONNECTIONS

How are computers changing the way people write, learn, and play? To find out, look at the Technology theme in **CONNECTIONS**, pages C2–C3. Then write a short paragraph about the history of computers and how they are being used today. Use pronouns to avoid repeating the word *computer* in your paragraph. Then check your writing for correct pronoun usage.

PRACTICE • 2

▶ **Part A** Rewrite the following sentences so that there are no pronoun shifts and no indefinite or missing antecedents.

1. Suddenly I was afraid because you couldn't tell whether the guy had a weapon or not.

 ____

2. Joan and Ella's party was no fun because she was so fussy.

 ____

3. I stuck the bills between two books, but unfortunately they got lost.

 ____

4. I love Delta blues musicians like Bukka White and Son House because they make you feel that feeling bad is all right.

 ____

5. Julie walked up to Tonya, and she began to sing.

 ____

▶ **Part B** In the following paragraph, some of the pronouns are used incorrectly. Others have indefinite or missing antecedents. Cross out these pronouns and replace them or rewrite as necessary.

Juanita asked me if I would help her and Neil as they moved some heavy bookshelves from one apartment to another. They aren't something I can do, however. I have a bad foot and a bad back, and it prevents me from doing any heavy work. I help them a lot, but you can't ever do enough for that guy. We used to be close friends, but since they moved in with each other, we have grown apart.

▶ *Answers begin on page 260.*

FOCUS USAGE: CHECKING PRONOUNS AND ANTECEDENTS

Pronoun shifts and errors with antecedents are common in writing. Pronoun-antecedent problems tend to happen for one of three reasons. Look for these three specific situations:

1. There are two nouns that could be the antecedent of a pronoun.

   Winston lent my brother a jacket that he didn't like.

   Rewrite: Winston didn't like the jacket, so he lent it to my brother.

2. A pronoun and its antecedent are too far away from one another, so the reader might need to be reminded of that antecedent.

   I loved my old skates. I used to skate with my friends, Sally and Jorge. We went every Saturday. I was sad when they wore out.

   Replace pronoun: I was sad when those skates wore out.

3. There is no antecedent at all.

   The toaster was on the wrong setting, and it popped out black and hard.

   Replace pronoun: The toaster was on the wrong setting, and the toast popped out black and hard.

EDITING PRACTICE

■ The paragraph below contains incorrect pronouns and pronouns with unclear antecedents. Edit the paragraph by correcting pronoun shifts and clarifying antecedents. One edit has been done for you.

There was no hot water in our apartment building for twenty days this month, and it didn't seem to bother ~~him~~ *the landlord* one bit. I figured that he would apologize because they owns it, but you can never predict what his reaction will be. The maintenance man said it broke last winter. A group of tenants got together and held back our rent payments.

► *Answers begin on page 261.*

PRE-GED PRACTICE

*Choose the **one best answer** for each item.*
***Items 1 to 5** refer to the following passage.*

(1)Fred Thomaston hired me to assist a chef named Charles, and he was the nicest guy I have ever met. (2)Charles kidded Fred just about every day because you could do that with a guy as easygoing as Fred. (3)I learned a lot of lessons from both of those men, but it didn't come easily. (4)The three of us felt a lot of pressure because they put out two hundred meals in the course of about four hours. (5)They kept coming back every day, so we were doing something right.

1. Sentence 1: Fred Thomaston hired me to assist a chef named Charles, and he was the nicest guy I have ever met.

What correction should be made to this sentence?
(1) change *me* to *mine*
(2) change *me* to *I*
(3) change *he* to *Charles*
(4) change *he* to *his*
(5) change *I* to *I've*

2. Sentence 2: Charles kidded Fred just about every day, because you could do that with a guy as easygoing as Fred.

What is the best way to correct this sentence?
(1) change *Charles* to *He*
(2) change *Charles* to *They*
(3) change *Fred* to *him*
(4) change *you* to *he*
(5) change *you* to *they*

3. Sentence 3: I learned a lot of lessons from both of those men, but <u>it didn't</u> come easily.

Which of the following is the best way to write the underlined portion of this sentence? If you think the original is the best way, choose (1).
(1) it didn't
(2) it doesn't
(3) they didn't
(4) I didn't
(5) the lessons didn't

4. Sentence 4: The three of us felt a lot of pressure because they put out two hundred meals in the course of about four hours.

What correction should be made to this sentence?
(1) change *they* to *there*
(2) change *they* to *they're*
(3) change *they* to *we*
(4) change *us* to *we*
(5) change *put* to *puts*

5. Sentence 5: <u>They kept</u> coming back every day, so we were doing something right.

Which of the following is the best way to write the underlined portion of this sentence? If you think the original is the best way, choose (1).
(1) They kept
(2) The customers kept
(3) Theirs kept
(4) They keep
(5) They will keep

► *Answers begin on page 261.*

Verbs: Simple Tenses

Every sentence contains at least one verb. Verbs can show physical action, as in the verbs *run*, *toss*, and *chew*. They can also show mental action, as in the verbs *dream*, *understand*, and *remember*. Verbs also can be used to describe states of being (He *is* nice.) or ask questions (*Is* he nice?). Sentences that are commands can even consist of only a verb (Run!). But it is impossible to write a complete sentence *without* a verb.

A verb's tense tells when the action occurred. Verbs in the *past tense* show actions that happened in the past. *Present tense* verbs show actions that are happening now or that happen regularly. *Future tense* verbs show actions that will happen in the future. Three different tenses of the verb *work* are used in the following examples:

> Joanne's father worked in the coal mines until last year.
>
> Joanne works there six days a week.
>
> However, she will work at a restaurant next year.

In the first sentence, the past tense is used. Joanne's father worked in the mines *once*, but he does not work there now. In the second sentence, the present tense is used. Joanne works in the mines *now*. In the last sentence, the future tense is used. Joanne does not work at a restaurant *yet*.

SIMPLE TENSES WITH REGULAR VERBS

Most verbs are *regular verbs*. Regular verbs always follow the same spelling rules for their endings. Here are the rules, along with some examples using the verb *stay*:

SIMPLE PRESENT, PAST, AND FUTURE TENSE IN REGULAR VERBS

PRESENT TENSE	verb has no special ending or ends in *-s* or *-es*: The guests stay until after dinner. Jamal stays late every night.
PAST TENSE	verb ends in *-d* or *-ed*: Last night he stayed until 10P.M.
FUTURE TENSE	verb follows the word *will* and has no special ending: He will stay late tonight if he can.

You may have noticed that present and past tense verbs can be identified by their spellings and endings. Future tense verbs, however, can be identified by the word *will*, which precedes the verb.

Find the verb in each sentence below. Can you tell whether it is in the past, present, or future tense?

Li Ling wants a new job.

In her old job, she called customers on the phone.

Soon she will finish her new training program.

In the first sentence, the present tense verb *wants* ends in *-s* and tells what Li Ling wants now. In the second sentence, the past tense verb *called* ends in *-ed* and tells what Li Ling did in the past. The action in the last sentence is expressed by the future tense verb *will finish*. The word *finish* follows the word *will* and has no special ending.

PRACTICE • 1

▶ **Part A** Write the following verbs in the two tenses indicated.

		Past	Future
1.	count	__________	__________
2.	save	__________	__________
3.	play	__________	__________
4.	thank	__________	__________
5.	wash	__________	__________
6.	enter	__________	__________

▶ **Part B** The verbs in the following paragraph should be in the past tense. Some of them are in the wrong tense. Cross out the incorrect verbs, and rewrite them in the past tense.

The first time Ruben washed and waxes his car, he loves the way it looks. The car looked great. That night, however, it will rain very hard. Suddenly, the car looked dull and old. Ruben just laughs. The next morning, he will wash the car again.

▶ *Answers begin on page 261.*

SIMPLE TENSES WITH IRREGULAR VERBS

Irregular verbs do not follow the regular rules for past tense endings. They do not end with *-d* or *-ed*. To form the past tense of irregular verbs, you must change their spelling. The most commonly used irregular verb (the verb *be*) is also probably the oddest. The chart below shows the three tenses of the verb *be*.

Tense	I	he, she, it	we, you, they
Present	*am*	*is*	*are*
Past	*was*	*was*	*were*
Future	*will be*	*will be*	*will be*

The spelling of this verb changes greatly from tense to tense. Study the forms of the verb *be* and the forms of the common irregular verbs listed in the chart below. It is not important to memorize them. Instead, refer back to these charts when needed. The more you use these verbs, the more easily you will be able to remember their forms.

SOME COMMON IRREGULAR VERBS		
Present	**Past**	**Future**
begin	began	will begin
bring	brought	will bring
catch	caught	will catch
come	came	will come
do, does	did	will do
drink	drank	will drink
drive	drove	will drive
eat	ate	will eat
get	got	will get
give	gave	will give
go, goes	went	will go
have, has	had	will have
hear	heard	will hear
know	knew	will know
lose	lost	will lose
make	made	will make
pay	paid	will pay
ride	rode	will ride
run	ran	will run
see	saw	will see
sit	sat	will sit
speak	spoke	will speak
take	took	will take
think	thought	will think
write	wrote	will write

PRACTICE • 2

■ Each of the following sentences is preceded by a verb in parentheses. Use the chart on page 162 to write the correct form of the verb in the blank to complete each sentence.

1. (come) Ten years ago, my family _______________ here from Vietnam.
2. (know) When we arrived, only my mother _______________ English.
3. (speak) She said, "Don't worry, soon you _______________ English."
4. (begin) I _______________ to learn English in school.
5. (take) Last year, I _______________ the GED and passed.
6. (have) Now I _______________ a job as a store manager.
7. (pay) My employers _______________ me a good salary.
8. (get) Soon I _______________ my own apartment.

FOCUS PRESENT TENSE SINGULAR AND PAST TENSE

To form the third person singular of present tense regular verbs, follow these rules:

FORMING THIRD PERSON SINGULAR VERBS

for most verbs	add *-s*	sit →	he *sits*
for verbs:			
• ending in *ch* or *sh*	add *-es*	catch →	she *catches*
• ending with a *y* that follows a vowel	add *-s*	say →	it *says*
• ending with a *y* that follows a consonant	change *-y* to *-ies*	carry →	he *carries*

► *Answers begin on page 261.*

In the past tense, each verb has only one form. This form is used with any subject. To form the past tense of regular verbs, follow these rules:

FORMING PAST TENSE VERBS

for most verbs	add *-ed*	wait → *waited*
for verbs:		
• ending with a silent *e*	add *-d*	hike → *hiked*
• ending with a *y* that follows a vowel	add *-ed*	stay → *stayed*
• ending with a *y* that follows a consonant	change *-y* to *-ied*	try → *tried*
• ending with a ***stressed*** vowel-consonant	double the consonant and add *-ed*	patrol → *patrolled*

stressed: emphasized: paTROL, not PAtrol

EDITING PRACTICE

■ In the paragraph below, some of the verbs are in the wrong tense. Others are spelled incorrectly. Edit this paragraph by crossing out the incorrect verbs and rewriting them correctly. The first one is done for you.

My son and I ~~go~~ *went* to the library last weekend. He wants a book about dinosaurs. I tryed to find one. I look and look, but I had no luck. Finally, I asks the librarian. He showed me the card catalog. We will find a great book. Now my son reades the book all the time.

CONNECTIONS

Read the excerpt from *Kaffir Boy* in the Health Matters theme in **CONNECTIONS,** pages C14–C15. Then, write a short paragraph about whether you think health care is important. Examine the verb tenses you used. Are all the verbs spelled correctly?

► *For more work with verb tenses, see pages 80–81 of Section 2. Answers begin on page 261.*

PRE-GED PRACTICE

Choose the ***one best answer*** *for each item.* ***Items 1 to 5*** *refer to the following passage.*

(1)Jesse come to the United States six years ago. (2)His sister is already here. (3) At first he lived with his sister and her husband. (4)He payed them money each month for rent. (5)Soon, he began to want his own apartment.

(6)Now Jesse has his own place. (7)He enjoys living on his own. (8)He knowes he can visit his family whenever he feels lonely.

1. Sentence 1: Jesse come to the United States six years ago.

What correction should be made to this sentence?

(1) change *come* to *comed*
(2) change *come* to *came*
(3) change *come* to *commed*
(4) change *come* to *comes*
(5) change *come* to *will come*

2. Sentence 2: His sister is already here.

What correction should be made to this sentence?

(1) change *is* to *am*
(2) change *is* to *be*
(3) change *is* to *will be*
(4) change *is* to *are*
(5) change *is* to *was*

3. Sentence 4: He payed them money each month for rent.

What correction should be made to this sentence?

(1) change *payed* to *will pay*
(2) change *payed* to *payyed*
(3) change *payed* to *payd*
(4) change *payed* to *paid*
(5) change *payed* to *pays*

4. Sentence 6: <u>Now Jesse has</u> his own place.

Which is the best way to write the underlined portion of this sentence? If you think the original is the best way, choose (1).

(1) Now Jesse has
(2) Now Jesse had
(3) Now Jesse have
(4) Now Jesse will have
(5) Now Jesse haves

5. Sentence 8: He knowes he can visit his family whenever he feels lonely.

What correction should be made to this sentence?

(1) change *knowes* to *will know*
(2) change *knowes* to *knows*
(3) change *knowes* to *knew*
(4) change *knowes* to *knowed*
(5) change *knowes* to *know*

► *Answers begin on page 261.*

LESSON 5

Verbs: Other Tenses

Try to speak using only the three simple verb tenses (past, present, and future). Sooner or later you will have difficulty expressing exactly when something happened, is happening, or will happen. Other verb tenses allow you to describe the time frame of an action in ways that the simple tenses cannot. In this lesson, you will learn about two other kinds of tenses: perfect tenses and continuous tenses.

PERFECT TENSES AND THE PAST PARTICIPLE

The *perfect tenses* are formed by adding a helping verb to the *past participle* of the main verb. For regular verbs, the past participle is exactly the same as the simple past tense. Look at these examples for the verb *play:*

Simple past tense: played **Past participle:** played

Irregular verbs may have different forms for the past participle. Use the chart on page 169 to become familiar with these forms. Refer back to it as often as you like.

Use the *perfect tenses* to show action that has a special circumstance. There are three perfect verb tenses: present perfect, past perfect, and future perfect.

PRESENT, PAST, AND FUTURE PERFECT TENSES

PRESENT PERFECT tense is formed with a helping verb (*have* or *has*) and the past participle of a main verb (see page 169). Use the present perfect tense:

- *to describe an action that occurred at some unspecified time in the past*

Those women have gone their separate ways.

- *to describe an action that started in the past and continues in the present*

Patrick has exercised for the last two weeks.

PAST PERFECT tense is formed with a helping verb (*had*) and the past participle of a main verb (see page 169). Use the past perfect tense:

- *to describe a past action that ended before another past action*

Joanie had visited us before we got the dog.

FUTURE PERFECT tense is formed with two helping verbs *(will have)* and the past participle of a main verb (see page 169). Use the future perfect tense:

- *to describe an action that will be ended before another future action*

I am sure that Doug will have played several dozen hands of poker before I get home.

PRACTICE • 1

▶ **Part A** Each of the following sentences is preceded by a verb in parentheses. In the blank space, write the verb in the correct perfect tense to complete each sentence.

1. (go) By next Monday, I _______________ to three different movies.
2. (hear) I don't know if many people your age _______________ of a comic movie actor named Buster Keaton.
3. (forget) I _______________ the title of Buster Keaton's first movie.
4. (think) Between them, Barry and Jim _______________ of four different Buster Keaton movies they would like to see.
5. (choose) Before yesterday's emergency, I _______________ a great movie to watch.

▶ **Part B** Each of the italicized verbs in the following paragraph should be written in one of the perfect tenses. Rewrite these verbs correctly.

Native Americans *lived* in North America for much longer than Europeans. When I learned this fact two weeks ago, I realized I *lived* in ignorance about the history of Native Americans all my life. Recently, I *discussed* this fact with anyone who is interested.

▶ *Answers begin on page 262.*

CONTINUOUS TENSES

The *continuous* (or progressive) *tenses* show action that is ongoing. There are three continuous tenses: the present continuous, the past continuous, and the future continuous.

PRESENT, PAST, AND FUTURE CONTINUOUS TENSES

PRESENT CONTINUOUS

tense is formed with two verbs: a helping verb (*am, is,* or *are*) and a main verb with an *-ing* ending. Use the present continuous tense to describe an action that:

- *is continuing*

  I am building a new house.

- *is happening at the moment*

  Right now the man from the construction crew is drilling a hole in the wall.

PAST CONTINUOUS

tense is also formed with two verbs: a helping verb (*was* or *were*) and a main verb with an *-ing* ending. Use the past continuous tense to describe an action that:

- *continued for some time*

  Charlene was talking for the entire ninety minutes.

- *continued at the same time another action was happening*

  Charlene was talking while the movie was playing on the screen.

- *continued until another action happened*

  Charlene and her mother were talking until the movie ended.

FUTURE CONTINUOUS

tense is formed with three verbs: two helping verbs (*will be*) and a main verb with an *-ing* ending. Use the future continuous tense to describe an action that:

- *will continue for some time*

  Tomorrow I will be driving for about twelve hours.

- *will continue at the same time another action is happening*

  Tomorrow I will be driving while you are relaxing at home.

- *will continue until another action happens*

  Tomorrow I will be driving until I get to Phoenix.

TENSES OF SOME COMMON IRREGULAR VERBS		
PRESENT (*Today I . . .*)	SIMPLE PAST (*Yesterday I . . .*)	PAST PARTICIPLE (*Many times I have . . .*)
am	was	been
are	were	been
begin	began	begun
bring	brought	brought
choose	chose	chosen
come	came	come
do	did	done
drink	drank	drunk
drive	drove	driven
eat	ate	eaten
fly	flew	flown
forget	forgot	forgotten
get	got	gotten
give	gave	given
go	went	gone
have	had	had
know	knew	known
lose	lost	lost
pay	paid	paid
ride	rode	ridden
run	ran	run
see	saw	seen
speak	spoke	spoken
take	took	taken
write	wrote	written

PRACTICE • 2

■ Write the following verbs in the tenses indicated.

VERBS	PRESENT CONTINUOUS	PAST CONTINUOUS	FUTURE CONTINUOUS
1. I fly			
2. you wash			
3. he questions			
4. we walk			
5. they study			

► *Answers begin on page 262.*

FOCUS USAGE: USING PAST PARTICIPLES CORRECTLY

Be careful when you use an irregular verb in a perfect tense. A common error is to use a helping verb plus the simple past tense instead of the past participle. For example:

Incorrect: I have drove that road many times.

Correct: I have driven that road many times.

The past participle of the irregular verb *drive* is *driven*, not *drove*. Use the table on page 169 if you are uncertain of the correct past participle form of an irregular verb.

EDITING PRACTICE

■ In the paragraph below, some of the verbs are incorrect. Edit the paragraph by crossing out the incorrect verbs and rewriting them correctly. The first one is done for you.

was watching

Last night while I ~~watch~~ the news, my girlfriend Anne was making a birthday card for her mother. She finished it by the time the news was over, but she fussed over it for another fifteen or twenty minutes. When I had asked her why she didn't leave it alone, she glared at me and was walking into the other room all upset. I think for the last few years she felt anxious about her mother's getting older.

CONNECTIONS

Did you know that the number of newspapers in the U.S. is declining? Read about it in the News Media theme in **CONNECTIONS**, pages C8–C9. How do you decide whether to buy a newspaper? Do headlines or pictures on the front page attract your interest? What kinds of words, types of stories, or celebrity names catch your eye and make you decide to buy? Write a few sentences to explain. Check your writing for the correct use of verb tenses.

▶ *Answers begin on page 262.*

PRE-GED PRACTICE

Choose the ***one best answer*** *for each item.*
Items 1 to 5 *refer to the following passage.*

(1)Before I moved here ten years ago, I was a resident of a big city. (2)I enjoyed myself there until I took a trip to the country with a friend. (3)I had loved it immediately and decided to move there. (4)It was so beautiful and peaceful, and the air was smelling so fresh. (5)Now I look forward to the time when I will leave this place and go back to the excitement of the city.

1. Sentence 1: Before I moved here ten years ago, I was a resident of a big city.

What correction should be made to this sentence?
(1) change *moved* to *had moved*
(2) change *moved* to *was moving*
(3) change *moved* to *am moving*
(4) change *was* to *had been*
(5) change *was* to *have been*

2. Sentence 2: I enjoyed myself there until I took a trip to the country with a friend.

What correction should be made to this sentence?
(1) change *enjoyed* to *was enjoying*
(2) change *enjoyed* to *have enjoyed*
(3) change *enjoyed* to *will enjoy*
(4) change *took* to *was taking*
(5) change *took* to *taken*

3. Sentence 3: I had loved it immediately and decided to move there.

What correction should be made to this sentence?
(1) change *had loved* to *was loving*
(2) change *had loved* to *loved*
(3) change *decided* to *have decided*
(4) change *decided* to *had decided*
(5) change *decided* to *were deciding*

4. Sentence 4: It was so beautiful and peaceful, and the air was smelling so fresh.

What correction should be made to this sentence?
(1) change the first *was* to *were*
(2) change the first *was* to *had been*
(3) change the first *was* to *will be*
(4) change *was smelling* to *had smelled*
(5) change *was smelling* to *smelled*

5. Sentence 5: Now I look forward to the time when I will leave this place and go back to the excitement of the city.

What correction should be made to this sentence?
(1) change *look* to *am looking*
(2) change *look* to *had looked*
(3) change *will leave* to *left*
(4) change *will leave* to *was leaving*
(5) change *will leave* to *leave*

▶ *Answers begin on page 262.*

LESSON 6

Subject-Verb Agreement

Every sentence contains a subject and a verb. As you have learned, the subject of a sentence is usually a noun or a pronoun. The verb usually describes an action or a state of being. An important part of good writing is making sure that these subjects and verbs are in agreement.

SUBJECT-VERB AGREEMENT IN ACTION SENTENCES

For *action sentences*—sentences where the verb describes an action—the subject and the verb in every sentence must agree, or match. Checking for agreement between subjects and verbs means making sure they agree in number. In other words, both must be singular (one person or thing is doing the action) or both must be plural (more than one person or thing is doing the action). Look at the sentences below:

Rob write about nature a lot.

Rob writes about nature a lot.

In the first sentence, the subject-verb agreement is incorrect. *Write* is a plural verb and does not agree with the singular subject *Rob*. The second sentence is correct. Both subject and verb are singular.

Present tense regular verbs show little difference in their singular and plural forms. The exception is the third person singular form. The third person singular ends in *-s*. Look at the following:

PRESENT SINGULAR	PRESENT PLURAL
I answer the phone.	We answer the phone.
You answer the phone.	You answer the phone.
He or she answers the phone.	They answer the phone.

In the six sentences above, only the third person singular verb changes. An *-s* is added. The other verbs have no special endings. The same is true if the subject is a noun rather than a pronoun. See the following examples:

Roberto (he) speaks on the phone.

The brothers (they) speak on the phone.

The first sentence contains a singular subject, *Roberto,* and a singular verb, *speaks*. The subject and the verb agree; they are both singular. The second sentence contains a plural subject, *brothers,* and a plural verb, *speak*. The subject and verb agree because they are both plural. Notice again, no special ending is added except to the third person singular verb.

FORMING PRESENT TENSE REGULAR VERBS

Add an *-s* to the third person singular verb. The other verb forms have no special ending.

PRACTICE • 1

▶ **Part A** In the following sentences, underline the subjects once and the verbs twice. Then write *S* in the blank space if the subject and verb are singular or *P* if they are plural.

_____ **1.** The men in the green car always yell at pedestrians.

_____ **2.** They say plenty about insects and other pests in this book.

_____ **3.** Every Sunday, Peter eats lunch with me.

_____ **4.** She throws that softball incredibly long distances.

_____ **5.** Most trees bend slightly in high winds.

▶ **Part B** In the following paragraph, you will find errors in subject-verb agreement. Cross out any verbs that do not agree with their subjects. Then rewrite the verbs correctly.

The people in this neighborhood runs everywhere. Nobody takes the time to walk anywhere. I wonders why this is true. My next-door neighbor always rush by me on his way to work. I think he should just get up a little earlier. I has told him that he should relax, but you knows he don't listen to me.

▶ *Answers begin on page 262.*

SUBJECT-VERB AGREEMENT IN DESCRIBING SENTENCES

The basic rules for subject-verb agreement are the same for sentences that describe a state of being as they are for sentences that show action. Either the subject and verb must be singular, or they must be plural. Take a look at the following sentences:

Janet looks happy this weekend.

The saxophones sound wonderful.

My grandmother feels content.

None of the verbs in the sentences above is an action verb. Each of these verbs helps the writer describe a state of being. In the first sentence, the singular subject *Janet* agrees with the singular verb *looks*. In the second sentence, the plural subject *saxophones* agrees with the plural verb *sound.* In the third sentence, the singular subject *grandmother* agrees with the singular verb *feels.* Here are some verbs that you will use in sentences that describe a state of being:

appear become seem feel taste smell look sound

For these verbs, the singular forms end in *-s*, and the plural forms have no special ending.

Often, however, you will use the verb *to be* in describing sentences. The verb *to be* is an exception to the rules above. As you learned in Lesson 4, this verb is highly irregular. Many writers become confused when they try to make the verb *to be* agree with a subject. The present and simple past tense forms of the verb *to be* are shown below:

SINGULAR		PLURAL	
Present	**Past**	**Present**	**Past**
I *am*	I *was*	we *are*	we *were*
you *are*	you *were*	you *are*	you *were*
he, she, it *is*	he, she, it *was*	they *are*	they *were*

I is the only subject that ever takes the verb form *am*. Notice that the singular subject *you* takes the same verb forms as the plural subject *you*: *are* in the present tense, *were* in the past tense. The following sentences use the verb *to be*:

She is on vacation from her job as a cook.

Janet's pies are the best in the world.

You were a great help to me.

PRACTICE • 2

▶ **Part A** In the following sentences, underline the subjects once and the verbs twice. Then write *S* in the blank space if the subject and verb are singular or *P* if they are plural.

_____ **1.** Music is a great pleasure in my life.

_____ **2.** The writing supplies are in the desk drawer.

_____ **3.** It becomes funnier after a few pages.

_____ **4.** We feel absolutely sure that we locked the house.

_____ **5.** He smells terrific with that cologne!

▶ **Part B** In the following paragraph, you will find errors in subject-verb agreement. Cross out any verbs that do not agree with their subjects. Then rewrite the verbs correctly.

Every night have been quiet since I've been here in Crawfordsville. John was nice enough to let me have the larger motel room. His room don't have nearly this much charm. During the day we is busy at the plant. I be a quality-control supervisor.

CONNECTIONS

Read the excerpt by the writer John Steinbeck in the Employment theme in **CONNECTIONS**, pages C4–C5. Steinbeck discusses the effects on his fingers of holding a pencil for many hours each day. Do you think holding a pencil is really the hardest part of a writer's work? Write a short paragraph describing what you find easy or difficult about writing. Then check your work for subject-verb agreement.

It is worth reviewing the forms of other irregular verbs (such as *do*, *have*, and *go*) to make sure that you won't make mistakes in subject-verb agreement.

▶ *For more work with irregular verbs, see pages 162–163.*
Answers begin on page 262.

FOCUS SPELLING: USING "-S" ENDINGS IN THE PERFECT AND CONTINUOUS TENSES

You form perfect tenses and continuous tenses of verbs by using a helping verb with the main verb. It is the helping verb that must agree with the subject. The past participles and the *-ing* forms of perfect and continuous tenses *never* change. The helping verb is some form of the verb *to be*. Here are some examples:

Present Continuous (helping verb = present tense of *to be*)

Thelma is listening for the sound of the train whistle.

I am listening for the sound of the train whistle.

Past Continuous (helping verb = past tense of the verb *to be*)

Harry was running around the block for an hour.

Harry and Kurt were running around the block for an hour.

Present Perfect (helping verb = present tense of *have*)

Mr. Mendoza has studied hard for his diploma.

The students have studied hard for their diplomas.

Past Perfect (helping verb = past tense of *have*)

Tracee had recorded three songs before the studio closed.

The other band had recorded two songs before the studio closed.

EDITING PRACTICE

■ The paragraph below contains errors in subject-verb agreement. Edit the paragraph by correcting the verbs that do not agree with their subjects. The first one is done for you.

Mr. Sanchez, according to his wife, has been thinking about going on a diet. However, I ~~hears~~ *hear* (from Mr. Sanchez himself) that he has no intention of doing any such thing. He likes the way he look. I believe the diet are just wishful thinking on her part. He does seem a little heavy to me, but they says that a man of Mr. Sanchez's height can carry a lot of weight.

▶ *Answers begin on page 263.*

PRE-GED PRACTICE

Choose the ***one best answer*** *for each item.* ***Items 1 to 5*** *refer to the following passage.*

(1)Baseball games sounds soothing and pleasant when they are broadcast on the radio. (2)Listeners has to use their imaginations to picture what is happening on the field. (3)As I listen to a ball game on the radio, all the parts of the field is visible in my mind. (4)On television, viewers sees only the small area that the camera can capture. (5)In my opinion, it are a great pleasure to lie in bed on a summer evening and listen to a ball game on the radio.

1. Sentence 1: Baseball games sounds soothing and pleasant when they are broadcast on the radio.

What correction should be made to this sentence?
(1) change *games* to *game*
(2) change *sounds* to *sound*
(3) change *sounds* to *sounds'*
(4) change *are* to *is*
(5) change *are* to *has*

2. Sentence 2: Listeners has to use their imaginations to picture what is happening on the field.

What correction should be made to this sentence?
(1) change *has* to *have*
(2) change *their* to *they're*
(3) change *their* to *his*
(4) change *is* to *are*
(5) change *Listeners* to *Listener*

3. Sentence 3: As I listen to a ball game on the radio, all the parts of the field is visible in my mind.

What correction should be made to this sentence?
(1) change *listen* to *listens*
(2) change *listen* to *listens'*
(3) change *is* to *am*
(4) change *is* to *are*
(5) change *parts* to *part's*

4. Sentence 4: On television, viewers sees only the small area that the camera can capture.

What correction should be made to this sentence?
(1) change *viewers* to *viewer's*
(2) change *sees* to *is seeing*
(3) change *sees* to *see*
(4) change *capture* to *captures*
(5) change *capture* to *have captured*

5. Sentence 5: In my opinion, it are a great pleasure to lie in bed on a summer evening and listen to a ball game on the radio.

What correction should be made to this sentence?
(1) change *are* to *am*
(2) change *are* to *is*
(3) change *it are* to *its*
(4) change *pleasure* to *plesure*
(5) change *listen* to *listens*

► *Answers begin on page 263.*

Subject-Verb Agreement with Special Subjects

In order to check for subject-verb agreement, you must first decide whether the subject is singular or plural. It is easy to decide whether most pronouns and nouns are singular or plural. A few are less obvious. For example, is *nobody* a singular or plural subject?

AGREEMENT WITH TRICKY SUBJECTS

It may surprise you to learn that the words below are *always* singular. Parts of many of these words ("body," "one," and "thing") give hints to the fact that they refer to *one* thing or person.

another	each	everything	no one	somebody
anybody	either	much	nothing	someone
anyone	everybody	nobody	one	something
anything	everyone	none	other	

In the sentence below, notice the singular verb form *wants*:

Nobody wants to come with me to the store.

If you think carefully about the meaning of the following words, common sense will tell you that they are *always* plural.

both few many several

In the following sentence, notice the plural verb form *plan*.

Few plan to vote for the candidate.

Some nouns, called *collective nouns,* represent groups of people or things. They seem to be plural because there is more than one individual in the group. However, they take a singular verb. This is because the group itself is counted as *one*. Here are some collective nouns:

army	choir	department	group	pack
audience	class	family	herd	public
band	crowd	flock	orchestra	team

In the following sentence, notice that the collective noun *audience* is counted as *one* and takes the singular helping verb *was*:

The audience was laughing throughout the entire performance.

Some nouns end in the letter *-s*, but they are not plural. Here are some of these words:

athletics	mathematics	news	series
electronics	measles	politics	United States

In the sentence below, notice the singular verb form *hopes*:

The United States hopes to finish first in the diving competition.

A few other nouns act in just the opposite manner. We think of them as *one thing*. However, they are technically plural and require plural verbs. Many of them describe objects that have two identical parts.

glasses	khakis	scissors	slacks	trousers
jeans	pants	shorts	tongs	tweezers

In the sentence below, notice that the noun *jeans* takes a plural verb.

Your favorite jeans were ruined at the laundromat.

PRACTICE • 1

■ In the following sentences, underline the subjects once and the verbs twice. Then make sure that each verb agrees with its subject. If a subject and verb do not agree, cross out the verb and rewrite it using the correct form.

1. A crowd appear in the street after every game.
2. Economics always confuse me.
3. Everyone are responsible for himself during this trip.
4. Sunglasses makes me look slightly more glamorous.
5. Nobody has permission to come near me.
6. Several people were injured.
7. Mathematics are difficult for some people.

► *Answers begin on page 263.*

AGREEMENT WITH COMPOUND SUBJECTS

Most sentences have a subject that is composed of one noun or one pronoun. However, some sentences have subjects made up of more than one noun or pronoun. A subject like this is called a *compound subject*.

Compound subjects can take either plural or singular verbs. The compound subject is considered plural or singular according to the connecting word that links the nouns or pronouns. For example:

> Lou and Marjorie know a lot about their town's history.
>
> The Monroes and the Baileys always take a summer trip together.
>
> Jeff, his girlfriend, and three other people want their coffees black.

In each of these sentences, the nouns or pronouns that make up the compound subject are connected by the word *and*. The word *and* connects these nouns and pronouns, making the subject plural. For this reason, each of the verbs above is plural.

Take a close look at each of the compound subjects above. As you look for the subject of a sentence, you sometimes need to separate the nouns and pronouns from other descriptive words around them. Words such as *the* in the second sentence and *his* and *three other* in the third sentence are not part of the subject.

Here are some more sentences with compound subjects. Can you identify the compound subjects? Are they singular or plural?

> The green chair and the pink sofa look horrible together!
>
> My mother and the man of my dreams are meeting tonight at 6P.M.
>
> The humidity and the heat are unbearable this summer.

In the first sentence, the compound subject is *green chair* and *pink sofa*. In the second sentence, the compound subject is *mother* and *man*. (The plural noun *dreams* is not part of the subject.) In the third sentence, the compound subject is *humidity* and *heat*. Because the nouns in all three sentences are connected by the word *and*, the compound subjects are all plural and take plural verb forms.

PRACTICE • 2

▶ **Part A** In the following sentences, underline the subjects once and the verbs twice. Then make sure that each verb agrees with its subject. If a subject and verb do not agree, cross out the verb and rewrite it using the correct form.

1. The trombones and the piano plays louder than the other instruments in the orchestra.
2. Sam Wilson and his parents are visiting us this Friday.
3. The stones and the seaweed is fun to collect.
4. Dogs and people gets along pretty well, in general.
5. She and the grocery store owner have lived together for years.
6. We and our cousins has an agreement to meet in ten years in Times Square in New York City.

▶ **Part B** In the following paragraph, you will find errors in subject-verb agreement. Cross out any verb that does not agree with its subject. Rewrite the verb correctly above.

The bushes and the grass is in need of some work. However, my niece and two cousins has conveniently disappeared. Denise, Scott, and David feels that this is a good time to walk over to the store for a pack of gum. Something tell me that nobody is going to hurry home, either. Well, anybody who is afraid of work can cook dinner instead.

CONNECTIONS

People around the world speak thousands of different languages. Would you like to learn a new language? Read about the use of language in the Language theme in **CONNECTIONS,** pages C12–C13. Then write a paragraph describing why speaking more than one language could be useful or just plain fun! In your paragraph, include at least two sentences containing compound subjects. Check your paragraph for subject-verb agreement when you are finished writing.

▶ *Answers begin on page 263.*

FOCUS USAGE: AGREEMENT WITH *"EITHER . . . OR"* OR *"NEITHER . . . NOR"*

Sometimes the nouns or pronouns in a compound subject are linked by the word pairs *either . . . or* or *neither . . . nor*. In these cases, the verb must agree with the noun or pronoun that is closer to it in the sentence. It can take a singular or a plural form. Look at these examples:

Either your parents or your sister is coming to get you.

Either your sister or your parents are coming to get you.

Either the sandwiches or the salad has to be eaten now.

Either the salad or the sandwiches have to be eaten now.

Notice how the verb in the first sentence agrees with the singular noun *sister* because *sister* is closer to the verb. In the second sentence, the verb must agree with the plural noun *parents*. The third and fourth sentences also are examples of how a compound subject could take either a singular or a plural verb. Remember in these cases to always make the verb agree with the subject that is closer to the verb.

EDITING PRACTICE

■ The paragraph below contains errors in subject-verb agreement. Edit the paragraph by correcting verbs that do not agree with their subjects.

Kyle and Mary agrees that having a telephone can be as much trouble as it is convenient. It's lucky for them that they do agree. Everyone in the world besides the two of them seem to feel that if a telephone rings, it must be answered. But if it is *your* telephone in *your* house, isn't it *your* choice whether or not you feels like talking to somebody? However, most people looks at you like you're crazy if you behaves like this. Neither Kyle nor Mary have that problem.

▶ *Answers begin on page 264.*

PRE-GED PRACTICE

*Choose the **one best answer** for each item.*
***Items 1 to 5** refer to the following passage.*

(1)Everybody have academic subjects in which he or she does well and others in which he or she does less well. (2)Mona and Terry was talking about how writing essays is fairly easy for them. (3)They feel that mathematics are the hardest subject unless statistics is counted as a separate subject. (4)However, the members of my math class feels confident that they have done well. (5)Personally, I hope that something happen so that I improve my writing skills.

1. Sentence 1: Everybody have academic subjects in which he or she does well and others in which he or she does less well.

What correction should be made to this sentence?
(1) change *have* to *has*
(2) change *subjects* to *subject's*
(3) change *does* to *do*
(4) change *does* to *did*
(5) change *does* to *dids*

2. Sentence 2: Mona and Terry was talking about how writing essays is fairly easy for them.

What correction should be made to this sentence?
(1) change *was* to *is*
(2) change *was* to *were*
(3) change *is* to *are*
(4) change *is* to *am*
(5) change *them* to *they*

3. Sentence 3: They feel that mathematics are the hardest subject unless statistics is counted as a separate subject.

What correction should be made to this sentence?
(1) change *are* to *were*
(2) change *are* to *is*
(3) change *is counted* to *are counted*
(4) change *is counted* to *am counted*
(5) change *is counted* to *count*

4. Sentence 4: However, the members of my math class feels confident that they have done well.

What correction should be made to this sentence?
(1) change *feels* to *feel*
(2) change *feels* to *felts*
(3) change *feels* to *feel's*
(4) change *have* to *has*
(5) change *done* to *do*

5. Sentence 5: Personally, I hope that something happen so that I improve my writing skills.

What correction should be made to this sentence?
(1) change *hope* to *hopes*
(2) change *hope* to *hoping*
(3) change *happen* to *happens*
(4) change *improve* to *improves*
(5) change *skills* to *skill's*

▶ *Answers begin on page 264.*

Subject-Verb Agreement and Sentence Word Order

In more complex sentences, identifying the subject and verb can be tricky. In this lesson, you will learn how to identify them and make sure they agree.

SUBJECT-VERB AGREEMENT WHEN THE SUBJECT FOLLOWS THE VERB

In checking for subject-verb agreement, it is usually best to identify the verb first. Then, ask *who* or *what* is performing the action or being described. This will help you find the subject. Once you have identified both the verb and the subject, you can check for agreement.

The subjects and verbs in these sentences are easy to identify because the verbs follow the subjects:

The car stopped at the stop sign.

We enjoyed the delicious meal.

However, in some sentences the verbs do not follow the subjects. This makes it trickier to identify them. Take a look at these sentences:

There goes my best friend.

Where is my wallet?

In the sky soared a black falcon.

These examples show three types of sentences in which the verb comes before the subject. In sentences beginning with the word *there*, the subject often follows the verb. The words *there* and *where* are not subjects. Rather, these words add information about the verbs.

Many questions are structured like backwards statements. It can help to reverse the question. Think about the second example above. This could be said, "My wallet is where?" This helps show that *wallet* (and not *where*) is the subject of the sentence.

Think about the example, "In the sky soared a black falcon." The subject is at the very end of the sentence. This is called a *reverse-order statement*. Again, the best strategy is to find the verb, then ask *who?* or *what?* In this case, *soared* is the verb. The sky did not soar, but the *falcon* did.

To check subject-verb agreement in the sentence below, first identify the subject and the verb.

Where is the newspapers?

In this sentence the verb is *is*—a singular form of the verb *to be*.

Then, reverse the question: "The newspapers is where?" Now it's easy to see that the subject is not *where*, but the plural noun *newspapers*. Since *is* is singular, it does not agree with this subject. Change it to the plural form of the verb, *are*. The corrected sentence should read:

Where *are* the newspapers?

PRACTICE • 1

▶ **Part A** In the following sentences, underline the subjects once and the verbs twice. Then make sure that each verb agrees with its subject. If a subject and verb do not agree, cross out the verb and rewrite it using the correct form.

1. Here is my favorite photograph of you.
2. What is the names of the puppies?
3. In the garden below the window stands the eerie statue.
4. There is no words for this feeling.
5. Why do you thinks she hung up on me?

▶ **Part B** In the following paragraph, there are errors in subject-verb agreement. Look for any verbs that do not agree with their subjects. Cross out the incorrect verbs, and rewrite them using the correct forms.

There is completely magical things about the ocean. For instance, there are the ocean's constant movement. In the tidal pools by the marsh are very warm salt water. There I feel at one with the natural world. Why doesn't lakes or ponds interest me more? I guess I like the expanse and motion of the sea.

▶ *Answers begin on page 264.*

SUBJECT-VERB AGREEMENT WITH PHRASES

Sometimes the subject and the verb in a sentence are separated by one or more phrases. Take a look at the following sentences:

> The violin with the dusty neck and the broken strings is mine.
>
> Two years in the attic aren't good for any instrument.
>
> The instructor of the music class helps me with my playing.

In each of these sentences, the subject and the verb are separated by a group of words or phrase. These phrases add description to the sentences, so they should not be removed. However, they can make it harder to identify the verb and subject.

In the first sentence, it might seem that the plural noun *strings* is the subject. However, if you identify the verb *is*, and ask yourself *who?* or *what?*, you will find the real subject, *violin*. The *violin*, not the *strings*, is mine. Since the subject *violin* is singular, the singular verb *is* is the correct form to use.

In Lesson 7, you learned that a compound subject is made up of two nouns or pronouns joined by the word *and*. There is a handful of phrases that can take the place of *and* and "interrupt" a sentence. These interrupting phrases include *along with, as well as, in addition to,* and *together with*. However, adding these phrases *does not* create a compound or plural subject. If the subject is singular, it takes a singular verb. If the subject is plural, it remains plural. Take a look at the following sentences:

> Tina and her four sisters want a party.
>
> Tina, in addition to her four sisters, wants a birthday party.
>
> Tina's parents, as well as her aunt, have planned a surprise party.

In the first sentence, *Tina and her four sisters* form a compound subject. This subject is plural and needs the plural verb form *want*. In the second sentence, *and* has been replaced by the interrupting phrase *in addition to*. Notice that this phrase does not create a compound subject. The subject is the singular *Tina* and takes the singular verb form *wants*. The third sentence also contains an interrupting phrase, *as well as*. There is no compound subject. The subject in this sentence is the plural *parents,* which agrees with the plural verb *have planned*.

Check these sentences for subject-verb agreement. Remember that the noun closest to the verb is *not* necessarily the subject.

The woman over there in the cotton skirt is my mother.

My mother, along with her two sisters, is here for a week.

In the first sentence, the verb *is* and the singular noun *woman* are in agreement. The subject and verb are separated by two phrases—*over there* and *in the cotton skirt*. In the second sentence, the verb *is* and the subject *mother* are both singular and in agreement. They are separated by the interrupting phrase, *along with her two sisters.*

PRACTICE • 2

▶ **Part A** In the following sentences, underline the subjects once and the verbs twice. Then make sure that each verb agrees with its subject. If a subject and verb do not agree, cross out the verb and rewrite it using the correct form.

1. The man in the expensive sunglasses are very mysterious.
2. The chart on the label of this jar of pickles is confusing.
3. These songs, as well as the one on the last album, is in the key of "C."
4. The best comedians in the world comes from Canada.
5. Three families, along with their four dogs, lives at this end of the road.

▶ **Part B** In the following paragraph, there are errors in subject-verb agreement. Cross out any verbs that do not agree with their subjects, and rewrite them using the correct forms.

The painters, as well as the carpenter and the plumber, is due to arrive on Wednesday. One of these workers are going to have to watch the others work for a while because everyone need to work in the same corner of the kitchen. The problem with this plan have to do with my checkbook. Some of my hard-earned dollars, as well as my groceries, is going to go to pay someone as he rests!

▶ *Answers begin on page 264.*

FOCUS PUNCTUATION: COMMAS WITH INTERRUPTING PHRASES

The four interrupting phrases that replace the word *and* on page 186 are always set off with commas when they appear between a subject and a verb. The commas can help remind you that these phrases do not affect the number of the subject and the verb. Look at the following sentences:

> This hammock, together with this novel, will be my entertainment.
>
> The potatoes, along with the corn, are fresh.

Descriptive phrases, however, are not set off by commas. Look at these examples:

> The book on the bed is very good.
>
> That book with the blue cover is great!

EDITING PRACTICE

■ The sentences below contain comma and subject-verb agreement errors. Edit the sentences by correcting any errors in these two areas.

> The men and the women, from the restaurant, is going skating at Webhannet Pond. Lynn, along with Patty and Lenore, say that she is going with them.

CONNECTIONS

Read about treasured cultural and historical documents in the Cultural theme in **CONNECTIONS**, pages C6–C7. Imagine that you were invited to place some personal documents in a time capsule that would be opened in 50 years. Write a few sentences about the documents you would choose and why you would choose them. Be sure your sentences use proper subject-verb agreement, especially those containing interrupting phrases.

▶ *Answers begin on page 265.*

PRE-GED PRACTICE

*Choose the **one best answer** for each item.*
***Items 1 to 5** refer to the following passage.*

(1)On the walls of this office there hangs many different photographs and items people have given to Julia. (2)The desk in the corner are piled high with papers, and I haven't the slightest idea how she works there. (3)The filing cabinets, along with two side tables and a huge bookcase, lines the walls and add to the clutter. (4)Why don't she try to reduce the volume of stuff in the room? (5)The smiling woman in the midst of the folders and the books haven't the slightest idea that there *is* a "mess" to be cleaned up!

1. Sentence 1: On the walls of this office there hangs many different photographs and items people have given to Julia.

What correction should be made to this sentence?
(1) change *hangs* to *hang*
(2) change *hangs* to *hanging*
(3) change *have given* to *has given*
(4) change *have given* to *had given*
(5) change *have given* to *have gave*

2. Sentence 2: The desk in the corner are piled high with papers, and I haven't the slightest idea how she works there.

What correction should be made to this sentence?
(1) change *are* to *is*
(2) change *are* to *were*
(3) change *haven't* to *hasn't*
(4) change *haven't* to *hadn't*
(5) change *works* to *work*

3. Sentence 3: The filing cabinets, along with two side tables and a huge bookcase, lines the walls and add to the clutter.

Which is the best way to write the underlined portion of this sentence? If you think the original is the best way, choose (1).
(1) cabinets, along with two side tables and a huge bookcase, lines
(2) cabinets, along with two side tables and a huge bookcase lines
(3) cabinets along with two side tables and a huge bookcase, lines
(4) cabinets, along with two side tables and a huge bookcase, line
(5) cabinets along with two side tables and a huge bookcase line

4. Sentence 4: Why don't she try to reduce the volume of stuff in the room?

What correction should be made to this sentence?
(1) change *don't* to *doesn't*
(2) change *don't* to *do*
(3) change *try* to *tries*
(4) change *try* to *tried*
(5) change *reduce* to *reduces*

5. Sentence 5: The smiling woman in the midst of the folders and the books haven't the slightest idea that there *is* a "mess" to be cleaned up!

What correction should be made to this sentence?
(1) add commas after *woman* and *books*
(2) change *haven't* to *hasn't*
(3) change *is* to *were*
(4) change *is* to *are*
(5) change *is* to *isn't*

► *Answers begin on page 265.*

LESSON 9

Action Verbs

Have you ever referred to someone as an active person—one who makes things happen? Or perhaps you've heard someone say, "I'm taking a passive role." Sentences can be described in the same way. Sentences are written in either the active or passive voice.

ACTIVE AND PASSIVE VOICE

The difference between these two "voices" is in the relationship between the subject and the verb. If the subject of the sentence *performs* the action of the verb, then the sentence is in the active voice. If the subject of the sentence *receives* the action of the verb, the sentence is in the passive voice.

Here are three pairs of sentences. Each sentence in the pair uses the same verb. The first sentence in each pair is in the active voice. The second sentence in each pair is in the passive voice.

Active: A barber cut my brother's hair yesterday.

Passive: My brother's hair was cut by a barber yesterday.

Active: The barber bent my brother's ear for nearly an hour.

Passive: My brother's ear was bent by this barber for nearly an hour.

Active: My brother enjoyed the haircut and the chat.

Passive: The haircut and the chat were enjoyed by my brother.

As you can see, sentences in the active voice do not need a helping verb or past participle. They use simple, perfect, or continuous verb tenses. In the active voice sentences, the *barber* and the *brother* perform the actions in their sentences. This is why the term "active" is used to describe these sentences.

Sentences in the passive voice have verbs constructed with a form of the verb *to be* and a **past participle.** In the passive voice sentences above, the subject receives the action of the verb. It does nothing by itself. This is why the term "passive" is used to describe these sentences.

past participle: a verb form usually made by adding *-ed* or *-en* to the present tense verb

When deciding whether a sentence is in the active or passive voice, ask whether the subject performs the action (active voice) or receives the action (passive voice). Also, look for a form of the verb *to be* followed by a past participle. Identify the voice in the sentences below:

The guitarist was cheered wildly.

Her guitar solo sent chills through me.

In the first sentence, the subject is *guitarist* and the verb is *was cheered*. The action of the verb is received by the subject, so this sentence is in the passive voice. Notice that the verb is constructed with a form of the verb *to be* (*was*) followed by a past participle (*cheered*). In the second sentence, the subject is *solo* and the verb is *sent*. The subject performs the action, so this sentence is in the active voice.

PRACTICE • 1

▶ **Part A** In the following sentences, underline the subjects once and the verbs twice. Then decide if the sentence is in the passive voice (*P*) or in the active voice (*A*). Write *P* or *A* in the space provided.

_____ **1.** The elementary schoolteacher was delighted by his class.

_____ **2.** Three of the children were given special attention after school.

_____ **3.** Many students spoke of their fondness for their teacher.

_____ **4.** In his classroom, a supportive atmosphere had been created.

_____ **5.** The school's principal was thrilled with this first-year teacher.

▶ **Part B** The following paragraph has sentences in both voices. Underline the subject of each sentence once and the verb twice. Place a *P* before each sentence that is in the passive voice and an *A* before each sentence that is in the active voice.

The set of oil paints was bought by Derek. It was wrapped up in colorful paper and ribbons by an employee of the art supplies store. Derek brought the gift home. It was left on the wooden table by the front door. Of course, I loved the surprise.

▶ *Answers begin on page 265.*

CHOOSING ACTION VERBS

As you write, you can structure your sentences in either the active or passive voice. As a general rule, you should choose the active voice. Sentences in the active voice tend to be livelier and more interesting than sentences in the passive voice. The active voice seems clearer and more direct because it is less wordy. Often, the wordiness of the passive voice makes a sentence sound awkward.

Take a look at these pairs of example sentences, and decide which one of each pair is clearer and more direct.

> The tuna sandwich was devoured by Katherine in a minute or two.
>
> Katherine devoured the tuna sandwich in a minute or two.

> Nothing had been eaten by her since the previous night.
>
> She had eaten nothing since the previous night.

> She was told by me that she should be more careful about her eating habits.
>
> I told her that she should be more careful about her eating habits.

The second sentence in each pair is in the active voice and is livelier and more direct. However, the active voice is not the only reason these sentences are livelier. They are also livelier because they use action verbs. *Action verbs* are verbs that describe actions. Often, when people write, they tend to use a form of the verb *to be* over and over again. This can make writing repetitive and boring. You can replace the verb *to be* with action verbs to improve your writing. Look at the sentence pairs below:

> Marian is a very fast runner.
>
> Marian runs very fast.

> Singing is fun for me.
>
> I love to sing.

In each pair, the second sentence has been rewritten to use an action verb rather than the verb *to be*. These verbs also provide variety and are more interesting.

Read these two descriptions. Which do you find more interesting? Why?

> Jorge is very tall. His eyes are green. His hair is brown. He is a night watchman in a big building downtown. He is very friendly and funny. When I see him he is always very nice to me.
>
> Jorge's head almost touches the seven-foot ceiling in his living room. His green eyes dance mischievously and his brown hair sparkles with sunny highlights. He works as a night watchman in a big building downtown. Jorge's friendly and funny personality charms everyone he meets. When I see him he always smiles and jokes with me.

The second is livelier and more interesting. It uses action verbs like *dance, sparkles, charms, smiles,* and *jokes.* Notice that using action verbs requires adding more imaginative details. This is a hidden advantage of using action verbs. Constructing sentences with them can help you discover more creative ways to describe something.

PRACTICE • 2

▶ **Part A** The following sentences use forms of the verb *to be.* Rewrite the sentences using action verbs.

1. The letter from Karen was very funny. ______________________________
2. There was laughter in the room. ______________________________
3. Some people were on the floor. ______________________________

▶ **Part B** Rewrite the following description using action verbs.

The building is old. It is on Main Street. It is four stories tall. It was a house many years ago, but now it's an office. The door and the shutters are green. The rest of the house is white. There is a garden in the back, but I don't know whose it is.

____

____

____

____

____

▶ *Answers begin on page 265.*

FOCUS USAGE: CHANGING PASSIVE TO ACTIVE VOICE

As you revise your own writing, you will probably come across sentences in the passive voice. You may decide that many of these sentences would be clearer and more effective in the active voice. To revise a sentence in the passive voice, rewrite it so that the performer of the action (the subject) comes first. Look at this example:

The celery was diced in about five seconds by the food processor.

The food processor diced the celery in about five seconds.

The easiest way to revise sentences in the passive voice is to first identify the verb. Then look for who or what could perform the action the verb describes. Rewrite the sentence so the performer becomes the subject and the verb becomes an action verb.

EDITING PRACTICE

■ The paragraph below contains sentences in both the active and passive voice. Label each sentence, and then edit the paragraph by revising sentences in the passive voice into the active voice.

The beach was visited by Ben and me last weekend. His car was taken for the trip. My own car (with three bad tires on it) didn't start. Ben's driving filled me with fear. Still, fun was had by both of us. Ben's hilarious attempts at swimming were watched by me with pleasure.

CONNECTIONS

Do you ever set a VCR to record a program while you're away? Or set a microwave to defrost a frozen dinner? These devices are made possible by microchips. Read about microchips in the Technology theme in **CONNECTIONS**, pages C2–C3. Then, think about the programmable devices you use. Write a short paragraph about whether these devices have made your life easier. See if you can write your paragraph in the active voice using action verbs.

► *Answers begin on page 265.*

PRE-GED PRACTICE

*Choose the **one best answer** for each item. **Items 1 to 5** refer to the following passage.*

(1)The tenant who lives next door is a real headache to me. (2)Every night, his television is played at top volume. (3)I have tried many ideas, including knocking on their door and calling him through the window. (4)I may call the landlord if the situation does not improve soon. (5)I, as well as my brother who live with me, hope to experience peace and quiet in the apartment.

1. Sentence 1: The tenant who lives upstairs is a real headache to me.

Which is the best way to write the underlined portion of the sentence? If you think the original is the best way, choose (1).

(1) is a real headache to me
(2) is a real headache to I
(3) are a real headache to me
(4) give me a real headache
(5) gives me a real headache

2. Sentence 2: Every night, his television is played at top volume.

Which is the best way to write the underlined portion of the sentence? If you think the original is the best way, choose (1).

(1) his television is played
(2) his television are played
(3) he play his television
(4) he plays his television
(5) He plays his television

3. Sentence 3: I have tried many ideas, including knocking on their door and calling him through the window.

Which is the best way to write the underlined portion of the sentence? If you think the original is the best way, choose (1).

(1) on their door and calling him
(2) on there door and calling him
(3) on they're door and calling him
(4) on his door and calling him
(5) on his door and calling them

4. Sentence 4: I may call the landlord if the situation does not improve soon.

Which is the best way to write the underlined portion of this sentence? If you think the original is the best way, choose (1).

(1) I may call the landlord
(2) I may call the Landlord
(3) The landlord may have to be called
(4) The landlord might have to be called
(5) The landlord may has to be called

5. Sentence 5: I, as well as my brother who live with me, hope to experience peace and quiet in the apartment.

What correction should be made to this sentence?

(1) remove the commas after *I* and *me*
(2) change *live* to *lives*
(3) change *live* to *live's*
(4) change *hope* to *hopes*
(5) replace *hope* with *is hoping*

► *Answers begin on page 265.*

LESSON 10

Adjectives and Adverbs

Another way to improve your writing is through the correct use of adjectives and adverbs.

USING ADJECTIVES AND ADVERBS

adjectives: words that describe nouns and pronouns

Usually, **adjectives** appear before the word they describe. The adjectives in the following sentences are underlined.

The clean shirt lay on the bookcase.

Even after fourteen years, I remember those delicious steaks.

The song sounds spooky and sexy.

The adjective *clean* describes the word *shirt*. In the second sentence, the adjective *fourteen* describes the word *years*, and *delicious* describes the word *steaks*. In the last sentence, the adjectives *spooky* and *sexy* both describe the noun *song*.

Adjectives describe nouns and pronouns by answering one of four questions: *which one?*, *what kind?*, *how much?*, and *how many?* Here is a chart showing how adjectives can answer these questions:

Which one?	that book	Johnson's office
What kind?	fresh fruit	fantastic movie
How much?	some gasoline	more money
How many?	four scars	few offers

adverbs: words that describe verbs, adjectives, and other adverbs

Adverbs can appear before or after the word they describe. Many adverbs end in the letters *ly*. The adverbs in the following sentences are underlined.

The child dreamed happily through the night.

I thought he was very nice.

The young athlete swam rather gracefully.

modifies: changes the meaning of another word by making it more specific

The adverb *happily* **modifies** the verb *dreamed*. It describes how the child dreamed. The adverb *very* modifies the adjective *nice*. The adverb *gracefully* modifies the verb *swam* by telling how the athlete performed the action. The adverb *rather* modifies the adverb *gracefully*.

Adverbs describe verbs, adjectives, and adverbs by answering one of four questions: *how?*, *when?*, *where?*, and *to what extent?* Here is a chart showing how adverbs can answer each of these questions:

How?	read thoughtfully	ate rudely
When?	arrived promptly	died yesterday
Where?	drove away	steps aside
To what extent?	barely cooked	almost ready

A common mistake is to use an adjective when an adverb should be used. Take a look at the following sentence and notice how it was corrected.

Incorrect: Joshua ran quick.

Correct: Joshua ran quickly.

PRACTICE • 1

▶ **Part A** In the following sentences, fill in the blank with an adjective that answers the question in parentheses.

1. He has received ________________ contract offers. (how many?)

2. After a hard practice, he needs to eat a ________ meal. (what kind?)

3. The __________________ shirt is his favorite. (which one?)

▶ **Part B** In the following sentences, circle the adverbs and draw arrows to the words that they modify.

1. The dancer was highly praised by the director.

2. The director spoke warmly of the dancer's movements.

3. Yesterday, she harshly criticized the troupe's most famous member.

▶ **Part C** In the following sentences, underline the adjectives and circle the adverbs. Then check to see if they are being used correctly. Cross out any that are incorrect and write the correct word above.

The sporty rental car rode quiet on the open highway. However, the steering wheel turned too easy, so the car was difficult to control.

▶ *Answers begin on page 266.*

COMPARING WITH ADJECTIVES AND ADVERBS

comparative form: the form of an adjective or an adverb used to compare *two* things

superlative form: the form of an adjective or adverb used to compare *three* or more things

Often in your writing you will want to compare two or more things. In these cases, you will need to use the **comparative form** or the **superlative form** of adjectives and adverbs. This chart shows how the basic form of adjectives and adverbs can change:

forms:	basic	comparative	superlative
adjective	smart	smarter	smartest
adverb	quickly	more quickly	most quickly

If you want to compare *two* persons, places, or things, you use the comparative form of an adjective or adverb. Add the ending *-er* to make the comparative form of a one-syllable adjective or adverb. For most adjectives and adverbs of two syllables or more, use the words *more* or *less* to make the comparative form. Look at the examples below:

Silk is smoother than cotton.

Kangaroos can jump higher than human athletes.

Steak is more expensive than chicken.

He treats customers less pleasantly than the other cashier.

If you want to compare *three or more* persons, places, or things, you must use the superlative form. Add the ending *-est* to make the superlative form of a one-syllable adjective or adverb. For an adjective or adverb of two syllables or more, use the words *most* or *least* before it. Here are some example sentences:

Of the three brothers, Charlie is the fastest talker.

I've seen many bad movies but this one was the most disappointing.

Of all the driving students, Bobbie drove least cautiously.

Many inexperienced writers make the mistake of using both the *-er* ending and *more* or *less* to form a comparative. Similarly, it is incorrect to use both the *-est* ending and the words *most* or *least* to form a superlative. Such constructions as *more harder, less colder, most fastest,* and *least driest* are always incorrect.

Take a look at the following examples of comparatives and superlatives:

I believe that Kate is a kinder person than Joe.

I think that Joe is more intelligent than Kate.

Among the three of us, I am the most artistic.

In the first two sentences, the comparative is used because two people are being compared. Because the third sentence compares more than two people, the superlative is used.

PRACTICE • 2

▶ **Part A** In the following sentences, underline the adjectives and circle the adverbs. Cross out any that are incorrect, and write them correctly above.

1. The rainier weather of the year arrived suddenly.
2. The long, steady storm raised reservoirs more dramatically than last month's storm.
3. We have had the most brownest lawns and driest forests in years.
4. To me, the pleasantest weather of all is a snowstorm.
5. My dog runs and leaps most enthusiastically than my cat.

▶ **Part B** In the following paragraph, some adjectives and adverbs are used incorrectly. Cross out any that are incorrect, and write them correctly above.

The city of Lowell, Massachusetts is more smaller than Boston. In the nineteenth and early twentieth centuries, it was one of the more important textile producers in the entire country. It fell on hard times in recent decades, but now is making one of the more impressive renewal efforts in all of New England.

▶ *Answers begin on page 266.*

FOCUS PUNCTUATION FOCUS: COMMAS IN A SERIES

Sometimes when you are writing you need to write two or three adjectives or adverbs in a series. There are specific rules for punctuating a series. Correct punctuation helps the reader avoid confusion.

COMMAS IN A SERIES

Use commas to separate three or more items from one another in a series. Look at these examples:

Adjectives: The fuzzy, friendly, black puppy lapped us.

Adverbs: The bird soared lazily, smoothly, and effortlessly above us.

Note that you *do not* need a comma between the last item in a series and the next word (*black puppy*, *effortlessly above*).

EDITING PRACTICE

■ The paragraph below contains incorrect adjectives and adverbs. Edit it by correcting any adjectives and adverbs that are used incorrectly.

The popular game of baseball is more extremely enjoyable to watch in person. The large, odd shaped, and very green field is impossible to appreciate on a television screen. You should go soonly to a local ballpark. Even the most small Little League field has a simpler and beautiful design. When the nine players scamper joyful onto the field, that simple design comes immediately to life.

CONNECTIONS

For centuries, people have played word games. Read about these games in the Entertainment theme in **CONNECTIONS**, pages C10-C11. Then play the tongue twister game with a friend. Each of you should write a tongue twister using a verb, a noun, adverbs, and adjectives all beginning with the same letter. For example, *Tom terrifically told two tantalizingly terrible tall tales*. Then try saying each other's twisters.

► *Answers begin on page 266.*

PRE-GED PRACTICE

*Choose the **one best answer** for each item.*
***Items 1 to 5** refer to the following passage.*

(1)The extraordinary painting *Moon Over Harlem* by William H. Johnson is the more stirring work of art I've ever seen. (2)In this painting, a woman lies dead on a littered Harlem street. (3)A large, burly, uniformed, policeman leads away one man. (4)Three other policemen seem to stare straight at you with shocked expressions. (5)Over this scene, an oranger moon rises in the black Harlem sky.

1. Sentence 1: The extraordinary painting *Moon Over Harlem* by William H. Johnson is the more stirring work of art I've ever seen.

Which is the best way to write the underlined portion of this sentence? If you think the original is the best way, choose (1).
(1) more stirring work of art
(2) most stirring work of art
(3) least stirring work of art
(4) stirringest work of art
(5) more stirringly work of art

2. Sentence 2: In this painting, a woman lies dead on a littered Harlem street.

Which is the best way to write the underlined portion of this sentence? If you think the original is the best way, choose (1).
(1) dead on a littered Harlem street
(2) dead on a more littered Harlem street
(3) dead on a most littered Harlem street
(4) deadly on a littered Harlem street
(5) deadly on a more littered Harlem street

3. Sentence 3: A large, burly, uniformed, policeman leads away one man.

Which is the best way to write the underlined portion of this sentence? If you think the original is the best way, choose (1).
(1) A large, burly, uniformed, policeman
(2) A large burly uniformed policeman
(3) A large, burly, uniformed policeman
(4) A large, burly uniformed policeman
(5) A larger, burly, uniformed policeman

4. Sentence 4: Three other policemen seem to stare straight at you with shocked expressions.

Which is the best way to write the underlined portion of this sentence? If you think the original is the best way, choose (1).
(1) with shocked expressions
(2) with shocked, expressions
(3) with more shocked expressions
(4) with most shocked expressions
(5) with most, shocked, expressions

5. Sentence 5: Over this scene, an oranger moon rises in the black Harlem sky.

Which is the best way to write the underlined portion of this sentence? If you think the original is the best way, choose (1).
(1) an oranger moon rises
(2) an oranger moon rise
(3) a more orange moon rises
(4) a more orange moon rise
(5) an orange moon rises

▶ *Answers begin on page 266.*

UNIT 2

Sentence Structure

In Unit 1, you learned about words and how they are used in sentences. In this unit, you will learn about different kinds of sentences and how they are constructed. You also will learn tips for avoiding common mistakes people make when they write sentences. Knowing more about sentence structure will help you write essays with clear, interesting, and varied sentences.

Compound Sentences

A simple sentence has one subject and one verb. You probably use a lot of simple sentences when you write. However, using varied sentence structures will make your writing lively and interesting.

IDENTIFYING A COMPOUND SENTENCE

In addition to simple sentences, you can use *compound sentences*. A compound sentence contains two complete thoughts that are related to one another. Each thought contains a subject and a verb and could stand alone as a simple sentence. Instead, the two thoughts are joined together by a comma and a connecting word. Take a look at the following examples:

> Finally the gloomy weather lifted, and we went for a bike ride.
>
> I listened to the radio all afternoon, but the bad music only worsened my mood.

Each sentence above contains two closely related ideas. In the first sentence, the first idea (*weather lifted*) and the second idea (*we went for a bike ride*) are related by cause and effect. In other words, the first action caused the second action.

The two ideas in a compound sentence must be related. If they are not, the two ideas belong in two separate sentences. For instance, the sentence *I listened to the radio all afternoon* should not be combined with the sentence *Jeopardy is my favorite television show*. There is no logical way to connect these two ideas.

Because a compound sentence combines two complete thoughts, it contains two subjects and two verbs. In the second example sentence, the first subject and verb are *I listened*, and the second subject and verb are *music worsened*. Notice how a comma separates the two thoughts. After the comma comes the connecting word. *And* is not the only connecting word that can be used. The words *but*, *nor*, *or*, *so*, and *yet* also can indicate how two ideas are related to one another.

You might assume that you can easily identify compound sentences by their length. However, compound sentences are not always longer than simple sentences. Take a look at the two sentences at the top of the next page.

The music from the orchestra, swelling upwards into every corner of the vast concert hall, filled Mrs. Kenny's heart with joy.

He brought the glass of water, and I drank it in a single gulp.

The first sentence is an extremely long simple sentence. However, the only subject is *music* and the only verb is *filled*. All the words between the commas describe the music. The second sentence is a relatively short compound sentence with two subjects and two verbs. The first subject and verb are *He brought*, and the second subject and verb are *I drank*. In order to correctly identify a compound sentence, you must examine it carefully. Look for two complete and related thoughts, as well as two subjects and two verbs.

PRACTICE • 1

■ In the following sentences, underline the subjects once and the verbs twice. Then decide if the sentences are compound or simple. Fill in each blank with a *C* if the sentence is compound, or an *S* if the sentence is simple.

_____ **1.** The construction workers arrived at 7:00A.M., and two hours later the sidewalk in front of the pharmacy was completely removed.

_____ **2.** Some men used shovels and a jackhammer, and others carried away pieces of stone and cement in wheelbarrows.

_____ **3.** The sidewalk was covered with piles of wood, gravel, and tools.

_____ **4.** Customers came to the pharmacy during the morning, but the store's entrance was blocked from time to time.

_____ **5.** One man became angry outside the entrance, but then he calmed down.

_____ **6.** This continued all through the day until quite late.

_____ **7.** The disruption brought some excitement to the neighborhood, yet nobody hopes for another day of it.

► *Answers begin on page 267.*

USING PARALLEL STRUCTURE

Some sentences are not compound sentences, but they contain some compound elements. In Lesson 7 you learned about compound subjects. Did you know that you also can write sentences with compound verbs or compound objects? Take a look at the following examples:

Compound Sentence: The door crashed open, and the dog jumped.

Compound Subject: The dog and I jumped at the sound of the crash.

Compound Verb: The door crashed open and slammed shut.

Compound Object: The loud crash scared the dog and me.

The first sentence contains two complete and related thoughts, as well as two subjects and two verbs. In the second sentence, both *dog* and *I* perform the single action of jumping. In the third sentence, the *door* performs two actions—crashing and slamming. In the fourth sentence, two words, *dog* and *me*, receive the action of the verb.

When you use compound elements in a sentence, you must make sure they have *parallel structure*. That is, they must be worded in similar ways. Here is a pair of sentences with compound verbs. The first sentence does not have parallel structure, but the second one does:

Not Parallel: Today I exercised, ate, and was reading a book.

Parallel: Today I exercised, ate, and read a book.

In the first sentence the verbs *exercised* and *ate* are in the past tense, but the third verb, *was reading,* is in the past continuous tense. In the second sentence, all the verbs are in the same tense.

Sometimes, using parallel structure is a better choice than writing a compound sentence. Look at the following:

Compound Sentence: The park is good for having a picnic and playing baseball, and often I find wildflowers.

Parallel Structure: The park is good for having a picnic, playing baseball, and finding wildflowers.

Compound Sentence: In the ocean I swam smoothly and calmly, and I had to be careful.

Parallel Structure: In the ocean I swam smoothly, calmly, and carefully.

Using a compound sentence for the ideas in each of these examples is awkward and unnecessary. Using parallel structure makes the sentences clearer and easier to read.

PRACTICE • 2

■ Revise the following compound sentences using parallel structure.

1. My teacher advised me to read and write, and I should study.

____

____

2. This past month I have read three books and written a ten-page autobiography, and I was researching a report on immigration.

____

____

3. A friend said that recently my writing seemed smoother and clearer, and it interests her more.

____

____

4. Writing well makes me feel happy and proud, and I am feeling more confident.

____

____

CONNECTIONS

The Employment theme in **CONNECTIONS,** pages C4–C5, gives information about jobs that require writing in order to perform the job well. Write two compound sentences that you might write if you were a nurse, an office manager, a bookkeeper, or a travel agent. Be sure to punctuate the sentences carefully.

► *Answers begin on page 267.*

FOCUS

PUNCTUATION: COMMAS AND SEMICOLONS WITH COMPOUND SENTENCES

Most compound sentences are connected with commas and a connecting word. However, you also can connect compound sentences with semicolons when the ideas are *very* closely related. If you use a semicolon to connect the thoughts in a compound sentence, you do not need a connecting word. However, a connecting word will make the relationship between the two thoughts clearer. Some connecting words you can use with a semicolon are: ***however, nonetheless,*** or ***nevertheless***. All three of the following compound sentences are correct.

I hate jazz, but my wife can't get enough of it.

I hate jazz; my wife can't get enough of it.

I hate jazz; however, my wife can't get enough of it.

Notice that the sentence with the connecting word *but* uses a comma and not a semicolon. Also, if you use a semicolon and a connecting word, you must use a comma after the connecting word.

EDITING PRACTICE

■ The paragraph below contains errors in parallel structure. Edit the paragraph by using correct parallel structure and combining some of the sentences into compound sentences.

Linda considered traveling to Chicago by train or plane, or she was thinking about driving. She was not terribly fond of flying. She was a little concerned about the safety of the train. There had been several train accidents lately. She thought driving might be the best way to go. She had never driven more than an hour by herself. She was interested in spending as much time as she could with her daughter in Chicago. She decided to overcome her fear and take the plane.

► *Answers begin on page 267.*

PRE-GED PRACTICE

Choose the ***one best answer*** *for each item.*
Items 1 to 4 *refer to the following passage.*

(1)At the beach various members of the family sunbathed, swam, and they were playing catch. (2)The sand dunes were wonderful for privacy, romantic walks, and to search for rare birds. (3)The water was freezing, nonetheless people went swimming. (4)Finally, the family picked up its belongings, carried them to the car, and they were riding home.

1. Sentence 1: At the beach various members of the family sunbathed, swam, and they were playing catch.

Which is the best way to write the underlined portion of this sentence? If you think the original is the best way, choose (1).

(1) sunbathed, swam, and they were playing catch
(2) sunbathed, swam, and played catch
(3) were sunbathing, swam, and they were playing catch
(4) sunbathed and swam, and they was playing catch
(5) sunbathed and swam, and plays catch

2. Sentence 2: The sand dunes were wonderful for privacy, romantic walks, and to search for rare birds.

Which is the best way to write the underlined portion of this sentence? If you think the original is the best way, choose (1).

(1) privacy, romantic walks, and to search for rare birds
(2) privacy and romantic walks, and to search for rare birds.
(3) privacy, to have romantic walks, and to search for rare birds
(4) privacy, romantic walks, and searches for rare birds
(5) privacy and romantic walking, and to search for rare birds.

3. Sentence 3: The water was freezing, nonetheless people went swimming.

What punctuation correction should be made to this sentence?

(1) The water was freezing nonetheless people went swimming.
(2) The water was freezing, nonetheless, people went swimming.
(3) The water was freezing; nonetheless, people went swimming.
(4) The water was freezing; nonetheless people went swimming.
(5) The water was freezing, and nonetheless people went swimming.

4. Sentence 4: Finally, the family picked up its belongings, carried them to the car, and they were riding home.

Which is the best way to write the underlined sentence? If you think the original is the best way, choose (1).

(1) Finally, the family picked up its belongings, carried them to the car, and they were riding home.
(2) Finally; the family picked up its belongings, carried them to the car, and they were riding home.
(3) Finally; the family picked up its belongings, carried them to the car, and rode home.
(4) Finally, the family picked up its belongings, carried them to the car, and rode home.
(5) Finally, the family picked up its belongings, carried them to the car, and was riding home.

► *Answers begin on page 267.*

Complex Sentences

Using compound sentences is one way to make your writing lively and interesting. Another way is to use *complex sentences*.

IDENTIFYING A COMPLEX SENTENCE

A complex sentence is a sentence that contains an independent clause and a dependent clause. A *clause* is a group of words that contains a subject and a verb. An *independent*, or main clause expresses a complete thought; it can stand on its own as a sentence. Some clauses cannot stand on their own as sentences. They are called *dependent clauses* because they depend on the rest of the sentence to give them their meaning. Look at the parts of the example sentence:

Independent Clause: He knew something about fishing though he wanted to know more.

Dependent Clause: He knew something about fishing though he wanted to know more.

You can see that the first clause could stand on its own as a sentence that makes sense. However, the second clause only makes sense if it is attached to the other idea in the sentence.

You can identify a complex sentence by trying to break the clauses into two complete sentences. If one of the clauses can stand alone (independent), but the other clause cannot (dependent), it is a complex sentence. Take a look at the following examples:

Two Clauses: When the doorbell rang

I gave my friend the package

Complex Sentence: When the doorbell rang, I gave my friend the package.

The first clause is dependent. It cannot stand on its own because it does not express a complete thought. The second clause is independent; it can stand on its own as a sentence. When these two clauses are put together, a complex sentence is formed.

Look at the following sentences. The independent clauses are underlined once. Notice that a dependent clause can come before or after the main clause. When the dependent clause comes first, a comma separates it from the independent clause.

> When I get home, <u>I want to wash the car</u>.
>
> <u>She refuses to buy an air conditioner</u> despite the fact that she is miserable in hot weather.
>
> Since you put it that way, <u>I'll buy you dinner</u>.
>
> <u>Juan has decided to look for a new job</u> even though the one he has now pays well.

PRACTICE • 1

■ In each of the following complex sentences, underline the *dependent* clause once and the connecting word twice.

1. Mr. Ramirez was not at work on Monday although he had never missed a day of work before.

2. He could not go to work because he needed to take his wife to the doctor.

3. Because she was suffering from the flu, Mrs. Ramirez felt as if she had been run over by a steamroller.

4. She was uncomfortable whenever she tried to sit or lie down.

5. After she went to the doctor, she felt better.

6. When his wife had completely recovered, Mr. Ramirez went back to work.

7. Since she was feeling better, she called her husband at his office.

8. If he could leave the factory by five o'clock, they would go to the movies.

► *Answers begin on page 268.*

USING CONNECTING WORDS

Complex sentences can improve your writing because they explain the relationship between two ideas to the reader. The connecting word communicates this information. The meaning of a complex sentence can change according to which connecting word you use. Take a look at the following sentences:

After they ate dinner, they had an important conversation.

While they had an important conversation, they ate dinner.

Before they had an important conversation, they ate dinner.

Whenever they ate dinner, they had an important conversation.

The meaning of each of these four sentences is different. The first sentence describes the order of two events. The important conversation was *after* dinner. The second sentence suggests that they did the two actions *at the same time*. The third sentence suggests that they talked *before* eating. The fourth sentence suggests that on many occasions they had important conversations *while* eating dinner.

Notice that in the first and fourth sentences, the main clause is *they had an important conversation*. In the second and third sentences, that idea is expressed in the dependent clause.

You can see that the connecting words that introduce dependent clauses are powerful because they show the relationship between two ideas in a sentence. The table below shows six different relationships between the two clauses in complex sentences. It also shows the connecting words that suggest each relationship.

RELATIONSHIP	CONNECTING WORDS	EXAMPLE
Cause and Effect	because, since, so that, in order that, as	Since you were late, I left without you.
Contrast	although, though, even though, despite the fact that, in spite of the fact that	Even though I hate science fiction, I will see the movie with you.
Time	before, once, as soon as, until, after, when, whenever, since, while	Before you eat that cookie, eat your peas.
Place	where, wherever	We were happy wherever we sat at the baseball game.
Condition	if, unless, whether	Unless you tell the truth, I will not respect you.
Comparison	as if, as though, like	The rabbit raced across the field as if he were frightened.

Look again at how the meaning of a sentence can change according to the connecting word used. Below are four ways of connecting the same two simple sentences: *She got her GED. She found a new job.* The main clauses are underlined in each.

Cause and Effect: She found a new job because she got her GED.

Contrast: Even though she found a new job, she got her GED.

Time: After she got her GED, she found a new job.

Condition: If she got her GED, she could find a new job.

PRACTICE • 2

▶ **Part A** In the following sentences, the incorrect connecting words are used. For each sentence, underline the *dependent* clause and choose a more appropriate connecting word.

1. As if there are so many banks in this city, it's hard to get good service from one.

2. After the bank is not busy, it does not have enough tellers serving the public.

3. Before they can get away with it, banks charge unfair fees to people without a lot of money.

4. I am switching banks though I can find one that has more respect for its customers.

▶ **Part B** In the following paragraph, incorrect connecting words are used in complex sentences. Identify the connecting words. Change these connecting words to correctly reflect the relationship between the ideas in the sentence. The first sentence has been done for you.

even though

The house I grew up in was small ~~as if~~ it didn't feel that way to me as a child. I had my own room so that I was nine years old. Then, I had to share my room with my brother whether his room was taken by the new baby. In that house, I was happy after I was spending my time. Although I have happy memories like this, I think I am unique.

▶ *Answers begin on page 268.*

PUNCTUATION: USING COMMAS TO SET OFF SUBORDINATE CLAUSES

subordinate: lower in rank or importance

Dependent clauses are also called *subordinate clauses* because they are **subordinate** to independent clauses. They can't stand alone as sentences. If a subordinate clause appears at the beginning of a sentence, a comma is used to set it off from the independent, or main clause. Take a look at the following sentences:

Though the playground was empty, it looked cheerful.

The playground looked cheerful though it was empty.

As you know, a dependent clause can either precede or follow a main clause. In the first sentence, the subordinate clause appears first; you place a comma after it. In the second sentence, the subordinate clause appears after the independent clause; a comma is not used.

EDITING PRACTICE

■ The paragraph below contains errors in the punctuation of subordinate and independent clauses. Edit the paragraph by correcting the punctuation.

Paper companies own huge tracts of land in the state of Maine, although not many people know it. You can drive on gravel roads in these areas, if you are willing to share the road with enormous trucks loaded with full-length trees. Because the companies own the roads the companies' truck drivers insist that you yield to them. This makes for an exciting ride, so long as you follow these unwritten rules.

CONNECTIONS

Take a look at Working World in the Health Matters theme in **CONNECTIONS,** pages C14–C15. What job would you like to have if you worked in a hospital? Write a paragraph explaining why you would like to have such a job. Use complex sentences. Check that you have used commas correctly.

► *Answers begin on page 268.*

PRE-GED PRACTICE

*Choose the **one best answer** for each item.*
***Items 1 to 4** refer to the following passage.*

(1)Because all bridges serve the same purpose, they look remarkably different from one another. (2)In order that you assume that all bridges are alike, think about how beautiful some bridges are. (3)Unless you have different taste from most people; you probably think that a small wooden bridge over a stream can be a handsome structure. (4)However, large bridges like the Golden Gate Bridge or the Brooklyn Bridge can be beautiful even though their materials (steel and stone) don't sound beautiful.

1. Sentence 1: Because all bridges serve the same purpose, they look remarkably different from one another.

What correction should be made to this sentence?
(1) insert *and* before *they*
(2) replace *Because* with *Though*
(3) remove the comma after *purpose*
(4) replace *Because* with *As if*
(5) replace *Because* with *Since*

2. Sentence 2: <u>In order that</u> you assume that all bridges are alike, think about how beautiful some bridges are.

Which is the best way to write the underlined portion of this sentence? If you think the original is the best way, choose (1).
(1) In order that
(2) When
(3) After
(4) Because
(5) Before

3. Sentence 3: Unless you have different taste from most people; you probably think that a small wooden bridge over a stream can be a handsome structure.

What correction should be made to this sentence?
(1) insert *the fact that* after *Unless*
(2) change *Unless* to *In order that*
(3) change *Unless* to *As if*
(4) replace the semicolon with a comma
(5) No correction is necessary.

4. Sentence 4: However, large bridges like the Golden Gate Bridge or the Brooklyn Bridge can be beautiful <u>even though</u> their materials (steel and stone) don't sound beautiful.

Which is the best way to write the underlined portion of this sentence? If you think the original is the best way, choose (1).
(1) even though
(2) because
(3) whether
(4) since
(5) while

► *Answers begin on page 268.*

Common Sentence Errors

As you may know, modifiers are descriptive words or phrases that modify other words or phrases in a sentence.

MISPLACED AND DANGLING MODIFIERS

One of the most common errors in writing occurs when modifiers are placed too far away from the word they modify or too close to a word they don't modify. These are called *misplaced modifiers.* Take a look at how the placement of a modifier can confuse or change the meaning of a sentence:

Misplaced Modifier: The woman spoke sternly to the toddler <u>with the umbrella</u>.

Correctly Placed Modifier: The woman <u>with the umbrella</u> spoke sternly to the toddler.

The phrase *with the umbrella* modifies the word *woman*. However, in the first example, the modifier is placed so far from the word *woman* that the sentence suggests that the toddler was carrying an umbrella. In the second sentence, it is clear that the phrase *with the umbrella* is identifying which *woman* spoke sternly to the toddler.

Another common error is a *dangling modifier*. This is a modifier that does not modify any of the words in a sentence. Here is an example:

Driving down the highway, the empty fields baked in the sun.

Were the *fields* or the *sun* driving down the highway? Grammatically, there are no other words that could be modified by the phrase *driving down the highway*. You can fix such dangling modifiers by adding a word or words that the modifier could logically modify. For instance, you could rewrite the sentence as:

Driving down the highway, <u>I saw</u> the empty fields baking in the sun.

You also could turn the dangling modifier into a dependent clause. However, you still need to make sure there is a word in the main clause that it modifies. The sentence would read as:

> While driving down the highway, I saw the empty fields baking in the sun.

The dangling modifier has been turned into the dependent clause *while driving down the highway.* A relationship of time is established. You know *when* the fields were seen.

PRACTICE • 1

▶ **Part A** Each sentence has a modifier in italics. In the space provided, write *C* if the modifier is placed correctly in the sentence. Write *M* if it is misplaced or *D* if it is a dangling modifier.

_____ **1.** The man was not a resident of the city *with the green jacket.*

_____ **2.** He turned the corner *with a suspicious look.*

_____ **3.** One detective suddenly spotted the missing evidence *with a sharp eye.*

_____ **4.** *Turning to the others,* he mentioned the wanted poster.

_____ **5.** *Waiting in the county jail,* no bail was set.

_____ **6.** At the trial, the man faced the judge *with a sad look.*

▶ **Part B** In the following paragraph, some of the modifiers are used incorrectly. Rewrite any sentences that contain such errors.

> Shouting at the top of their lungs, the demonstration caught the attention of the whole town. One woman stood on the shoulders of a statue with a bullhorn and gave a short speech. There she was noticed by just about everyone. Listening to her, tension filled the air. Local merchants watched outside their stores with frowning faces.

▶ *Answers begin on page 269.*

SENTENCE FRAGMENTS AND RUN-ON SENTENCES

Sentence fragments are groups of words that may look a lot like sentences, but they are incomplete. They lack at least one of the three requirements for a complete sentence: a subject, a verb, and the expression of a complete thought. Fragments can begin with capital letters and end with periods. Take a look at the following example:

> I knew Scott well. Because we had been close friends since sixth grade.

Although it contains a subject, *we,* and a verb, *had been*, the second sentence does not express a complete thought. The connecting word *because* implies a cause-and-effect relationship, but we don't know what it is. There are two different ways to fix a sentence fragment like this:

Solution 1: I knew Scott well. We had been close friends since sixth grade.

Solution 2: I knew Scott well because we had been close friends since sixth grade.

In the first solution, the connecting word was removed. The second sentence is now a complete sentence. In the second solution, the connecting word is used to form one complex sentence.

A *run-on sentence* is a string of two or more sentences that are incorrectly joined as one sentence. Take a look at the following example:

> Four people rushed into the water to help the elderly man he was struggling in the waves.

This run-on sentence incorrectly joins two complete thoughts as one. You could rewrite this run-on sentence in four different ways:

Solution 1: Four people rushed into the water to help the elderly man. He was struggling in the waves.

Solution 2: Four people rushed into the water to help the elderly man; he was struggling in the waves.

Solution 3: The elderly man was struggling in the waves, so four people rushed into the water to help.

Solution 4: Four people rushed into the water to help the elderly man, since he was struggling in the waves.

The first solution simply breaks the run-on sentence into two sentences. The second connects the two thoughts with a semicolon. The third solution links the two thoughts with a comma and the connecting word *so*. In the last solution, one half of the run-on sentence is now the dependent clause *since he was struggling in the waves.*

PRACTICE • 2

▶ **Part A** In the space provided, write *C* if the sentence is correctly written. Write *F* if it is a sentence fragment or *R* if it is a run-on sentence.

_____ **1.** Dozing comfortably in a hammock as a nice cool breeze comes up.

_____ **2.** Hoping to spend my weekend at the lake.

_____ **3.** I'll go for a dip I'll take the boat out once or twice.

_____ **4.** There is a tiny island I want to explore, but there are dangerous rocks all around it.

_____ **5.** The rocks are jagged they are in shallow water.

_____ **6.** Maybe I could wade in I'll have to be careful.

▶ **Part B** The following paragraph contains sentence fragments and run-on sentences. Rewrite the sentences correctly.

The wedding took place on Chicago's South Side there were about one hundred and twenty guests there. Played piano at the reception, since she's my sister. The guy she married is terrific I wish, however, that he weren't from Chicago if he were from the East, my sister and he would live here, and I could see them more often. Mixed feelings, I guess you could say.

CONNECTIONS

Some languages not only sound different from English but look different, too. The Languages theme in **CONNECTIONS**, pages C12–C13, discusses other types of alphabets. Would you like to write in ideograms or syllabic symbols? Do you think it would be easier or harder than English? Write one paragraph explaining your answers. When you have finished writing, check over your paragraph for sentence fragments and run-on sentences. Correct any errors you find.

▶ *Answers begin on page 269.*

FOCUS PUNCTUATION: USING PUNCTUATION TO CORRECT SENTENCE FRAGMENTS AND RUN-ONS

Punctuation plays an important role in correcting sentence fragments and run-on sentences. Many fragments can be corrected by joining them with another sentence. Often, a comma will be used with a connecting word to join the two parts of the newly-formed sentence. This is what was done in the following example:

Sentence Fragment: My grandmother made me raspberry jam. Because I love it so much.

Solution: Because I love it so much, my grandmother made me raspberry jam.

The fragment becomes a dependent clause joined to an independent clause. A comma is used because the dependent clause precedes the main clause. Remember that you do not use a comma when the dependent clause follows the main clause.

In the case of run-on sentences, semicolons, periods, or commas with connecting words can be used to make one or two correct sentences. Look at how these three punctuation marks offer different solutions:

Run-on Sentence: I opened the drawer there was a mouse.

Solution 1: I opened the drawer, and there was a mouse.

Solution 2: I opened the drawer; there was a mouse.

Solution 3: I opened the drawer. There was a mouse.

EDITING PRACTICE

■ The paragraph below contains some sentences with misplaced and dangling modifiers. Others contain fragments and run-on sentences. Rewrite the paragraph to correct these errors.

Keiko was inexperienced with apartment repairs she didn't know anything about refinishing floors. Moving in on the first weekend of April, the floors needed to be done first. The woman kindly offered to help her in the neighboring apartment.

▶ *Answers begin on page 269.*

PRE-GED PRACTICE

Choose the ***one best answer*** *for each item.* ***Items 1 to 5*** *refer to the following passage.*

(1)Traveling across the country, overdeveloped areas with strip malls fill the landscape. (2)Outside every city in the country, fast-food restaurants, budget motels, and industrial parks. (3)A person can get really depressed with an interest in ecology. (4)However, get off the interstates and the main roads, you will find more interesting places. (5)Put camping gear in your car you can travel pretty cheaply.

1. If you rewrote Sentence 1, starting after Traveling across the country, the next words should be
   (1) overdeveloping areas with strip malls fill the landscape.
   (2) areas that are overdeveloped with strip malls fill the landscape.
   (3) overdeveloped areas with strip malls filling the landscape.
   (4) all I see are overdeveloped areas with strip malls filling the landscape.
   (5) the landscape with overdeveloped areas of strip malls.

2. Sentence 2: Outside every city in the country, fast-food restaurants, budget motels, and industrial parks.

   What correction should be made to this sentence?
   (1) replace *Outside* with *Beside*
   (2) replace the first comma with a semicolon
   (3) begin the sentence with *Fast-food restaurants, budget motels, and industrial parks* and end it with *outside every city in the country.*
   (4) insert *are there* at the end of the sentence
   (5) insert *the landscape is littered* after the first comma

3. Sentence 3: A person can get really depressed with an interest in ecology.

   Which is the best way to write the underlined portion of this sentence? If you think the original is the best way, choose (1).
   (1) can get really depressed with an interest in ecology.
   (2) with an interest in ecology can get really depressed.
   (3) with ecology, a person can get really depressed.
   (4) can get really depressed, with an interest in ecology.
   (5) with an interest can get really depressed in ecology.

4. Sentence 4: However, get off the interstates and the main roads, you will find more interesting places.

   What correction should be made to this sentence?
   (1) replace *roads, you* with *roads you*
   (2) replace *However, get* with *However, if you get*
   (3) replace *However, get* with *However, although you get*
   (4) replace *roads, you* with *roads, or you*
   (5) No correction is necessary.

5. Sentence 5: Put camping gear in your car you can travel pretty cheaply.

   Which is the best way to write the underlined portion of this sentence? If you think the original is the best way, choose (1).
   (1) car you
   (2) car. That way you
   (3) car. So you
   (4) car, you
   (5) car. When

► *Answers begin on page 269.*

UNIT 3

Mechanics

Mechanics are the rules for spelling words and using punctuation marks and capital letters. Punctuation and capitalization can emphasize an idea or signal the beginning of a new idea. They also can show that a specific person, place, or thing is being discussed. Using mechanics properly helps you write clearly so that your ideas can be easily understood.

LESSON 14

Using Punctuation

Punctuation helps your reader understand your writing. Using correct punctuation is one of the ways to make your writing clear and effective.

USING END PUNCTUATION

The *period* is used at the end of sentences that make statements or give commands. Here are some examples:

> I read a biography of Malcom X this summer.
>
> Today the wind has stirred up dust and leaves.

The *question mark* is used at the end of sentences that ask a *direct question*. Direct questions require an answer. Look at these examples:

> Are you planning to get your hair cut this week?
>
> Why do you want to see that movie?

Be careful to distinguish direct questions from *indirect questions*. Indirect questions are statements that refer to questions. Use a period with statements like these:

> I began by asking her where she was last Monday.
>
> Mr. Harrington wouldn't tell me why he was closing the store early.

The *exclamation point* is used at the end of sentences that express strong emotions and are not direct questions. Here are two sentences that use exclamation points correctly:

> What a fabulous apartment!
>
> This is the best meal I have ever eaten!

Quotation marks are used at the beginning *and* the end of direct speech. Direct speech consists of words and sentences that someone actually said or might say. Here are two examples:

> I asked her, "Where were you last Monday?"
>
> He said, "The cat ate it all."

Direct speech is always introduced with a comma. The punctuation at the end of the sentence is placed before the closing quotation marks.

PRACTICE • 1

▶ **Part A** The following sentences lack end punctuation. Write the correct form of end punctuation for each sentence.

1. What is your opinion of this airline
2. We are flying from Atlanta to San Diego
3. What a view there is out the left windows
4. Aren't they serving dinner on this flight
5. I'm sure someone is picking us up at the airport
6. Now, *that's* turbulence
7. Have you ever been there before
8. I asked a friend of mine who lives in San Diego to show us around
9. The weather should be much warmer there than in Atlanta
10. I can't wait to get there

▶ **Part B** In the following paragraph, some end punctuation is used incorrectly. Correct the punctuation at the end of any questions, exclamations, commands, or statements.

Have you ever thought about supporting small businesses instead of huge corporations. If you think about it, it's quite easy to make it work! Most people simply aren't aware of the way "chain" stores put "mom and pop" stores out of business, If you feel that smaller, independent stores offer valuable services that larger stores don't, then you might consider giving your business to a small business? If people don't choose to support small businesses now, we may soon have only large chain stores?

▶ *Answers begin on page 269.*

USING COMMAS

The comma is the most frequently used punctuation mark. You use commas to set off, or separate, words or phrases from one another in a sentence. Here are some rules that govern the use of commas:

RULES FOR USING COMMAS

- *Use commas to separate items in a list or a series.*

  Please be careful removing the desk, the chairs, and the lamps.

- *Use commas to separate two or more adjectives that describe the same thing.*

  This long, gloomy, deserted street gives me the creeps.

- *Use a comma before a connecting word to join two independent clauses into a compound sentence.*

  The woman challenged the parking ticket, but the judge did not agree.

- *Use a comma to set off a dependent clause that appears at the beginning of a sentence.*

  When you reach the corner, you are almost to our house.

  Before they reached the restaurant, Zia discovered she had forgotten her purse.

- *Use a comma to set off elements that interrupt a sentence.*

  The freeway, rather than the state road, is the quicker route.

  I've known you, Maureen, for fifteen years now.

- *Use commas to separate each part of a date or place name.*

  On January 23, 1992, they were reunited with their parents.

  I drove as far as Pittsburgh, Pennsylvania, this morning.

- *Use commas before direct speech.*

  She said, "We'll have to turn back."

  I asked the police officer, "Which way is the public library?"

PRACTICE • 2

The following sentences lack commas. Insert the commas where they belong in each sentence.

1. I think I was in the town of Vergennes Vermont in July 1983.

2. Jane isn't Vergennes near Middlebury Bristol and Burlington?

3. In the summer of that year my younger brother Jim was traveling through the Green Mountains.

4. I swam in a small peaceful pond and I fished in a river near Bristol.

5. When I arrived in a town called Ripton I thought I was at the top of Bread Loaf Mountain.

6. I was only half way there however.

7. Down a dirt road in Ripton is the cabin where Robert Frost the famous American poet lived.

8. I said "I like Harlem Renaissance poetry."

9. However I've never been to Harlem.

10. Instead I drive to the mountains the beach and the lake.

11. The car which is only six years old has over 150,000 miles on it.

CONNECTIONS

The timeline in the Technology theme in **CONNECTIONS**, pages C2–C3, shows the development of computers. Use the information from the timeline to write a paragraph that traces the history of computers. Be careful to use end punctuation and commas correctly.

► *Answers begin on page 269.*

FOCUS PUNCTUATION: OVERUSING COMMAS

Overusing commas can weaken your writing. Never insert a comma into a sentence without a specific reason. Here are some rules to help you:

OVERUSING COMMAS

Do not use a comma to:

- *separate a compound verb or a compound subject.*

  Incorrect: I walked outside to the car, and drove away.

  Correct: I walked outside to the car and drove away.

  Incorrect: My friend, and his dog watched us.

  Correct: My friend and his dog watched us.

- *join two independent clauses without a connecting word.*

  Incorrect: The car windows were open, the rain soaked the seats.

  Correct: The car windows were open, <u>and</u> the rain soaked the seats.

  Correct: The car windows were open. The rain soaked the seats.

  Correct: The car windows were open; the rain soaked the seats.

- *separate a subject and a verb.*

  Incorrect: Last night Joey and Vincent, went to the ball game.

  Correct: Last night Joey and Vincent went to the ball game.

EDITING PRACTICE

■ In the paragraph below, some commas and end punctuation are incorrect. Rewrite the paragraph so that these errors are corrected.

Do you think professional athletes, get paid too much. During their first year on a major league baseball team most players get paid over $100,000. I don't understand why they get paid that when an electrician gets about $30,000? Of course they still demand a pay raise.

► *Answers begin on page 270.*

PRE-GED PRACTICE

Choose the ***one best answer*** *for each item.*
Items 1 to 5 *refer to the following passage.*

(1)There has been a lot of interest in the writers and artists of the Harlem Renaissance in the past several years! (2)The Harlem Renaissance took place during the 1920s in New York, and it involved writers painters actors musicians dancers and intellectuals. (3)Both Zora Neale Hurston, and Langston Hughes worked in Harlem. (4)Did you know that the essay *When Harlem Was the Rage* is by Langston Hughes. (5)Since many Harlem Renaissance artists have become popular again one can buy their books and look at their artworks.

1. Sentence 1: There has been a lot of interest in the writers and artists of the Harlem Renaissance in the past several years!

What correction should be made to this sentence?

(1) replace the exclamation mark after *years* with a period
(2) insert a comma after *writers*
(3) insert a comma after *Renaissance*
(4) insert a comma after *Harlem*
(5) No correction is necessary.

2. Sentence 2: The Harlem Renaissance took place during the 1920s in New York, and it involved writers painters actors musicians dancers and intellectuals.

What correction should be made to this sentence?

(1) insert a comma after *New York, and*
(2) replace *1920s in* with *1920s. In*
(3) replace *writers painters actors musicians dancers* with *writers, painters, actors, musicians, dancers,*
(4) replace *Harlem Renaissance* with *Harlem, Renaissance*
(5) No correction is necessary.

3. Sentence 3: Both Zora Neale Hurston, and Langston Hughes worked in Harlem.

What correction should be made to this sentence?

(1) insert a comma after ***Both***
(2) insert a comma after ***worked***
(3) replace ***Harlem.*** with ***Harlem!***
(4) remove the comma after ***Hurston***
(5) replace the comma after ***Hurston*** with a semicolon

4. Sentence 4: Did you know that the essay *When Harlem Was the Rage* is by Langston Hughes.

What correction should be made to this sentence?

(1) replace the period after *Hughes* with an exclamation mark
(2) insert a comma after ***know***
(3) insert a comma after *Harlem*
(4) replace the period after *Hughes* with a question mark
(5) No correction is necessary.

5. Sentence 5: Since many Harlem Renaissance artists have become popular again one can buy their books and look at their artworks.

What correction should be made to this sentence?

(1) replace the period after *artworks* with an exclamation point
(2) insert a comma after *artists*
(3) insert a comma after *again*
(4) insert a comma after *books*
(5) No correction is necessary.

► *Answers begin on page 270.*

LESSON 15

Other Punctuation Rules

Commas and periods are the punctuation marks you will use most frequently. However, these are not the only ones you will need to write well. You also will use semicolons and quotation marks.

COLONS AND SEMICOLONS

A *colon* (:) means, "take note of the words that follow." Because of this, it is sometimes used to signal a list. Here are a few examples:

I invited: Maggie, Laura, Jon, Darrel, and Denton.

My desk drawer contains everything I need: pencils, pens, paper, erasers, paper clips, a stapler, tape, and a pocket dictionary.

A colon also is used after the salutation in a business letter:

Dear Ms. Maxvill: *or* To Whom It May Concern:

A colon is used to write the time of day:

3:35 4:15

The *semicolon* (;) is used to separate two independent clauses from one another when there is no connecting word. Look at these examples:

The clarinets played a soft melody; the cellos played rich, long notes below the melody.

I have known Sal for a long time; we have not always gotten along.

Had the writer used a connecting word such as *and, but, or, nor, so,* or *yet* after the first clause, a comma would have been the correct punctuation. However, since there is no connecting word, a semicolon is the correct punctuation. Use a semicolon only when the relationship between the two clauses is absolutely clear. If you think a reader might be confused by the relationship, use a comma and a connecting word between the independent clauses.

A semicolon is *never* used to separate a dependent clause from an independent clause. Always use a comma in sentences such as this:

After I met Alan, I wanted to learn more about him.

PRACTICE • 1

▶ **Part A** The following sentences are missing commas, colons, and semicolons. Insert the correct punctuation mark in each sentence.

1. The filth in the house was unbelievable I decided it was time to get out the vacuum cleaner.
2. When I discovered I had no vacuum cleaner bags I remembered why I hadn't vacuumed earlier.
3. I went to the hardware store for the following items vacuum cleaner bags a Venetian blind and a ball of strong twine.
4. Because the vacuum cleaner bags were the wrong size I had to return them.
5. I spent a day cleaning the house it was worth it.
6. I cleaned all of these rooms the kitchen the bedroom the bathroom the living room and the study.
7. Before I cleaned the kitchen I cleaned the bathroom.
8. I never knew that cleaning was such hard work it really takes it out of you.
9. Since I had worked so hard I treated myself to a nice dinner.
10. Here's what I ate steak a baked potato a salad and a glass of wine.

▶ **Part B** In the following paragraph, there are some punctuation errors. Add, delete, or change punctuation marks as necessary.

Our flight was scheduled to leave at 5;33 in the evening: at 5:00 we were not even near the airport. Furthermore, we had a trunk full of stuff that needed to be checked. Four suitcases, three cardboard boxes with household goods, several small Christmas packages, and a child's bicycle. I asked the taxi driver whether there was another route, he looked at me, shook his head, and chuckled to himself.

▶ *Answers begin on page 270.*

QUOTATION MARKS, DASHES, AND PARENTHESES

Quotation marks are most often used to show a person's exact words. The quotation marks are placed at the beginning and at the end of these words. Take a look at the following examples:

Kenneth said, "I'm sorry," as soon as he walked in the door.

Henry answered, "The way you left this shop last night ought to make you sorry."

When a quotation appears in the middle of a sentence, as in the first example, it must be set off with two commas. Notice that the comma at the end of the quotation is placed before the second quotation mark. The period at the end of the second example also goes before the second quotation mark. Commas and periods at the end of quotations are *always* placed before the second quotation mark.

Also use quotation marks to set off unusual expressions, such as slang words:

People speak about getting "tight" in the movies of the 1930s.

The young people in the room thought the music was "cool."

In type, you may see a *dash* (— or --). A dash is used to set off words that show a sudden shift in thought. A dash also can be used to set off words that interrupt the main thought of a sentence. Here are some examples:

I was at the grocery store at noon—or was it the bakery?

The play—I shouldn't dignify it with that term—was so boring that I wanted to run screaming out of the theater.

nonessential: not of primary or central importance

Parentheses are used to add nonessential words and phrases to a sentence. Often these words and phrases explain something or give an example. Use parentheses instead of dashes when you do not wish to stress the additional words. Look at the following sentences:

I got my first job (on a highway crew) when I was 17.

These groceries (cereal, vegetables, bread, and milk) should last through the weekend.

Be careful not to use parentheses too often. They can be confusing if they appear in writing too frequently.

PRACTICE • 2

▶ **Part A** Some of the following sentences contain punctuation errors. If you think a sentence is correct, write *C* in the space provided. If a sentence is incorrect, write *I* in the space and correct all punctuation errors.

_____ **1.** We took the kids to the Acton Fair last night: all of us had a great time.

_____ **2.** One guy at a booth said to Marie: Let me draw your picture, lovely lady.

_____ **3.** Since it was cheap only three dollars; she went ahead with it; he drew really well.

_____ **4.** Here's what we got for the admission price: two free rides and coupons for a dollar off at the cotton candy stand.

_____ **5.** The cotton candy–if you could call it that–was burned and bad.

_____ **6.** I saw–that the sky–was turning black.

_____ **7.** Marie said,"Let's get out of here before it pours".

_____ **8.** We all (the kids, the dog, and Marie and I) piled into the car.

▶ **Part B** In the following paragraph, there are punctuation errors. Correct all the punctuation errors you find.

My friend Jamie and I, were talking about the words—we used in school years ago—to express enthusiasm over something. For instance, when something was really good, we said it was wicked. We laughed, and Jamie said—Do you remember what we used to call pretty girls? He reminded me that we had called them fine. We talked about how it's hard to keep up with slang words if you're not young: they change extremely quickly.

▶ *Answers begin on page 271.*

FOCUS USAGE: DIRECT AND INDIRECT QUOTES

In writing, you use quotation marks when you are representing a speaker's exact words. These exact words are called a *direct quotation*. Here are two examples—correctly punctuated—of direct quotations:

Patrick Henry said, "Give me liberty, or give me death."

"There is a chance of showers today," said the meteorologist.

However, sometimes you will elect to use *indirect quotations* when you write. An indirect quotation rewords what someone says. Indirect quotations are not punctuated with quotation marks. Here are the direct quotations above reworded as indirect quotations:

Patrick Henry said that he would prefer death to a life without liberty.

The meteorologist said that we might have showers today.

EDITING PRACTICE

■ The paragraph below contains punctuation errors. Rewrite the paragraph so that all the errors are corrected.

The old shoe factory (where my great-grandfather worked was on Bridge Street in Springvale, it was demolished in 1967. Before the town decided to tear down this old wooden building: my father took pictures of it. I remember my father saying I'm sorry to see it go the morning the wrecking ball smashed it to bits.

CONNECTIONS

The Entertainment theme in **CONNECTIONS**, pages C10–C11, includes an excerpt from the book, *Alice's Adventures in Wonderland*. Notice how it uses punctuation for direct speech. Write your own short piece of dialogue, humorous or otherwise. Remember to use quotation marks, commas, and any other necessary punctuation.

► *Answers begin on page 271.*

PRE-GED PRACTICE

Choose the one best answer for each item.
Items 1 to 4 refer to the following passage.

(1)As Ruben studies old photographs of Yuma (his favorite city)—he is becoming very knowledgeable about the city's history. (2)He has learned that the city has had these names; Colorado City, Arizona City, and Yuma. (3)The name Yuma—from a Spanish word meaning "smoke"—was probably chosen because local Native Americans tried to make it rain by creating smoke clouds. (4)I love the history of Yuma because it is like a puzzle, says Ruben.

1. Sentence 1: As Ruben studies old photographs of Yuma (his favorite city)—he is becoming very knowledgeable about the city's history.

Which of the following is the best way to write the underlined portion of this sentence? If you think the original is the best way, choose (1).

(1) city)—he
(2) city), he
(3) city): he
(4) city: he
(5) city; he

2. Sentence 2: He has learned that the city has had these names; Colorado City, Arizona City, and Yuma.

What correction should be made to this sentence?

(1) Remove the commas after *Colorado City* and *Arizona City.*
(2) Replace the semicolon after *names* with a dash.
(3) Replace the semicolon after *names* with a colon.
(4) Replace the semicolon after *names* with a comma.
(5) No correction is necessary.

3. Sentence 3: The name Yuma—from a Spanish word meaning "smoke"—was probably chosen because local Native Americans tried to make it rain by creating smoke clouds.

Which of the following is the best way to write the underlined portion of this sentence? If you think the original is the best way, choose (1).

(1) Yuma—from a Spanish word meaning "smoke"—was
(2) Yuma from a Spanish word meaning "smoke"—was
(3) Yuma from a Spanish word meaning "smoke" was
(4) Yuma: from a Spanish word meaning "smoke"—was
(5) Yuma; from a Spanish word meaning "smoke"—was

4. Sentence 4: I love the history of Yuma because it is like a puzzle, says Ruben.

What correction should be made to this sentence?

(1) Replace the comma after *puzzle* with a semicolon.
(2) Insert a semicolon after *Yuma.*
(3) Replace both of the commas after *Yuma* and *puzzle* with parentheses.
(4) Insert quotation marks at the beginning of the sentence and before *says.*
(5) No correction is necessary.

► *Answers begin on page 271.*

LESSON 16

Capitalization

CAPITALIZING IN SENTENCES AND QUOTATIONS

In writing, there must be a capital letter at the beginning of every complete sentence. It doesn't matter if the sentence is a statement, a command, a question, or an exclamation. They all require capital letters. Here are some examples:

Our dog has been missing for three or four days.

Go to the police precinct, and inform them that he disappeared.

Do you know where the police precinct is?

Never mind because there's our dog right now!

Notice that in the second example sentence a capital letter is *not* used at the beginning of the second independent clause. You should never use capital letters to begin clauses within sentences.

In Lesson 15, page 234, you learned about direct quotations. If a direct quotation is a complete sentence, you should capitalize the first word of the quotation. This is true no matter where in your sentence the quotation appears. Look at the following examples:

My boss said, "Your patience and willingness to learn make you a valuable asset to any company."

"Thank you for the compliment," I replied.

If, however, the direct quotation is not a complete sentence, you do not need to capitalize the first word. Look at this example:

I was glad that my boss had talked about my "patience and willingness to learn."

Sometimes a direct quotation is broken into two parts. You should *not* capitalize the first word of the second part unless it is the beginning of a new sentence. Here are two examples:

"I've gone around the world," he said, "and I haven't found a better place to live than right here in Topeka, Kansas."

"This is my puppy," she said. "His name is Brodie."

PRACTICE • 1

▶ **Part A** Some of the following sentences contain capitalization errors. If the capitalization in a sentence is correct, write *C* in the space provided. If the capitalization is incorrect, write *I*. Cross out any incorrect words and rewrite them in the correct form.

_____ **1.** A few people were discussing whether there was any difference between jazz and the blues.

_____ **2.** One of my friends said, "to me they are the same thing."

_____ **3.** my wife, of course, agreed with his "Expert opinion."

_____ **4.** "In my opinion," I said, "Jazz is cool and blues is hot."

_____ **5.** we then listened to some jazz and some blues records.

_____ **6.** Afterwards, my wife said, "let's get something to eat."

_____ **7.** "It would be nice," I said, "If we can find some place that's still open."

_____ **8.** We all got in the car and went downtown.

_____ **9.** At the restaurant, my wife changed her mind and agreed that "Blues is hot."

▶ **Part B** In the following paragraph, there are errors in the use of capital letters. Identify and change any letters that are incorrect.

Some people can't stand admitting that they are wrong, and My uncle is one of them. The other day he told me, "you can't burn regular unleaded gas in that car. Use super unleaded." well, I did some research in my owner's manual just to prove him wrong. When I showed him the evidence in black and white, he still said that my car would run "Very poorly" if I used regular unleaded gas.

▶ *Answers begin on page 271.*

CAPITALIZING PROPER NOUNS

Proper nouns name a *specific* person, place, thing, or idea. They must be capitalized no matter where they appear in a sentence. Some proper nouns contain more than one word, and you must capitalize each key word. Words such as *and, or, the, a, an*, and prepositions of four or fewer letters should not be capitalized unless they are the first word of a title. Here are some examples:

Names of People: Horace, Kareem Abdul Jabaar, Terry McMillan, Robert Redford, Elvis Presley, Cher, Joan Chen, Rosie Perez, Andy Garcia

Names of Places: Portugal, Asia, the Rocky Mountains, Lake Superior, the Everglades, Los Angeles, Rwanda, Oak Street, Baxter State Park, the Pacific Northwest, Wells Beach

Titles of Individuals: President Mandela, Doctor Gutierrez, Ms. Dunston, Uncle Paul, Chief Joseph, General Powell

Names of Organizations, Institutions, Companies, and Products: National Association for the Advancement of Colored People (NAACP), National Booksellers Association, National Hockey League, Ohio State University, Nasson College, First Baptist Church, Ford Motor Company, Bath Iron Works, Panasonic™

Names of Historical Events, Special Events, and Calendar Items: the Korean War, the Crusades, the Holocaust, World War II, the Rose Bowl Parade, Columbus Day, Kwanzaa, Wednesday, December

Names of Ethnic Groups, Nationalities, Languages, and Religions: African American, Hispanic, Chinese, Vietnamese, Gaelic, Dutch, Swahili, Spanish, English, Protestant, Islam, Buddhism

Titles of Works (Books, Movies, Paintings, Songs, etc.): *The Art of War, Jurassic Park,* Van Gogh's *Sunflowers, Moon over Miami*

CONNECTIONS

In the News Media theme in **CONNECTIONS**, pages C8–C9, you'll find out about the newspaper industry and some people's views on the press. Read each of the quotations on page C8. Then create a newspaper title to match any two. Make sure your titles have the correct letters capitalized.

► *Answers begin on page 272.*

▶ **Part A** Some of the following sentences contain capitalization errors. If the capitalization in a sentence is correct, write *C* in the space provided. If the capitalization is incorrect, write *I*. Cross out and correct any incorrect words.

_____ **1.** My buddy nick told me that *true lies* is playing at the movie theater in downtown tulsa.

_____ **2.** I asked if he meant the criterion theater or the capital theater, but he only knew that it was the one on south street.

_____ **3.** We were only in the city for the weekend, so we skipped the movie and went to three museums instead.

_____ **4.** In front of the museum, we saw Mayor Jefferson and the Presidents of several local organizations having pictures taken.

_____ **5.** the museum was featuring works by artists from oklahoma.

_____ **6.** All of the artists were born after the civil war.

_____ **7.** On sunday, we went to the oklahoma state fair.

_____ **8.** We ate Mexican food and drank soft drinks.

_____ **9.** Then we went back to the big plains motel where we were staying.

_____ **10.** Someone said garth brooks was staying there; I didn't see him.

▶ **Part B** In the following paragraph, there are errors in the use of capital letters. Identify and correct these errors.

In my new job at american cyanamid, we get all major holidays off, including thanksgiving, new year's day, independence day, and labor day. I start work a Week from Tuesday. My Supervisor told me that my friend audrey works in the plant at Southborough.

▶ *Answers begin on page 272.*

FOCUS USAGE: WHEN TO USE PROPER NOUNS

Words that name specific people, places, and things are *proper nouns*. The naming makes the noun specific. For example, if you use a noun like *boy*, you would not capitalize it. It is a common noun and has a general meaning. However, if you use the name of the boy (*Ricardo*, for instance), that is a proper noun and should be capitalized.

Imagine that you are writing about a person approaching the receptionist in a medical office. The person says, "I'm here to see the doctor." You would be correct in not capitalizing the word *doctor*. If the person said, "I'm here to see Doctor Simpson," then writing *Doctor* with a capital letter would be correct. The word *Doctor*, when used this way, is the title of a specific person. You would also use a capital letter if the person used the title to directly address the physician, such as, "Hello, Doctor, how are you?"

Deciding whether to use a proper noun or a common noun when you write is a matter of deciding how specific you want to be. Proper nouns are more specific than common nouns and therefore give more detail.

EDITING PRACTICE

■ The paragraph below contains capitalization errors. Edit the paragraph by fixing the errors.

According to today's *new york times*, computers in restaurants are "Changing the way diners, waiters, kitchen staff, and Management interact." Not only is this true in Fast Food restaurants across the Country, but also at small, independently-owned restaurants in las vegas, cincinnati, and flagstaff, arizona. however, one restaurant owner quoted in the *times* is not going along with this trend. "we prefer," She said, "to keep the personal connection between the kitchen and the dining room staff."

► *Answers begin on page 272.*

PRE-GED PRACTICE

*Choose the **one best answer** for each item. **Items 1 to 5** refer to the following passage.*

(1)The new york world's fair of 1965 continued for seven months. (2)It was held on more than six hundred acres of land in queens, one of the city's five boroughs. (3)Patrons could view exhibits arranged by companies like general electric, eastman kodak, and parker pens. (4)"The fair," according to Robert Moses, its organizer, "aims to be universal." (5)The fair featured pavilions and restaurants from countries such as venezuela and egypt.

1. Sentence 1: The new york world's fair of 1965 continued for seven months.

What correction should be made to this sentence?
(1) Replace *months* with *Months.*
(2) Replace *new york* with *New York.*
(3) Replace *new york world's fair* with *New York World's Fair.*
(4) Replace *world's fair* with *World's Fair.*
(5) No correction is necessary.

2. Sentence 2: It was held on more than six hundred acres of land in queens, one of the city's five boroughs.

What correction should be made to this sentence?
(1) Replace *six hundred acres* with *Six Hundred Acres.*
(2) Replace *city's* with *City's.*
(3) Replace *city's five boroughs* with *City's Five Boroughs.*
(4) Replace *queens* with *Queens.*
(5) No correction is necessary.

3. Sentence 3: Patrons could view exhibits arranged by companies like general electric, eastman kodak, and parker pens.

Which of the following is the best way to write the underlined portion of this sentence? If you think the original is the best way, choose (1).
(1) companies like general electric, eastman kodak, and parker pens
(2) companies like General Electric, Eastman Kodak, and Parker Pens
(3) Companies like General electric, Eastman kodak, and Parker pens
(4) Companies like General Electric, Eastman Kodak, and Parker Pens
(5) companies like general Electric, eastman Kodak, and parker Pens

4. Sentence 4: "The fair," according to Robert Moses, its organizer, "aims to be universal."

Which of the following is the best way to write the underlined portion of this sentence? If you think the original is the best way, choose (1).
(1) Robert Moses, its organizer, "aims
(2) Robert Moses, its organizer, "Aims
(3) robert moses, its organizer, "aims
(4) robert moses, its organizer, "Aims
(5) robert Moses, its organizer, "Aims

5. Sentence 5: The fair featured pavilions and restaurants from countries such as venezuela and egypt.

What correction should be made to this sentence?
(1) Replace *fair* with *Fair.*
(2) Replace *pavilions* with *Pavilions.*
(3) Replace *countries* with *Countries.*
(4) Replace *venezuela and egypt* with *Venezuela and Egypt.*
(5) No correction is necessary.

► *Answers begin on page 273.*

Spelling

In general, one of the best ways to improve your spelling is to read. The more you read, the more familiar you will be with how words are spelled. However, there also are rules you can learn.

GENERAL SPELLING RULES

Study the following rules and their exceptions. You also can refer back to Lesson 1, page 142, for a review of spelling rules for plural nouns, as well as to Lessons 4 and 5, pages 160 and 166, for a review of spelling rules for verbs.

WORDS WITH *ie* AND *ei*

There is a traditional rhyme that helps you remember how to spell these words—"Put *i* before *e*, except after *c* or when sounded like *a*, as in *neighbor* and *weigh*." Here are some examples:

relief, view, field   perceive, receive   vein, their

Exceptions: either, neither, seize, weird, height, leisure, foreign, forfeit, ancient, species, science, financier

WORDS THAT END IN *-cede, -ceed*

There are only three words in the English language that end in *-ceed*: *proceed*, *succeed*, and *exceed*. All other words with the long *e* sound followed by *d* are spelled *-cede*. Here are some examples:

precede, recede, secede

WORDS WITH PREFIXES

A *prefix* is a group of letters added to the beginning of a word. Adding prefixes never requires you to change the spelling of the root word. Here are some examples:

dis + honor = dishonor   un + real = unreal

WORDS WITH SUFFIXES

A *suffix* is a group of letters added to the end of a word. Usually, you can add a suffix without changing the spelling of the root word. Here are some examples:

thought + less = thoughtless   comfort + able = comfortable

WORDS WITH SPECIAL SUFFIXES

- *If a word ends with the letter* e, *and the suffix begins with a consonant, just add the suffix.*

  hope + ful = hopeful   **Exceptions:** wise/wisdom, awe/awful, true/truly

- *If a word ends with the letter* e, *and the suffix begins with a vowel, you must drop the final* e *before adding the suffix.*

  hope + ing = hoping   **Exceptions:** see/seeing, agree/agreeing

- *If a consonant comes before the letter* y, *you must change the* y *to* i *before adding the suffix.*

  floppy + er = floppier   sleepy + ly = sleepily

  Exceptions: dry/dryly   If the suffix is *ing*: copy/copying

- *If a vowel comes before the letter y, you do not change the y.*

  gray + er = grayer   **Exceptions:** dry/dryly, day/daily, pay/paid

PRACTICE • 1

The following sentences contain misspelled words. Cross out any words that are misspelled. Then write the correctly spelled word above the incorrect one.

1. Sometimes haveing a car in the city doesn't make your life easyer.
2. When I boughte a used car, I thought it would be great.
3. Of course, that was before I payed the first of many parking tickets.
4. One summons was unfair, and I decided on challengeing it in court.
5. I was confident about wining, knoing that the parkeing meeter had been broken.
6. I was pleasantely surprised when I immediatly one.
7. Of course, don't be decieved into thinking that tickets are the only hassle of haveing a car in the city!

▶ *Answers begin on page 273.*

SPELLING POSSESSIVES AND CONTRACTIONS

Many spelling mistakes occur because of incorrectly used apostrophes. Apostrophes are used with nouns to show possession. They also are used in contractions to show that letters are missing.

On page 150, you worked with *possessive nouns*. Recall that you use an apostrophe and an *s* with most singular nouns (common and proper) to show possession. Here is an example:

The dog's paw is bandaged.

With most possessive plural nouns, you use an apostrophe after the final *s* to show possession:

The leaves' colors were glorious last autumn.

A *contraction* joins two words into one. In the process, one or more letters are left out. An apostrophe marks the missing letters. Look at these examples:

They didn't know who sang that love song.

What's the name of that video that you've been talking about?

In the first sentence, the contraction *didn't* is made from the words *did not*. The *o* is left out and an apostrophe marks its place. In the second sentence *you've* (*you have*) omits the letters *ha*. An apostrophe marks this omission.

Here are some common contractions:

CONTRACTION	WORDS	CONTRACTION	WORDS	CONTRACTION	WORDS
I'm	I am	they've	they have	aren't	are not
you're	you are	I'll	I will	couldn't	could not
he's	he is	you'll	you will	wouldn't	would not
she's	she is	he'll	he will	shouldn't	should not
it's	it is / it has	she'll	she will	hasn't	has not
we're	we are	we'll	we will	haven't	have not
they're	they are	they'll	they will	who's	who is
I've	I have	don't	do not	what's	what is
you've	you have	doesn't	does not	where's	where is
we've	we have	isn't	is not		

Using a lot of contractions tends to give writing an informal tone. Not using any can make writing sound very formal. When you write, you should consider your purpose and audience and then decide when and where contractions are appropriate.

PRACTICE • 2

■ In the following sentences, you will find misspelled words, including misspelled contractions and possessives. Cross out any misspelled words and rewrite them correctly.

1. My friends son, Anthony, is a little less than two year's old, I beleive.
2. Whenever I see him, I cant understand how he couldve grown so much.
3. Im sure that if I saw him daily, his' growth would'nt be so surprising.
4. Still, its as if one day he was crawling and the next day hes not walking but *runing* around!
5. Both of his parents, of course, coul'dnt be more athleteic.
6. They're first meeting was on a basketball court in Detroit, and their cars license plate says, "BBALL."
7. Ive not yet made up my own mind about haveing children.
8. Isnt it wierd how confused you can be about big life decisions?
9. My husband wants a child, but I feel were better off waiting.

CONNECTIONS

Writers improve their skills through practice, just like athletes and musicians. Read about writing in the Employment theme in **CONNECTIONS**, pages C4–C5. Then choose four words from those pages that you have difficulty spelling correctly. Write four sentences using one of these words each time.

▶ *Answers begin on page 273.*

SPELLING: FREQUENTLY MISSPELLED WORDS

Below are some words that often present spelling problems. It will be worthwhile for you to learn these spellings.

a lot	deposit	hurried	necessary	separate
accept	difference	imaginary	niece	several
accomplish	doubt	immigrant	often	sight
ache	eight	increase	once	special
achieve	embarrass	innocence	opinion	straight
application	English	interfere	ought	tenant
assistance	excellent	interest	peace	thorough
balance	experience	island	piece	through
because	familiar	judgment	personal	tomorrow
between	foreign	knew	please	toward
breath	fourteen	know	possess	unnecessary
breathe	friend	language	prepare	usual
careful	general	library	probably	view
certain	governor	license	promise	visitor
choose	great	loose	quiet	voice
chose	grocery	lose	quite	weak
comfortable	half	marriage	raise	wear
communicate	healthy	match	receipt	week
courtesy	height	mortgage	restaurant	which
daily	hospital	muscle	right	whole

EDITING PRACTICE

■ The paragraph below contains spelling errors. Edit the paragraph by correcting all the misspelled words.

When Doreen became intrested in a positon in one of the towns office's, it was nesessary for her to fill out an aplication for employement. She was quiet surprised when she looked closly and saw that it was writen in Spanish. She asked if there were any applicationes in english, and the clerk said, "Weve got applications in four diffrent languges, but we just ran out of the English ones!"

► *Answers begin on page 273.*

PRE-GED PRACTICE

*Choose the **one best answer** for each item.*
***Items 1 to 5** refer to the following passage.*

(1)I cant understand why I'm paid a lot less money than bankers and lawyers. (2)I guess it's simply that thier experience and skills are valued more. (3)I know that a bankers judgment is important because money is at stake. (4)However, I also posess skills and succeed at doing important things. (5)It would'nt be a bad idea to raise the pay of all people who work hard and are capable.

1. Sentence 1: I cant understand why I'm paid a lot less money than bankers and lawyers.

Which is the best way to write the underlined portion of this sentence? If you think the original is the best way, choose (1).

(1) I cant understand why I'm paid a lot less
(2) I cant understand why I'm paid alot less
(3) I can't understand why I'm paid alot less
(4) I can't understand why I'm payed a lot less
(5) I can't understand why I'm paid a lot less

2. Sentence 2: I guess its simply that thier experience and skills are valued more.

Which is the best way to write the underlined portion of this sentence? If you think the original is the best way, choose (1).

(1) thier experience
(2) thier expereince
(3) their expereince
(4) their experience
(5) they're experience

3. Sentence 3: I know that a bankers judgment is important because money is at stake.

Which is the best way to write the underlined portion of this sentence? If you think the original is the best way, choose (1).

(1) bankers judgment is
(2) banker's judgment is
(3) banker's judgement is
(4) bankers judgement is
(5) bankers judgment are

4. Sentence 4: However, I also posess skills and succeed at doing important things.

Which is the best way to write the underlined portion of this sentence? If you think the original is the best way, choose (1).

(1) posess skills and succeed
(2) possess skill's and succeed
(3) posess skills and succede
(4) posses skills and succede
(5) possess skills and succeed

5. Sentence 5: It would'nt be a bad idea to raise the pay of all people who work hard and are capable.

Which is the best way to write the underlined portion of this sentence? If you think the original is the best way, choose (1).

(1) It would'nt be a bad idea to raise
(2) It wouldnt be a bad idea to raise
(3) It wouldn't be a bad idea to raise
(4) It wouldn't be a bad idea to rayse
(5) It would'nt be a bad idea to rayse

► *Answers begin on page 274.*

LESSON 18

Tricky Spelling Words

Although spelling rules are useful, there are always exceptions to these rules. Other words are frequently misused because of confusion about their meaning. By studying these words and using them in your writing, you can learn to use and spell them correctly.

HOMONYMS

Sometimes two words sound alike but are spelled differently and have different meanings. These words are called *homonyms*. Homonyms can pose spelling problems. However, studying the spellings and meanings of homonyms will help you use these words properly. The chart on the next page shows some commonly confused homonyms, along with their meanings and example sentences. Refer to the chart as you work on the practice items below.

PRACTICE • 1

■ In each of the following sentences, there are two homonyms in parentheses. Circle the correct homonym.

1. No matter how hard I concentrated, I couldn't seem to (hear/here) the bass guitar as the band played.
2. (Who's/Whose) singing the background harmony?
3. Doesn't music like this have any (affect/effect) on you?
4. The band is talented, but (their/they're) equipment is pretty old.
5. As far as the club was concerned, the musicians (passed/past) the audition.
6. After the audition, we were supposed to (meat/meet) at the restaurant.
7. Everyone agreed (accept/except) Maude.
8. She said she would be an (our/hour) late.

► *Answers begin on page 274.*

HOMONYMS	MEANINGS	EXAMPLE SENTENCES
accept **except**	receive excluding	I accept this gift. I like them all except that one.
affect **effect**	to influence a result	Did their criticism affect you? The effect of the flood was obvious.
bare **bear**	naked an animal; to endure	I diapered the baby's bare bottom. The bear stood on his hind legs. I can't bear this pain.
fare **fair**	price of travel just; an exhibit	Bus fare is fifty cents. The judge's decision was not fair. The fair includes a fun house.
for **four**	a preposition a number	Buy this pie for me. Can you eat four pies?
hear **here**	to perceive with the ear in this place	I hear a bell. Come here immediately.
hour **our**	a unit of time belonging to us	Be there in an hour. Our car is muddy.
meat **meet**	animal flesh join	I eat meat at least once a week. Meet me in Kansas City.
passed **past**	past tense of *to pass* time that has gone by	He passed the salt. That was in the past.
peace **piece**	calmness a part or portion	I would like some peace and quiet. I had a small piece of pie.
root **route**	growth under the surface a way of travel	This tooth's root has rotted. This is the best route to get there.
steal **steel**	take without permission iron	I could steal your heart. The sink was stainless steel.
there **their** **they're**	in that place belonging to them contraction of *they are*	Don't sit there. I ate their dinner. They're an hour late.
two **to** **too**	a number toward also, excessive	LeShan speaks two languages. He went to the jukebox. Bob is here, too. His hair is too long.
whose **who's**	possessive pronoun contraction of *who is* or *who has*	Whose hat is this? Who's coming tonight? Who's got an extra key?

FREQUENTLY MISUSED WORDS

There are some pairs of words that are often confused with one another, though they are not homonyms. Study the differences between the words in each pair below.

lie / lay These two irregular verbs are often confused with one another. Remember the different meaning of the two verbs. *Lie* means "to rest or recline." *Lay* means "to place or put" something. You *lie* down to take a nap. The magazine *lies* on the counter. You *lay* the book on the table.

sit / set This pair of words is often confused in the same way that *lie* and *lay* are. The verb *sit* means "to rest in place." A person "*sits* down." The verb *set* means "to place or fix something in position." It always takes an object. One "*sets* dishes on a table," "*sets* the hands of a watch," or "*sets* a date."

among / between These two prepositions are often used incorrectly. Use the word *between* when two people, things, or ideas are being discussed. Use the word *among* if three or more are being discussed. For instance, two people could come to an agreement *between* themselves; however, a roomful of people would have to come to an agreement *among* themselves.

that / who and whom A common mistake in speech and writing is to use the word *that* when *who* or *whom* is correct. *Who* and *whom* always refer to people. The word *that*, on the other hand, refers to **inanimate** objects, ideas, and animals. For example, you would be correct in saying, "He is the person *who* knows the most." You would use the word *that* correctly in a sentence such as, "This is the lamp *that* I like the most."

inanimate: nonliving

can / may It is mistakenly assumed that these two words are interchangeable, but they are not. The word *can* conveys the idea of "ability." For instance, you would say, "This athlete has trained for a month so that he *can* run ten miles." On the other hand, the word *may* conveys the idea of "permission." It would be correct to say, "You *may* take five dollars out of my purse."

fewer / less The correct use of this pair of words depends on the nature of the thing being described. If you are describing something that can be counted, the word *fewer* is correct—for instance, "fewer books" or "fewer calories." However, if you are describing something that can't be divided or counted in this way, use the word *less*—for instance, "less fat" or "less pain." Remember, if you can count the units, use *fewer*.

PRACTICE • 2

■ In each of the following sentences, there are two words in parentheses. Circle the word that best completes the sentence.

1. You (can/may) do well in this job if you put your mind and your heart into it.

2. Please (lie/lay) this on the table for me.

3. (Among/Between) the whole group of you, I want to find maybe a dozen solid individuals.

4. These are the people (that/who) will stick with the program, even when the work gets difficult.

5. The person who has to (lay/lie) down and complain after he or she breaks a sweat is *not* the person I'm seeking.

6. I'll be honest with you: there are (fewer/less) people of that quality in this room than you might think.

7. You (can/may) borrow my car for the weekend.

8. Don't (sit/set) on that bench until it is dry.

9. We received (fewer/less) rain this month than last month.

CONNECTIONS

Doctors and other health professionals depend upon good communication to help their patients. Read the Health Matters theme in **CONNECTIONS**, pages C14–C15. Then write a short paragraph about why you think communication is an important part of health care. Use at least three of the homonyms and frequently misused words discussed in this lesson in your paragraph. After you finish writing, check to make sure that you have used these words correctly.

▶ *Answers begin on page 274.*

FOCUS USAGE HIGHLIGHT: MISUSED WORDS

Here are more misused words that you should study.

uninterested / disinterested The adjective *uninterested* means "lacking interest." If a person is *uninterested*, he or she may become bored. The adjective *disinterested* means "impartial or objective." In other words, a person might be chosen to settle an argument because he or she is *disinterested*.

immoral / amoral The word *immoral* means "not moral." On the other hand, the word *amoral* means "being neither moral nor immoral." For instance, a person may behave in an *immoral* manner. However, acts of nature, like hurricanes, are *amoral* events.

emigrate / immigrate Emigrate means "to *leave* a country for good." Immigrate means "to *come* to a country to live." For example, a person could leave Vietnam and come to the United States to live. That person has *emigrated* from Vietnam. He or she has *immigrated* to the United States.

infer / imply The word *imply* means "to express indirectly." Thus, a person might *imply* that her brother is a liar by questioning, "Oh, is that the way it happened?" The word *imply* always has to do with an indirect expression of meaning. On the other hand, the word *infer* means "to draw a conclusion based on evidence." Thus, in the example above, the brother (after hearing his sister's question) might well *infer* that she believed him to be a liar.

EDITING PRACTICE

■ The following paragraph contains spelling and usage errors. Edit the paragraph by correcting all of the errors you find.

They're is alot to be said for excepting another individual exactly the way he or she is. This sort of fareness and understanding among two people is harder than it sounds. Many people are effected by the actions of others. I know I was hurt when my coworker inferred to my boss that I was lazy. Too tell a deliberate lie about someone is an amoral act in my opinion.

► *Answers begin on page 274.*

PRE-GED PRACTICE

*Choose the **one best answer** for each item.*
***Items 1 to 5** refer to the following passage.*

(1)In this neighborhood there are several different emigrant groups, such as Dominicans and Russians. (2)There are Cubans, Haitians, Syrians, Yemenis, and Italians here, to. (3)There are fewer Italians than there were ten years ago, but you still see many older Italian residents. (4)In the passed two decades the neighborhood has changed a lot. (5)Now sidewalks are filled with merchants lying their wares on carts and tables.

1. Sentence 1: In this neighborhood there are several different emigrant groups, such as Dominicans and Russians.

Which is the best way to write the underlined portion of this sentence? If you think the original is the best way, choose (1).

(1) neighborhood there are several different emigrant groups
(2) neighborhood there are several different immigrant groups
(3) neighborhood they're are several different immigrant groups
(4) nieghborhood there are several different emigrant groups
(5) neighborhood their are several different immigrant groups

2. Sentence 2: There are Cubans, Haitians, Syrians, Yemenis, and Italians here, to.

Which is the best way to write the underlined portion of this sentence? If you think the original is the best way, choose (1).

(1) and Italians here, to
(2) and Italians here, two
(3) and Italians hear, to
(4) and Italians here, too
(5) and Italians hear, too

3. Sentence 3: There are fewer Italians than there were ten years ago, but you still see many older Italian residents.

Which is the best way to write the underlined portion of this sentence? If you think the original is the best way, choose (1).

(1) There are fewer Italians than there
(2) There are fewer Italians than their
(3) There are less Italians than their
(4) Their are fewer Italians than there
(5) They're are less Italians than there

4. Sentence 4: In the passed two decades the neighborhood has changed a lot.

Which is the best way to rewrite this sentence? If you think the original is the best way, choose (1).

(1) in the passed two
(2) in the passed too
(3) in the passed to
(4) in the past to
(5) in the past two

5. Sentence 5: Now sidewalks are filled with merchants lying their wares on carts and tables.

Which is the best way to write the underlined portion of this sentence? If you think the original is the best way, choose (1).

(1) with merchants lying their wares
(2) with merchants lying thier wares
(3) with merchant's laying their wares
(4) with merchants laying their wares
(5) with merchants laying thier wares

► *Answers begin on page 274.*

Writing Skills Review

*Choose the **one best answer** for each item. **Items 1 to 10** refer to the following passage.*

(1)I find traveling by car is much more enjoyably than traveling by airplane. (2)In airplane travel, you waste half your time not traveling, for instance, you wait in lines and get tickets stamped and sit on the runway. (3)Also, after you buy your ticket, you no longer had any control over your trip. (4)If a place before your final destination interested you suddenly, she couldn't investigate it. (5)In other words there are no pleasant surprises to airplane travel.

(6)On the other hand, in an automobile you go slow enough to see details of the scenery. (7)Can take a tempting dirt road off the main road. (8)You are in control, you can decide if and when to stop for entertainment or rest. (9)Plus, you can get to exactly the place you want to go: 432 McDonald street in Fresno, for instance. (10)An airplane cannot be as exact; they will take you only to another airport!

1. Sentence 1: I find traveling by car is much more enjoyably than traveling by airplane.

What correction should be made to this sentence?
(1) change *traveling* to *travelling*
(2) change *is* to *are*
(3) change *is* to *was*
(4) insert a comma after *enjoyably*
(5) change *enjoyably* to *enjoyable*

2. Sentence 2: In airplane travel, you waste half your time not traveling, for instance, you wait in lines and get tickets stamped and sit on the runway.

What is wrong with Sentence 2?
(1) It is a fragment.
(2) It is a run-on sentence.
(3) It contains a misplaced modifier.
(4) The subject and verb don't agree.
(5) There is nothing wrong with Sentence 2.

3. Sentence 3: Also, after you buy your ticket, you no longer had any control over your trip.

What correction should be made to this sentence?
(1) take out the comma after *also*
(2) change *after* to *before*
(3) change *had* to *have*
(4) change *had* to *has*
(5) change *your* to *you're*

4. Sentence 4: If a place before your final destination interested you suddenly, she couldn't investigate it.

What correction should be made to this sentence?
(1) change *interested* to *interest*
(2) change *suddenly* to *sudden*
(3) change *couldn't* to *cannot*
(4) take out the comma after *suddenly*
(5) change *she* to *you*

5. Sentence 5: In other words there are no pleasant surprises to airplane travel.

What correction should be made to this sentence?
(1) place a comma after *words*
(2) change *there* to *their*
(3) change *are* to *is*
(4) place a comma after *no*
(5) change *pleasant* to *pleasent*

6. Sentence 6: On the other hand, in an automobile you go slow enough to see details of the scenery.

What correction should be made to this sentence?
(1) change *go* to *went*
(2) change *slow* to *slower*
(3) change *slow* to *slowly*
(4) place a comma after *enough*
(5) change *scenery* to *senery*

7. Sentence 7: Can take a tempting dirt road off the main road.

What is wrong with Sentence 7?
(1) It lacks a subject.
(2) It lacks a verb.
(3) It has a misplaced modifier.
(4) The verb is in the wrong tense.
(5) Nothing is wrong with Sentence 7.

8. Sentence 8: You are in control, you can decide if and when to stop for entertainment or rest.

What correction should be made to this sentence?
(1) add the word *Since* before the first *you*
(2) add the word *however* after the comma
(3) add the word *but* after the comma
(4) add the word *then* after the comma
(5) add the word *first* after the comma

9. Sentence 9: Plus, you can get to exactly the place you want to go: 432 McDonald street in Fresno, for instance.

What correction should be made to this sentence?
(1) change *Plus* to *Also*
(2) change *want* to *wanted*
(3) change *street* to *Street*
(4) take out the comma after *Fresno*
(5) change the period to a question mark

10. Sentence 10: An airplane cannot be as exact; they will take you only to another airport!

What correction should be made to this sentence?
(1) change *cannot* to *could not*
(2) change *you* to *me*
(3) change the semicolon to a comma
(4) change *they* to *it*
(5) change *they* to *he*

***Items 11 to 21** refer to the following passage.*

(1)How would I describe my life these past five years. (2)I am starting a new career and lived in a new home with my family.

(3)First of all, a new job because of my new skills. (4)Now I earn more than minimum wage, to take home to my family. (5)The job challenges me and gives me security, there are good people around me.

(6)I moved from Charlotte to a small town about a hundered miles away. (7)Now my family and I lives in a roomy three-bedroom apartment. (8)It is near my job and my childrens school.

(9)My family is more large than it was five years ago! (10)My husband and I have two children now, and us are in good health. (11)My life has been happier and more fulfilling when the children were born.

11. Sentence 1: How would I describe my life these past five years.

What correction should be made to this sentence?
(1) change *would* to *could*
(2) change *describe* to *describes*
(3) insert a comma after *describe*
(4) change the period to a question mark
(5) change the period to an exclamation point

12. Sentence 2: I am starting a new career and lived in a new home with my family.

Which is the best way to write the underlined portion of this sentence? If you think the original is the best way, choose (1).
(1) am starting a new career and lived
(2) are starting a new career and lived
(3) was starting a new career and lived
(4) am starting a new career and am living
(5) am starting a new career and was living

13. Sentence 3: First of all, a new job because of my new skills.

Which is the best way to write the underlined portion of this sentence? If you think the original is the best way, choose (1).
(1) First of all, a new job
(2) First of all a new job
(3) First of all, my new job
(4) First, a new job,
(5) First of all, I got a new job

14. Sentence 4: Now I earn more than minimum wage, to take home to my family.

What correction should be made to this sentence?
(1) change *earn* to *earned*
(2) change *earn* to *earns*
(3) insert a comma after *earn*
(4) change *than* to *then*
(5) take out the comma after *wage*

15. Sentence 5: The job <u>challenges me and gives me security, there are good people</u> around me.

Which is the best way to write the underlined portion of this sentence? If you think the original is the best way, choose (1).

(1) challenges me and gives me security, there are good people
(2) challenges and gives me security, and there are good people
(3) challenges and gives me security, they are good people
(4) challenges and gives me security there are good people
(5) challenges, gives me security, there are good people

16. Sentence 6: I moved from Charlotte to a small town about a hundered miles away.

What correction should be made to this sentence?

(1) change *moved* to *move*
(2) change *moved* to *moves*
(3) insert a comma after *Charlotte*
(4) insert a comma after *town*
(5) change *hundered* to *hundred*

17. Sentence 7: <u>Now my family and I lives</u> in a roomy three-bedroom apartment.

Which is the best way to write the underlined portion of this sentence? If you think the original is the best way, choose (1).

(1) Now my family and I lives
(2) Now my family and me lives
(3) Now my family and me live
(4) Now I and my family lives
(5) Now my family and I live

18. Sentence 8: It is near my job and my childrens school.

What correction should be made to this sentence?

(1) change *is* to *were*
(2) change *is* to *was*
(3) insert a comma after *job*
(4) change *childrens* to *children's*
(5) change *childrens* to *childrens'*

19. Sentence 9: My family is more large than it was five years ago!

What correction should be made to this sentence?

(1) change *is* to *are*
(2) change *is* to *be*
(3) change *more large* to *larger*
(4) change *more large* to *more larger*
(5) change *it* to *they*

20. Sentence 10: My husband and I have two children now, and us are in good health.

What correction should be made to this sentence?

(1) change *I* to *me*
(2) change *have* to *has*
(3) change *have* to *haves*
(4) change *us* to *we*
(5) change *us* to *our*

21. Sentence 11: My life has been happier and more fulfilling when the children were born.

What correction should be made to this sentence?

(1) change *happier* to *happily*
(2) change *has been* to *is being*
(3) change *more fulfilling* to *fulfillinger*
(4) change *when* to *since*
(5) change *were born* to *was born*

***Items 22 to 26** refer to the following paragraph.*

(1)I love winter; its my favorite season. (2)When it snows I help my kids build a snowman in the yard. (3)When the kids come inside from playing in the snow, there cheeks and noses are rosy. (4)To warm them up, I gave them hot cocoa. (5)My daughter always counts the marshmallows to see if her brother got more than her did.

22. Sentence 1: I love winter; its my favorite season.

What correction should be made to this sentence?
(1) change *winter* to *Winter*
(2) change the semicolon to a comma
(3) change *its* to *it's*
(4) change *its* to *its'*
(5) change *season* to *Season*

23. Sentence 2: When it snows I help my kids build a snowman in the yard.

What correction should be made to this sentence?
(1) insert a comma after *snows*
(2) change *kids* to *kid's*
(3) change *my* to *mine*
(4) insert a comma after *build*
(5) insert a comma after *snowman*

24. Sentence 3: When the kids come inside from playing in the snow, there cheeks and noses are rosy.

What correction should be made to this sentence?
(1) insert a comma after *inside*
(2) take out the comma after *snow*
(3) change *there* to *their*
(4) insert a comma after *and*
(5) change *rosy* to *rosey*

25. Sentence 4: To warm them up, I gave them hot cocoa.

What correction should be made to this sentence?
(1) change the first *them* to *they*
(2) take out the comma after *up*
(3) change the comma to a colon
(4) change *gave* to *give*
(5) change *cocoa* to *coco*

26. Sentence 5: My daughter always counts the marshmallows to see if her brother got more than her did.

What correction should be made to this sentence?
(1) change *counts* to *count*
(2) change *counts* to *counted*
(3) insert a comma after *marshmallows*
(4) change *got* to *had*
(5) change the second *her* to *she*

► *Answers begin on page 274.*

SECTION THREE • Answers and Explanations

UNIT 1

LESSON 1

Practice 1, page 143

Part A

1. ideas **2.** wishes **3.** cities **4.** pencils
5. leaves **6.** bottoms **7.** boxes **8.** boys

Part B

The following nouns should be underlined: room, furniture, chairs, bookcases, table, bench, bureau, couch, bed, middle, floor, boxes, guitar, room, atmosphere, gloom, mystery

Plural ≠ Singular: rooms, furniture, chair, bookcase, tables, benches, bureaus, couches, beds, middles, floors, box, guitars, rooms, atmospheres, glooms, mysteries

Practice 2, page 145

Part A

1. windows' **2.** goose's **3.** witch's **4.** stories'
5. Thomas's **6.** mouse's **7.** senator's **8.** Zaire's

Part B

The following nouns should be underlined: newspapers, methods, cities, "personality," newspapers, readers, community's, mood, atmosphere, stories', photographs', luck, paper, citys', side, side, balance

Corrections: city's, newspaper's, stories, photographs, city's

Editing Practice, page 146

Josie enrolled in a ~~Community College~~ *community college* in Toledo and started school in ~~september~~ *September*. She is taking three ~~courses'~~ *courses* and is doing well in all of them. One of ~~Josies'~~ *Josie's* best ~~qualitys~~ *qualities* is her eagerness. She says her education will be like an ~~insurance's~~ *insurance* policy for her ~~familys~~ *family's* future.

CONNECTIONS, page 146

President, person; *United States*, place; *Commander-in-Chief*, person; *Army*, thing; *Navy*, thing; *States*, places; *Executive Government*, thing.

Pre-GED Practice, page 147

1. (4) The noun *Athletes* should be plural possessive. Choice (1) contains the plural *Athletes* without the possessive. Choice (3) contains the singular possessive, *Athlete's*. The plural noun *bodies* is misspelled in Choices (2) and (5).
2. (3) *Basketball players* is not a proper noun so it is not capitalized. Choices (1), (2), (4), and (5) use incorrect capitalization.
3. (2) *Gymnasts* should be plural but not possessive. Choices (1) and (4) contain incorrect possessives. The singular form *frame* in Choice (3) is incorrect, as is the plural form of *fat* in Choice (5).
4. (1) *Men* is the plural of man and does not need an *s*. Choices (2), (3), and (5) are incorrect since *Men* and *athletes* don't need apostrophes. Choice (2) incorrectly contains an *s* at the end of *Men*. *Athletes* should be plural, so Choice (4) is incorrect.
5. (3) *People* is a plural noun without an *s* at the end. Choices (1) and (2) use an incorrect *s* and apostrophe. *Players* should be plural and not possessive, so Choices (4) and (5) are incorrect.

LESSON 2

Practice 1, page 149

Part A

1. Pronoun *she*, antecedent *Kathy*.
2. Pronoun *it*, antecedent *flag*.
3. Pronoun *he*, antecedent *tomcat;* pronoun *them*, antecedent *mice*.

Part B

1. him **2.** I I **3.** them

Practice 2, page 151

Part A

1. Please let me know what your decision is.
2. Her ambition is upsetting to him for some reason.
3. They took their chances when they adopted that grumpy dog.
4. Martha did her share of the driving, but I didn't do mine.
5. There is something strange in your salad, and you probably shouldn't look too closely at it.
6. The officer gave them his word, but they didn't trust him.

Part B

The day I *(S)* took my *(P)* driver's test was the worst day of my *(P)* life. My *(P)* wife was very supportive, but I [S] was nervous. I [S] wouldn't let her [O] come with me [O] to the test. My [P] friend Jerry loaned me [O] his [P] car, and we [S] went together. Of course, he [S] didn't tell me [O] that his [P] car was on its [P] last legs. Halfway to the test center, it [S] stalled. We [S] finally got it [O] started, but we [S] were late, and my [P] appointment was rescheduled for next month.

Editing Practice, page 152

The other day Reiko decided ~~her~~ *she* would like to go to a baseball game. She called her friend Fujio because she knew that ~~him~~ *he* enjoyed baseball. He said ~~him~~ *he* would love to go. ~~Their~~ *They* wondered if they should take ~~her's~~ *her* car or his car. Finally, it was decided by the two of ~~they~~ *them* to take the subway.

CONNECTIONS, page 152

Answers will vary. Here is a sample:

1. She was born a slave but escaped to freedom.
2. Her daring rescues helped slaves escape.
3. She was nicknamed "Moses."

Answer: Harriet Tubman

Pre-GED Practice, page 153

1. (1) A possessive is needed here, so *your* is correct. *Yours* is a possessive pronoun when used alone, not before a noun, so Choice (2) is incorrect. *Me* is correct, so Choices (3) and (4) are incorrect. In Choice (5), *its* is incorrect.
2. (4) The possessive pronoun *your* should be replaced by the object pronoun *you*. *I* is the correct subject pronoun, so Choices (1) and (2) are incorrect. *Your* should be replaced by an object pronoun, so Choices (3) and (5) are incorrect.
3. (5) *Its* is the possessive form of "it." *Its'* is not a word. The possessive pronoun *your* is correct, so Choices (1) and (2) are incorrect. Choice (3) contains the incorrect possessive *her*. Choice (4) incorrectly uses *it's*, a contraction for "it is."
4. (3) *Brothers'* should be replaced by the plural non-possessive, *brothers*. *Your* is the correct possessive pronoun, so Choices (1) and (2) are incorrect. *Theys* is not a word and the possessive *their* is not needed, so Choices (4) and (5) are incorrect.
5. (2) *You and I* is a compound subject, so the subject pronoun *I* is correct. *My* is a possessive pronoun, so both Choices (1) and (3) are incorrect. The second *you* should not be *your*, so Choice (4) is incorrect. Choice (5) contains the incorrect possessive *its*.

LESSON 3

Practice 1, page 155

Part A

1. Pronoun, *his*; antecedent, *Lawrence*.
2. Pronoun, *his*; antecedent, *he*.
3. Pronoun, *they*; antecedent, *Ginnie* and *Patty*.

Part B

The following pronouns should be circled:
Their; its; It

CONNECTIONS, page 156

Answers will vary. Here is a sample:

The first computer was built in 1942. Thirty-two years later, the first microcomputers were built. By 1976, they had become portable. Soon, they became very common.

Practice 2, page 157

Part A

1. Suddenly I was afraid because I couldn't tell whether the guy had a weapon or not.
2. Joan and Ella's party was no fun because Ella was so fussy.
3. Even though I stuck the bills between two books, they unfortunately got lost.
4. I love Delta Blues musicians like Bukka White and Son House because they make me feel that feeling bad is all right.
5. Julie walked up to Tonya and began to sing.

Part B

Juanita asked me if I would help her and Neil as they moved some heavy bookshelves from one apartment to another. ~~They aren't~~ *The job isn't* something I can do, however. I have a bad foot and a bad back, and ~~it prevents~~ *these injuries prevent* me from doing any heavy work. I help ~~them~~ *Juanita and him* a lot, but ~~you~~ *I* can't ever do enough for that guy. ~~We~~ *He and I* used to be close friends, but since ~~they~~ *he* moved in with ~~each other~~ *her*, ~~we~~ *he and I* have grown apart.

Editing Practice, page 158

There was no hot water in our apartment building for twenty days this month, and it didn't seem to bother ~~him~~ *the landlord* one bit. I figured that he would apologize because they own ~~it~~ *the building*, but ~~you~~ *I* can never predict what his reaction will be. The maintenance man said ~~it~~ *the boiler* broke last winter. A group of tenants got together and held back our rent payments.

Pre-GED Practice, page 159

1. (3) Using *Charles* instead of *he* will eliminate the vague pronoun reference. *Me* is the correct object pronoun, so Choices (1) and (2) are incorrect. Choice (4) incorrectly changes *he* to the possessive *his*. The use of the contraction *I've* in Choice (5) is unnecessary.
2. (4) Changing *you* to *he* eliminates the pronoun shift that was present in this sentence. The proper nouns *Charles* and *Fred* are necessary, so Choices (1), (2), and (3) are incorrect. In Choice (5), replacing *you* with *they* does not eliminate the pronoun shift.
3. (5) The pronoun *it* is incorrect in number. In Choices (1) and (4) the pronouns don't agree in number with their antecedents. Choice (2) incorrectly changes the verb tense. The pronoun *they* in Choice (3) is correct in number, but it is unclear.
4. (3) The pronoun *they* disagrees in person with its antecedent *three of us*; it should be replaced by *we*. Choices (1), (2), and (4) are grammatical errors. Choice (5) incorrectly changes the verb to *puts*.
5. (2) *They* is vague. *The customers* is much clearer. In Choice (3), the possessive pronoun *theirs* is incorrect. Choices (4) and (5) contain errors in verb tense and do not eliminate the vague pronoun reference.

LESSON 4

Practice 1, page 161

Part A

		past	future
1.	count	counted	will count
2.	save	saved	will save
3.	play	played	will play
4.	thank	thanked	will thank
5.	wash	washed	will wash
6.	enter	entered	will enter

Part B

The first time Ruben washed and ~~waxes~~ *waxed* his car, he ~~loves~~ *loved* the way it ~~looks~~ *looked*. The car looked great. That night, however, it ~~will rain~~ *rained* very hard. Suddenly, the car looked dull and old. Ruben just ~~laughs~~ *laughed*. The next morning, he ~~will wash~~ *washed* the car again.

Practice 2, page 163

1.	came	2.	knew	3.	will speak	4.	began
5.	took	6.	have	7.	pay	8.	will get

Editing Practice, page 164

My son and I went to the library last weekend. He ~~wants~~ *wanted* a book about dinosaurs. I ~~tryed~~ *tried* to find one. I ~~look~~ *looked* and ~~look~~ *looked*, but I had no luck. Finally, I ~~asks~~ *asked* the librarian. He showed me the card catalog. We ~~will find~~ *found* a great book. Now my son ~~reades~~ *reads* the book all the time.

CONNECTIONS, page 164

Answers will vary. Here is a sample:

My great-grandfather died in the flu epidemic that swept Europe in 1918. Today, he could have been cured. It is important to go on improving health care. We also need to make sure it is available to all who need it.

Pre-GED Practice, page 165

1. (2) *Come* is an irregular verb, and its past tense form is *came*. Choice (1), *comed*, and Choice (3), *commed*, are not words. Choice (4), *comes,* is in the present tense. Choice (5), *will come*, is in the future tense.
2. (5) The sentence should be in the past tense. The sentence should read, "His sister was already here." None of the other choices are in the past tense.
3. (4) *Pay* is an irregular verb. The past tense form is *paid*. Choice (1), *will pay*, is in the future tense. Choices (2) and (3) are misspellings. Choice (5), *pays*, is in the present tense.

4. (1) *Has* is in the present tense singular. Choice (3), *have*, is present tense, but it is the plural form. Choices (2) and (4) are in the wrong tense, and Choice (5) is not a word.
5. (2) To form the present tense singular of *know*, just add an *s*. Choice (1), *will know*, is in the future tense. Choice (3), *knew*, is in the past tense. Choice (4), *knowed*, is not a word. Choice (5), *know*, is not third-person singular.

LESSON 5

Practice 1, page 167

Part A

1. will have gone 2. have heard
3. have forgotten 4. have thought 5. had chosen

Part B

Native Americans have lived in North America for much longer than Europeans. When I learned this fact two weeks ago, I realized I had lived in ignorance about the history of Native Americans all my life. For the past two weeks, I have discussed this fact with anyone who is interested.

Practice 2, page 168

Part A

	Past Continuous	Present Continuous	Future Continuous
1.	was flying	am flying	will be flying
2.	were washing	are washing	will be washing
3.	was questioning	is questioning	will be questioning
4.	were walking	are walking	will be walking
5.	were studying	are studying	will be studying

Editing Practice, page 170

Last night while I ~~watch~~ *was watching* the news, my girlfriend Anne was making a birthday card for her mother. She ~~finished~~ *had finished* it by the time the news was over, but she fussed over it for another fifteen or twenty minutes. When I ~~had asked~~ *asked* her why she didn't leave it alone, she glared at me and ~~was walking~~ *walked* into the other room all upset. I think for the last few years she ~~felt~~ *has felt* anxious about her mother's getting older.

CONNECTIONS, page 170

Answers will vary. Here is a sample:

First I look at the front page to see if it is interesting and easy to read. I also look at the sports pages and the business section.

Pre-GED Practice, page 171

1. (4) The second action should be in the past perfect. The simple past tense *moved* is correct. Using the present perfect *have been* is incorrect.
2. (1) The verb *enjoyed* should be in the past continuous. The present perfect *have enjoyed* is incorrect. The simple past tense verb *took* does not need to be changed.
3. (2) The simple past is the correct tense to use here. *Was loving* is in the past continuous. The simple past tense verb *decided* does not need to be changed.
4. (5) The past continuous, *was smelling*, is incorrect. *It* is the third-person singular, so *was* is correct.
5. (1) The present continuous is the correct tense. *Had looked* is in the past perfect tense. The simple future tense *will leave* is correct.

LESSON 6

Practice 1, page 173

Part A

1. P; men always yell
2. P; They say
3. S; Peter eats
4. S; She throws
5. P; trees bend

Part B

The people in this neighborhood ~~runs~~ *run* everywhere. Nobody takes the time to walk anywhere. I ~~wonders~~ *wonder* why this is true. My next-door neighbor always ~~rush~~ *rushes* by me on his way to work. I think he should just get up a little earlier. I ~~has~~ *have* told him that he should relax, but you ~~knows~~ *know* he ~~don't~~ *doesn't* listen to me.

Practice 2, page 175

Part A

1. S; Music is
2. P; supplies are
3. S; It becomes
4. P; We feel
5. S; He smells

Part B

Every night ~~have~~ has been quiet since I've been here in Crawfordsville. John was nice enough to let me have the larger motel room. His room ~~don't~~ doesn't have nearly this much charm. During the day we ~~is~~ are busy at the plant. I ~~be~~ am a quality-control supervisor.

CONNECTIONS, page 175

Answers will vary. Here is a sample:

The most difficult part of writing is looking at an empty sheet of paper and thinking what I will say first. The more I write, the easier it gets.

Editing Practice, page 176

Mr. Sanchez, according to his wife, has been thinking about going on a diet. However, I ~~hears~~ hear (from Mr. Sanchez himself) that he has no intention of doing any such thing. He likes the way he ~~look~~ looks. I believe the diet ~~are~~ is just wishful thinking on her part. He does seem a little heavy to me, but they ~~says~~ say that a man of Mr. Sanchez's height can carry a lot of weight.

Pre-GED Practice, page 177

1. (2) The verb must be in its plural form, *sound*. Choice (1) would involve also changing *they are*. *Sounds'*, Choice (3), adds an incorrect apostrophe to the verb. Choices (4) and (5) are incorrect because the verb *are* agrees with the subject *they*.
2. (1) The verb must be changed to its plural form, *have*. *Their* is the correct possessive pronoun, so Choices (2) and (3) are incorrect. The verb *is* agrees with *what*, so Choice (4) is incorrect. Changing *listeners* to *listener* would create disagreement with *their imaginations*, so Choice (5) is incorrect.
3. (4) The verb *is* must be changed to its plural form, *are*. *Listen* agrees with the pronoun *I*, so Choices (1) and (2) are incorrect. *Am* is a singular form of the verb *to be*, so Choice (3) is incorrect. Choice (5) is incorrect because *parts* is plural, not possessive.
4. (3) The verb *sees* must be changed to its plural form, *see*. *Viewer's* is an incorrect possessive, so Choice (1) is incorrect. If the verb tense were present continuous, the correct helping verb would be *are*, not *is*, so Choice (2) is incorrect. In Choice (4), *capture* does not need an *s*. The helping verb *have* doesn't agree with *camera*, so Choice (5) is incorrect.
5. (2) The verb *are* must be changed to *is*. *Am* does not agree with *it*, so Choice (1) is incorrect. The possessive *its* is incorrect, so Choice (3) is incorrect. In Choice (4), *plesure* is incorrectly spelled. There is no *s* needed at the end of *listen*, so Choice (5) is incorrect.

LESSON 7

Practice 1, page 179

1. crowd ~~appear~~ appears
2. Economics ~~confuse~~ confuses
3. Everyone ~~are~~ is
4. Sunglasses ~~makes~~ make
5. Nobody has
6. people were
7. Mathematics ~~are~~ is

Practice 2, page 181

Part A

1. The trombones and the piano ~~plays~~ play
2. Sam Wilson and his parents are visiting
3. The stones and the seaweed ~~is~~ are
4. Dogs and people ~~gets~~ get
5. She and the grocery store owner have lived
6. We and our cousins ~~has~~ have

Part B

The bushes and the grass ~~is~~ are in need of some work. However, my niece and two cousins ~~has~~ have conveniently disappeared. Denise, Scott, and David ~~feels~~ feel that this is a good time to walk over to the store for a pack of gum. Something ~~tell~~ tells me that nobody is going to hurry home, either. Well, anybody who is afraid of work can cook dinner instead.

CONNECTIONS, page 181

Answers will vary. Here is a sample:

Neither my Dad nor my mother speak any language but English, but my grandparents speak Chinese. My grandparents live in Taiwan, and I would love to visit them. My aunt in mainland China has invited me as well.

Editing Practice, page 182

Kyle and Mary ~~agrees~~ *agree* that having a telephone can be as much trouble as it is convenient. It's lucky for them that they do agree. Everyone in the world besides the two of them ~~seem~~ *seems* to feel that if a telephone rings, it must be answered. But if it is *your* telephone in *your* house, isn't it *your* choice whether or not you ~~feels~~ *feel* like talking to somebody? However, most people ~~looks~~ *look* at you like you're crazy if you ~~behaves~~ *behave* like this. Neither Kyle nor Mary ~~have~~ *has* that problem.

Pre-GED Practice, page 183

1. (1) The subject *everybody* is singular, so the verb must be *has*. In Choice (2), *subject's* is misspelled. *Does* is the correct singular form, so Choices (3), (4), and (5) are incorrect.
2. (2) The compound subject *Mona and Terry* is plural, so the verb must be *were talking*. The verb *is talking* is singular, so Choice (1) is incorrect. The verb *is* agrees with its subject, so Choices (3) and (4) are incorrect. *Them* is correct, so Choice (5) is incorrect.
3. (2) The verb must be the singular *is*. *Were* is also a plural verb, so Choice (1) is incorrect. *Are counted* and *count* are plural verb forms, so Choices (3), (4), and (5) are incorrect.
4. (1) The subject *members* is plural, so the verb must be *feel*. Choice (2), *felts*, is not a word. The apostrophe in *feel's* is wrong, so Choice (3) is incorrect. Choice (4) is incorrect since *have* agrees with the pronoun *they*. *Done* is a correct past participle, so Choice (5) is incorrect.
5. (3) The subject *something* is singular, so the verb must be *happens*. *Hope* agrees with the subject *I*, so Choices (1) and (2) are incorrect. *Improve* agrees with the subject *I*, so Choice (4) is incorrect. Choice (5) is incorrect because *skills* should not be possessive.

LESSON 8

Practice 1, page 185

Part A

1. is photograph
2. ~~is~~ *are* names
3. stands statue
4. is words
5. do you ~~thinks~~ *think*

Part B

There ~~is~~ *are* completely magical things about the ocean. For instance, there ~~are~~ *is* the ocean's constant movement. In the tidal pools by the marsh ~~are~~ *is* very warm salt water. There I feel at one with the natural world. Why ~~doesn't~~ *don't* lakes or ponds interest me more? I guess I like the expanse and motion of the sea.

Practice 2, page 187

Part A

1. man ~~are~~ *is*
2. chart is
3. songs ~~is~~ *are*
4. comedians ~~comes~~ *come*
5. families ~~lives~~ *live*

Part B

The painters, as well as the carpenter and the plumber, ~~is~~ *are* due to arrive on Wednesday. One of these workers ~~are~~ *is* going to have to watch the others work for a while because everyone ~~need~~ *needs* to work in the same corner of the kitchen. The problem with this plan ~~have~~ *has* to do with my checkbook. Some of my hard-earned dollars, as well as my groceries, ~~is~~ *are* going to go to pay someone as he rests!

Editing Practice, page 188

The men and the women, from the restaurant, ~~is~~ are going skating at Webhannet Pond. Lynn, along with Patty and Lenore, ~~say~~ says that she is going with them.

CONNECTIONS, page 188

Answers will vary. Here is a sample:

I would put my grandmother's ring and a family tree that my grandfather drew. It shows our family history and where my brothers, sisters, and cousins live today.

Pre-GED Practice, page 189

1. (1) The compound subject is plural, so the verb must be *hang*. Choice (2), *hanging*, is a participle that would need the verb *are* to complete it. Choices (3), (4), and (5) are incorrect because *have given* correctly agrees with *people*.
2. (1) The subject *desk* is singular, so the verb must be *is*. Choice (2) is incorrect because the verb *were* is not singular. *Haven't* is the correct verb for the subject *I*, so Choices (3) and (4) are incorrect. *Works* agrees with *she*, so Choice (5) is incorrect.
3. (4) The subject *cabinets* is plural, so the verb must be *line*. The interrupting phrase should be set off with two commas. Choices (1), (2), and (3) contain the incorrect singular form *lines*. Choice (5) is missing both commas.
4. (1) The subject *she* is singular, so the verb must be *doesn't try*. In Choice (2), *do* is not a correct third-person singular form. *Try* is correct, so Choices (3) and (4) are incorrect. *Reduces* is not used after *to*, so Choice (5) is incorrect.
5. (2) The subject *woman* is singular, so the verb must be *hasn't*. The prepositional phrase does not need to be set off by commas, so Choice (1) is incorrect. *Is* is the correct form of the verb *to be*, so Choices (3), (4), and (5) are incorrect.

LESSON 9

Practice 1, page 191

Part A

1. P; schoolteacher was delighted
2. P; Three were given
3. A; students spoke
4. P; atmosphere had been created
5. A; principal was thrilled

Part B

P; The set of oil paints was bought by Derek. P; It was wrapped up in colorful paper and ribbons by an employee of the art supplies store. A; Derek brought home the gift. P; It was left on the wooden table by the front door. A; Of course, I loved the surprise.

Practice 2, page 193

Part A

Sentences will vary. Here are some samples:

1. Karen wrote a very funny letter.
2. Laughter filled the room.
3. Some people fell onto the floor.

Part B

Descriptions will vary. Here is a sample:

The building on Main Street has stood for many years. Its four stories tower over the small house next door. Once, people lived in the building, but now they only work there. Someone has painted the building white with green shutters. A garden sprawls across the backyard but I don't know who keeps it up.

Editing Practice, page 194

The following sentences from the paragraph have been numbered.

1. P; Possible revision: Ben and I visited the beach last weekend.
2. P; Possible revision: We took his car for the trip.
3. A
4. A
5. P; Possible revision: Still, we both had fun.
6. P; Possible revision: I watched Ben's hilarious attempts at swimming with pleasure.

CONNECTIONS, page 194

Answers will vary. Here is a sample:

I use three programmable items every day. My clock-radio wakes me up in the morning. My telephone has my father's number programmed into it. My television remembers my favorite channels.

Pre-GED Practice, page 195

1. (5) The sentence would be improved by using the action verb *gives*. Choices (1), (2), and (3) use forms of the verb *to be*. In addition, Choice (2) replaces *me* with the subject pronoun *I*, and in Choice (3), *are* does not agree with the subject *tenant*. In Choice (4), the verb *give* does not agree with the subject *tenant*.
2. (4) The original sentence would be improved by revising into the active voice. Choices (1) and (2) are in the passive voice. In addition, the verb *are* in Choice (2) does not agree with the subject *television*. In Choice (3), the verb *play* doesn't agree with the subject *he*. *He* does not need to be capitalized, so Choice (5) is incorrect.

3. (4) *Their* does not agree with its antecedent (the neighbor) and the singular pronoun *him*. In Choice (2), *there* is not a possessive pronoun. In Choice (3), the incorrect contraction *they're* is used. Choice (5) does not correct the disagreement and creates a new disagreement between *them* and *him*.
4. (1) The original sentence is the best choice. *Landlord* does not need capitalization, so Choice (2) is incorrect. Choices (3), (4), and (5) use wordy constructions in the passive voice. In addition, in Choice (5), *may has* is an incorrect verb form.
5. (2) The verb *live* should be changed to agree with *brother*. The interrupting phrase should be set off with commas, so Choice (1) is incorrect. *Lives* does not require an apostrophe, so Choice (3) is incorrect. *Hopes* and *is hoping* do not agree in number with the subject *I*, so Choices (4) and (5) are incorrect.

LESSON 10

Practice 1, page 197

Part A

Answers will vary. Here are some sample answers:

1. He has received *several* contract offers.
2. After a hard practice, he needs to eat a *large* meal.
3. The *blue* shirt is his favorite.

Part B

1. The adverb *highly* modifies *praised*.
2. The adverb *warmly* modifies *spoke*.
3. The adverbs *yesterday* and *harshly* modify *criticized*.

Part C

The sporty rental car rode ~~quiet~~ quietly on the open highway. However, the steering wheel turned too ~~easy~~ easily, so the car was difficult to control.

Practice 2, page 199

Part A

1. The ~~rainier~~ rainiest weather of the year arrived suddenly.
2. The long, steady storm raised reservoirs more dramatically than last month's storm.
3. We have had the ~~most~~ brownest lawns and driest forests in years.
4. To me, the ~~pleasantest~~ most pleasant weather of all is a snowstorm.
5. My dog runs and leaps ~~most~~ more enthusiastically than my cat.

Part B

The city of Lowell, Massachusetts is ~~more~~ smaller than Boston. In the nineteenth and early twentieth centuries, it was one of the ~~more~~ most important textile producers in the entire country. It fell on hard times in recent decades, but now is making one of the ~~more~~ most impressive renewal efforts in all of New England.

Editing Practice, page 200

The popular game of baseball is more extremely enjoyable to watch in person. The large, ~~odd~~ oddly shaped, and very green field is impossible to appreciate on a television screen. You should go ~~soonly~~ soon to a local ballpark. Even the ~~most small~~ smallest Little League field has a ~~simpler~~ simple and beautiful design. When the nine players scamper ~~joyful~~ joyfully onto the field, that simple design comes immediately to life.

CONNECTIONS, page 200

Tongue twisters will vary. Here is a sample:
The sixth sheik's sixth sheep is sick.

Pre-GED Practice, page 201

1. (2) The superlative adjective *most stirring* modifies *work*. Choice (1) uses the comparative *more*. Choice (3) does not make sense since the writer has described the painting as *extraordinary*. Choice (4) is wrong because the superlative cannot be formed by adding *-est*. Choice (5) incorrectly uses a comparative adverb form.
2. (1) The original sentence is correct. Choices (2) and (3) are incorrect because they misuse the adjective *littered*. Choice (4) incorrectly uses *deadly* as an adverb to modify *lies*.

Choice (5) incorrectly uses both *deadly* and the comparative form of *littered*.

3. (3) You do not need a comma between the last item of a series (*uniformed*) and *policeman*. Choices (1) and (4) incorrectly place commas. Choice (2) contains no commas at all when they are needed. Choice (5) contains the unnecessary comparative adjective *larger*.
4. (1) The adjective *shocked* correctly modifies the noun *expressions*. Choices (2) and (5) contain unnecessary commas. Choices (3) and (4) have unnecessary comparative or superlative forms of *shocked*.
5. (5) The adjective *orange* modifies *moon*. *Oranger* is not a word, so Choices (1) and (2) are incorrect. Choices (3) and (4) are incorrect because they have an unnecessary comparative form of *orange*. Choices (2) and (4) are also incorrect because *moon* does not agree in number with the verb *rise*.

UNIT 2
LESSON 11
Practice 1, page 205

1. C; The construction workers arrived at 7:00 A.M., and two hours later the sidewalk in front of the pharmacy was completely removed.
2. C; Some men used shovels and a jackhammer, and others carried away pieces of stone and cement in wheel barrows.
3. S; The sidewalk was covered with piles of wood, gravel, and tools.
4. C; Customers came to the pharmacy during the morning, but the store's entrance was blocked from time to time.
5. C; One man became angry outside the entrance, but then he calmed down.
6. S; This continued all through the day until quite late.
7. C; The disruption brought some excitement to the neighborhood, yet nobody hopes for another day of it.

Practice 2, page 207

Revisions will vary. Here are some samples:

1. My teacher advised me to read, write, and study.
2. This past month I have read three books, written a ten-page autobiography, and researched a report on immigration.
3. A friend said that recently my writing seemed smoother, clearer, and more interesting.
4. Writing well makes me feel happy, proud, and more confident.

CONNECTIONS, page 207

Answers will vary. Here are two sample sentences using parallel structure:

1. Today we booked a package tour to Mexico, a flight to Hawaii, and a Caribbean cruise.
2. On the night shift, I give my patients their medication and check if they need water.

Editing Practice, page 208

Revisions will vary. Here is a sample:

Linda considered traveling to Chicago by train, ~~or~~ plane, or automobile ~~she was thinking about driving~~. She was not terribly fond of flying, but she ~~She~~ was a little concerned about the safety of the train. There had been several train accidents lately. She thought driving might be the best way to go, but she ~~She~~ had never driven more than an hour by herself. She was interested in spending as much time as she could with her daughter in Chicago, so she ~~She~~ decided to overcome her fear and take the plane.

Pre-GED Practice, page 209

1. (2) The three verbs should be in parallel structure in the simple past tense. Choices (1), (3), (4), and (5) contain verbs in different tenses.
2. (4) The three objects of the preposition *for*—*privacy, walks,* and *search*—should be put into parallel structure. The objects in Choices (1), (2), (3), and (5) are not parallel. The tenses of their objects are different.
3. (3) This is a compound sentence that should be separated by a semicolon. The connecting word should be followed by a comma. Choices (1) and (2) incorrectly combine compound sentences into one sentence. Choices (4) and (5) do not follow the connecting word with a comma.
4. (4) The introductory phrase is separated from the rest of the sentence by a comma, and the three verb phrases are in parallel structure. Choices (1), (2), and (5) do not contain parallel structure. Choices (2) and (3) separate the introductory phrase with a semicolon.

LESSON 12

Practice 1, page 211

1. Mr. Ramirez was not at work on Monday although he had never missed a day of work before.
2. He could not go to work because he needed to take his wife to the doctor.
3. Because she was suffering from the flu, Mrs. Ramirez felt as if she had been run over by a steamroller.
4. She was uncomfortable whenever she tried to sit or lie down.
5. After she went to the doctor, she felt better.
6. When his wife had completely recovered, Mr. Ramirez went back to work.
7. Since she was feeling better, she called her husband at his office.
8. If he could leave the office by five o'clock, they would go to the movies.

Practice 2, page 213

Part A

Possible revisions:

1. ~~As if~~ *Although* there are so many banks in this city, it's hard to get good service from one.
2. ~~After~~ *Unless* the bank is not busy, it does not have enough tellers serving the public.
3. ~~Before~~ *Because* they can get away with it, banks charge unfair fees to people without a lot of money.
4. I am switching banks ~~though~~ *as soon as* I can find one that has more respect for its customers.

Part B

Revisions will vary. Here is a possible revision:

The house I grew up in was small ~~as if~~ *even though* it didn't feel that way to me as a child. I had my own room ~~so that~~ *until* I was nine years old. Then, I had to share my room with my brother ~~whether~~ *because* his room was taken by the new baby. In that house, I was happy ~~after~~ *wherever* I was spending my time. ~~Although~~ *Because* I have happy memories like this, I think I am unique.

Editing Practice, page 214

Revisions will vary. Here is a possible revision:

Paper companies own huge tracts of land in the state of Maine, although not many people know it. You can drive on gravel roads in these areas~~,~~ if you are willing to share the road with enormous trucks loaded with full-length trees. Because the companies own the roads, the companies' truck drivers insist that you yield to them rather than share with them. This makes for an exciting ride~~,~~ so long as you follow these unwritten rules.

CONNECTIONS, page 214

Answers will vary. Here is a sample:

If I worked in a hospital, I would choose to be a physical therapist. When people have an operation or injure themselves, physical therapists play an important role in helping them to regain their strength. Since you get to watch a person's physical improvement, being a physical therapist would be a very rewarding job.

Pre-GED Practice, page 215

1. (2) The connecting word *though* correctly suggests that the two clauses are in contrast to one another. Choice (1) does not suggest a contrast. Choice (3) is incorrect because a comma should separate the dependent clause from the subordinate clause. Choices (4) and (5) incorrectly suggest connections between the two clauses.
2. (5) The connecting word *before* establishes a time relationship between the clauses. Choices (1), (2), (3), and (4) incorrectly suggest connections between the two clauses.
3. (4) The connecting word *unless* correctly suggests that the ideas in the two clauses are related by a condition, so a comma should link the two clauses. Choices (1), (2), and (3) incorrectly suggest connections between the two clauses. Choice (5) is incorrect.
4. (1) The connecting words *even though* correctly suggest that the two clauses are in contrast to one another. Choices (2), (3), (4), and (5) incorrectly suggest connections between the two clauses.

LESSON 13

Practice 1, page 217

Part A

1. M **2.** M **3.** M **4.** C **5.** D **6.** M

Part B

Rewritten paragraphs will vary. Here is a sample revision:

Shouting at the top of their lungs, the demonstrators caught the attention of the whole town. One woman with a bullhorn stood on the shoulders of a statue and gave a short speech. There she was noticed by just about everyone. Listening to her, people noticed how tension filled the town square. Local merchants with frowning faces watched from outside their stores.

Practice 2, page 219

Part A

1. F **2.** F **3.** R **4.** C **5.** R **6.** R

Part B

Revisions will vary. Here is a possible revision:

The wedding took place on Chicago's South Side. There were about one hundred and twenty guests there. I played piano at the reception since the bride's my sister. The guy she married is terrific. I wish, however, that he weren't from Chicago. If he were from the East, my sister and he would live here, and I could see them more often. I have mixed feelings, I guess you could say.

CONNECTIONS, page 219

Answers will vary. Here are two sample answers.

Writing in ideograms or syllabic symbols would be much slower than writing English. Each word would have to be learned separately.

Editing Practice, page 220

Revisions will vary. Here is a possible revision:

Keiko was inexperienced with apartment repairs. She didn't know anything about refinishing floors. Since she was moving in on the first weekend of April, the floors needed to be done first. The woman in the neighboring apartment kindly offered to help her.

Pre-GED Practice, page 221

1. (4) The dangling modifier *traveling* has been corrected so that it modifies *I*. The modifier *traveling* still refers to the *areas* in Choices (1), (2), and (3), and *traveling* refers to the *landscape* in Choice (5).
2. (5) The subject *landscape* and the verb *is littered* have been added to correct the sentence fragment. Choices (1), (2), (3), and (4) still create sentence fragments.
3. (2) The misplaced modifier *with an interest in ecology* has been moved closer to the word it modifies, *person*. Choices (1), (4), and (5) still contain misplaced modifiers. Choice (3) contains a comma-spliced run-on sentence.
4. (2) The run-on sentence has been corrected by turning the first part into a dependent clause using the connecting word *if*. Choices (1), (4), and (5) are still run-on sentences. Choice (3) is grammatically correct, but the connecting word, *although*, is not appropriate.
5. (2) This run-on sentence has been divided into two simple sentences. Choice (1) is a run-on sentence. Choice (4) is a comma-splice run-on sentence. The second sentences in Choices (3) and (5) are sentence fragments.

UNIT 3

LESSON 14

Practice 1, page 225

Part A

1. What is your opinion of this airline?
2. We are flying from Atlanta to San Diego.
3. What a view there is out the left windows!
4. Aren't they serving dinner on this flight?
5. I'm sure someone is picking us up at the airport.
6. Now, *that's* turbulence!
7. Have you ever been there before?
8. I asked a friend of mine who lives in San Diego to show us around.
9. The weather should be much warmer there than in Atlanta.
10. I can't wait to get there!

Part B

Have you ever thought about supporting small businesses instead of huge corporations? If you think about it, it's quite easy to make it work. Most people simply aren't aware of the way "chain" stores put "mom and pop" stores out of business. If you feel that those smaller, independent stores offer valuable services that larger stores don't, then you might consider giving your business to a small business. If people don't choose to support small businesses now, we may soon have only large chain stores?.

Practice 2, page 227

1. I think I was in the town of Vergennes, Vermont, in July 1983.
2. Jane, isn't Vergennes near Middlebury, Bristol, and Burlington?

3. In the summer of that year, my younger brother Jim was traveling through the Green Mountains.
4. I swam in a small, peaceful pond, and I fished in a river near Bristol.
5. When I arrived in a town called Ripton, I thought I was at the top of Bread Loaf Mountain.
6. I was only halfway there, however.
7. Down a dirt road in Ripton is the cabin where Robert Frost, the famous American poet, lived.
8. I said, "I like Harlem Renaissance poetry."
9. However, I've never been to Harlem.
10. Instead I drive to the mountains, the beach, and the lake.
11. The car, which is only six years old, has over 150,000 miles on it.

CONNECTIONS, page 227

Answers will vary. Here is a sample:

I would enjoy working with computers as a graphic artist. Not only would I be able to use my creative skills, but I also would be able to make my work easier by using a computer. Because of computer technology, now is the perfect time to be a graphic artist!

Editing Practice, page 228

Do you think professional athletes, get paid too much? During their first year on a major league baseball team, most players get paid over $100,000. I don't understand why they get paid that when an electrician gets about $30,000. Of course they still demand a pay raise!

Pre-GED Practice, page 229

1. (1) The simple sentence ends in a period. Choices (2), (3), and (4) insert unnecessary commas.
2. (3) The elements of a series are separated by commas. Choice (1) inserts a comma after a connecting word. Choice (2) creates a second sentence without a subject. Choice (4) inserts an unnecessary comma. Choice (5) does not insert commas in the series.
3. (4) *Zora Neale Hurston and Langston Hughes* is a compound subject. Choices (1) and (2) insert unnecessary commas. No strong emotion is being expressed in the sentence, so Choice (3) is incorrect. The semicolon in Choice (5) creates two sentence fragments.
4. (4) This direct question should end with a question mark. The sentence is a question, so Choice (1) is incorrect. Choices (2) and (3) insert unnecessary commas. Choice (5) does not indicate a question.
5. (3) There should be a comma after *again* to separate the two clauses. No strong emotion is being expressed, so Choice (1) is incorrect. Choices (2) and (4) insert unnecessary commas. Choice (5) does not insert a comma after the dependent clause.

LESSON 15

Practice 1, page 231

Part A

1. The filth in the house was unbelievable; I decided it was time to get out the vacuum cleaner.
2. When I discovered I had no vacuum cleaner bags, I remembered why I hadn't vacuumed earlier.
3. I went to the hardware store for the following items: vacuum cleaner bags, a Venetian blind, and a ball of strong twine.
4. Because the vacuum cleaner bags were the wrong size, I had to return them.
5. I spent a day cleaning the house; it was worth it.
6. I cleaned all of these rooms: the kitchen, the bedroom, the bathroom, the living room, and the study.
7. Before I cleaned the kitchen, I cleaned the bathroom.
8. I never knew that cleaning was such hard work. It really takes it out of you.
9. Since I had worked so hard, I treated myself to a nice dinner.

10. Here's what I ate steak a baked potato a salad and a glass of wine.

Part B

Our flight was scheduled to leave at 5;33 in the evening. at 5:00 we were not even near the airport. Furthermore, we had a trunk full of stuff that needed to be checked, Four suitcases, three cardboard boxes with household goods, several small Christmas packages, and a child's bicycle. I asked the taxi driver whether there was another route, he looked at me, shook his head, and chuckled to himself.

Practice 2, page 233
Part A

1. I; We took the kids to the Acton Fair last night all of us had a great time.
2. I; One guy at a booth said to Marie: Let me draw your picture, lovely lady.
3. I; Since it was cheap only three dollars; she went ahead with it; he drew really well.
4. C
5. C
6. I; I saw—that the sky—was turning black.
7. I; Marie said, "Let's get out of here before it pours",
8. C

Part B

My friend Jamie and I, were talking about the words—we used in school years ago—to express enthusiasm over something. For instance, when something was really good, we said it was wicked. We laughed, and Jamie said—Do you remember what we used to call pretty girls? He reminded me that we had called them fine. We talked about how it's hard to keep up with slang words if you're not young, they change extremely quickly.

Editing Practice, page 234

The old shoe factory (where my great-grandfather worked was on Bridge Street in Springvale, it was demolished in 1967. Before the town decided to tear down this old wooden building: my father took pictures of it. I remember my father saying I'm sorry to see it go the morning the wrecking ball smashed it to bits.

CONNECTIONS, page 234
Answers will vary. Be sure you used quotation marks, commas, and other necessary punctuation.

Pre-GED Practice, page 235

1. (2) A comma should separate the dependent clause from the independent clause. Choices (1), (3), (4), and (5) do not include this comma.
2. (3) A colon after *names* sets off the items in the list. Choice (1) removes necessary commas. Choices (2), (4), and (5) use incorrect punctuation to precede a list.
3. (1) The phrase that interrupts the main thought should be set off with dashes. Removing the first dash, as in Choice (2), or both as in Choice (3), means there is no indication of the beginning (or end) of the interruption. The colon in Choice (4) should be used before a list. The semicolon in Choice (5) indicates two independent clauses.
4. (4) The direct quote should have quotation marks on either end of it, and a comma should appear inside the end quotation marks. Choices (1), (2), (3), and (5) fail to recognize that the sentence contains direct speech.

LESSON 16

Practice 1, page 237
Part A

1. C
2. I; One of my friends said, "to me they are the same thing."

3. I; ~~my~~ *My* wife, of course, agreed with his "~~Expert~~ *expert* opinion."

4. I; "In my opinion," I said, "~~Jazz~~ *jazz* is cool and blues is hot."

5. I; ~~we~~ *We* then listened to some jazz and some blues records.

6. I; Afterwards, my wife said, "~~let's~~ *Let's* get something to eat."

7. I; "It would be nice," I said, "~~If~~ *if* we can find someplace that's still open."

8. C

9. I; At the restaurant, my wife changed her mind and agreed that "~~Blues~~ *blues* is hot."

Part B

Some people can't stand admitting that they are wrong, and ~~My~~ *my* uncle is one of them. The other day he told me, "~~you~~ *You* can't burn regular unleaded gas in that car. Use super unleaded." ~~well,~~ *Well* I did some research in my owner's manual just to prove him wrong. When I showed him the evidence in black and white, he still said that my car would run "~~Very~~ *very* poorly" if I used regular unleaded gas.

CONNECTIONS, page 238

Answers will vary.

Practice 2, page 239

Part A

1. I; My buddy ~~nick~~ *Nick* told me that ~~*true lies*~~ *True Lies* is playing at the movie theater in downtown ~~tulsa~~ *Tulsa*.

2. I; I asked if he meant the ~~criterion theater~~ *Criterion Theater* or the ~~capital theater~~ *Capital Theater*, but he only knew that it was the one on ~~south street~~ *South Street*.

3. C

4. I; In front of the museum, we saw Mayor Jefferson and the ~~Presidents~~ *presidents* of several local organizations having pictures taken.

5. I; ~~the~~ *The* museum was featuring works by artists from ~~oklahoma~~ *Oklahoma*.

6. I; All of the artists were born after the ~~civil war~~ *Civil War*.

7. I; On ~~sunday~~ *Sunday*, we went to the ~~oklahoma state fair~~ *Oklahoma State Fair*.

8. C

9. I; Then we went back to the ~~big plains motel~~ *Big Plains Motel* where we were staying.

10. I; Someone said ~~garth brooks~~ *Garth Brooks* was staying there; I didn't see him.

Part B

In my new job at ~~american cyanamid~~ *American Cyanamid*, we get all major holidays off, including ~~thanksgiving~~ *Thanksgiving*, ~~new year's day~~ *New Year's Day*, ~~independence day~~ *Independence Day*, and ~~labor day~~ *Labor Day*. I start work a ~~Week~~ *week* from Tuesday. My ~~Supervisor~~ *supervisor* told me that my friend ~~audrey~~ *Audrey* works in the plant at Southborough.

Editing Practice, page 240

According to today's ~~*new york times*~~ *New York Times*, computers in restaurants are "~~Changing~~ *Changing* the way diners, waiters, kitchen staff, and ~~Management~~ *management* interact." Not only is this true in ~~Fast Food~~ *fast food* restaurants across the ~~Country~~ *country*, but also at small, independently-owned restaurants in ~~las vegas~~ *Las Vegas*, ~~cincinnati~~ *Cincinnati*, and ~~flagstaff~~ *Flagstaff*, ~~arizona~~ *Arizona*. ~~however~~ *However*, one restaurant owner quoted in the ~~*times*~~ *Times* is not going along with this trend. "~~we~~ *We* prefer," ~~She~~ *she* said, "to keep the personal connection between the kitchen and the dining room staff."

Pre-GED Practice, page 241

1. (3) The place, *New York,* and special event, *World's Fair,* are capitalized. In Choice (1), *months* is not capitalized because it is not a proper noun. Choices (2), (4), and (5) fail to recognize the full title of the event.
2. (4) *Queens* is a specific place that must be capitalized. Choices (1), (2), and (3) confuse proper nouns with common nouns. Choice (5) does not recognize the proper noun.
3. (2) Each word in the names of the three companies that appear at the end of the sentence must be capitalized. Choices (1) and (5) do not capitalize the names. Choices (3) and (4) capitalize a common noun.
4. (1) The name, *Robert Moses,* is capitalized. However, the first word of the second part of the quotation is not capitalized. Choices (3), (4), and (5) do not capitalize the name correctly. Choices (2), (4), and (5) capitalize the second part of the quotation.
5. (4) The word *fair* is not a proper noun here. However, the two countries must be capitalized. Choices (1), (2), and (3) capitalize common nouns. Choice (5) does not capitalize the names of the countries.

LESSON 17

Practice 1, page 243

1. Sometimes ~~haveing~~ *having* a car in the city doesn't make your life ~~easyer~~ *easier*.
2. When I ~~boughte~~ *bought* a used car, I thought it would be great.
3. Of course, that was before I ~~payed~~ *paid* the first of many parking tickets.
4. One summons was unfair, and I decided on ~~challengeing~~ *challenging* it in court.
5. I was confident about ~~wining~~, ~~knoing~~ *winning, knowing* that the parking meter had been broken.
6. I was pleasantly surprised when I ~~immediatly~~ *immediately* ~~one~~ *won*.
7. Of course, don't be ~~decieved~~ *deceived* into thinking that tickets are the only hassle of ~~haveing~~ *having* a car in the city!

Practice 2, page 245

1. My ~~friends~~ *friend's* son, Anthony, is a little less than two ~~year's~~ *years* old I ~~beleive~~ *believe*.
2. Whenever I see him, I ~~cant~~ *can't* understand how he ~~couldve~~ *could've* grown so much.
3. ~~Im~~ *I'm* sure that if I saw him daily, ~~his'~~ *his* growth ~~would'nt~~ *wouldn't* be so surprising.
4. Still, ~~its~~ *it's* as if one day he was crawling and the next day ~~hes~~ *he's* not walking but ~~runing~~ *running* around!
5. Both of his parents, of course, ~~coul'dnt~~ *couldn't* be more ~~athleteic~~ *athletic*.
6. ~~They're~~ *Their* first meeting was on a basketball court in Detroit, and their ~~cars~~ *car's* license plate says, "BBALL."
7. ~~Ive~~ *I've* not yet made up my own mind about ~~haveing~~ *having* children.
8. ~~Isnt~~ *Isn't* it ~~wierd~~ *weird* how confused you can be about big life decisions?
9. My husband wants a child, but I feel ~~were~~ *we're* better off waiting.

CONNECTIONS, page 245

Answers will vary.

Editing Practice, page 246

When Doreen became ~~intrested~~ *interested* in a positon in one of the town ~~office's~~ *offices*, it was ~~nesessary~~ *necessary* for her to fill out an ~~aplication~~ *application* for ~~employement~~ *employment*. She was ~~quiet~~ *quite* surprised when she looked ~~closly~~ *closely* and saw that it was ~~writen~~ *written* in Spanish.

She asked if there were any ~~applicationes~~ *applications* in ~~english~~ *English*, and the clerk said, "~~Weve~~ *We've* got applications in four ~~diffrent~~ *different* ~~languges~~ *languages*, but we just ran out of the English ones!"

Pre-GED Practice, page 247

1. (5) In Choices (1) and (2), *can't* is misspelled. In Choices (2) and (3), *a lot* is misspelled. In Choice (4), *paid* is misspelled.
2. (4) In Choices (1), (2), and (5), *their* is misspelled. In Choices (2) and (3), *experience* is misspelled.
3. (2) *Banker's* is possessive and must have an apostrophe, so Choices (1), (4), and (5) are incorrect. Also, in Choices (3) and (4), *judgment* is misspelled.
4. (5) In Choices (1), (3), and (4), *possess* is misspelled. In Choice (2), *skills* is misspelled. In Choices (3) and (4), *succeed* is misspelled.
5. (3) In Choices (1), (2), and (5), *wouldn't* is misspelled. In Choices (4) and (5), *raise* is misspelled.

LESSON 18

Practice 1, page 248

1. hear	**2.** Who's	**3.** effect	**4.** their
5. passed	**6.** meet	**7.** except	**8.** hour

Practice 2, page 251

1. can	**2.** lay	**3.** Among	**4.** who	**5.** lie
6. fewer	**7.** may	**8.** sit	**9.** less	

CONNECTIONS, page 251

Answers will vary.

Editing Practice, page 252

~~They're~~ *There* is ~~alot~~ *a lot* to be said for ~~excepting~~ *accepting* another individual exactly the way he or she is. This sort of ~~fareness~~ *fairness* and understanding ~~among~~ *between* two people is harder than it sounds. Many people are ~~effected~~ *affected* by the actions of others. I know I was hurt when my coworker ~~inferred~~ *implied* to my boss that I was lazy. ~~Too~~ *To* tell a deliberate lie about someone is an ~~amoral~~ *immoral* act in my opinion.

Pre-GED Practice, page 253

1. (2) The groups of people are living in *this* country, so *immigrants* is the correct word. In Choices (1) and (4), *emigrants* is used. In Choice (3), the incorrect contraction *they're* is used. In Choice (5), the incorrect possessive *their* is used.
2. (4) In Choices (3) and (5), the homonym *hear* is used. In Choices (1), (2), and (3), the incorrect homonym *too* is used.
3. (1) Italian people can be counted as individuals, so *fewer* is correct in this sentence. Choices (3) and (5) incorrectly use *less*. Choices (2), (4), and (5) use the incorrect homonym *there*.
4. (5) The word *past* refers to time that has gone by. Choices (1), (2), and (3) use *passed*. Choices (2), (3), and (4) incorrectly use the homonym *two*.
5. (4) *Laying* is correct for the merchants are placing their wares on display. In Choices (1) and (2), the incorrect *lying* is used. In Choice (3), *merchants* is spelled with an unnecessary apostrophe. In Choice (5), the homonym *their* is used incorrectly.

WRITING SKILLS REVIEW

Pages 254–258

1. (5) *Enjoyable* is an adjective, which is correct in this sentence. *Enjoyably* is an adverb, which is incorrect.
2. (2) This is a run-on sentence. It could be corrected by breaking it into two sentences.
3. (3) *Have* is the correct verb tense. Choice (1) would cause a punctuation error. Choices (2), (4), and (5) are grammatically incorrect.
4. (5) The pronoun should be *you* and not *she*. All other choices are incorrect.
5. (1) The phrase *in other words* needs to be set off with a comma. Choices (2) and (3) are grammatically incorrect. Choice (4) would cause a punctuation error. Choice (5) would cause a spelling error.
6. (3) *Slowly* is an adverb modifying the verb *go*, which is correct in this sentence. Choices (1) and (2) are grammatically incorrect. Choice (4) would cause a punctuation error. Choice (5) would cause a spelling error.
7. (1) This is a sentence fragment with no subject.
8. (1) *Since* is a connecting word that would make this a correct complex sentence contain-

ing a dependent clause and an independent clause. Choices (2), (4), and (5) are grammatically incorrect. Choice (3) is incorrect for the meaning of the word *but* would make the sentence nonsensical.

9. (3) *Street* should be capitalized because it is part of a proper noun. Choice (1) would be acceptable but would not correct the spelling error cited above. Choice (2) would cause a grammatical error. Choices (4) and (5) would cause punctuation errors.

10. (4) *Airplane* is singular so it takes the pronoun *it*. Choice (1) would be acceptable but would not correct the grammatical error in the sentence. Choice (2) would cause confusion in the comparison. Choice (3) would cause a punctuation error. Choice (5) is incorrect.

11. (4) A question mark is the correct punctuation for this sentence. Choice (1) would be an acceptable change but would not correct the punctuation error addressed above. Choice (2) would cause a grammatical error. Choices (3) and (5) would cause punctuation errors.

12. (4) The verbs *am starting* and *am living* are parallel, and both should be in the present continuous tense. All the other choices would cause grammatical errors.

13. (5) The fragment is missing the subject, *I*, and the verb, *got*. All the other choices would leave this sentence as a fragment.

14. (5) The pair of prepositional phrases *to take home* and *to my family* do not need to be separated from the rest of this sentence. Choices (1), (2), and (4) are grammatically incorrect. Choice (3) would cause a punctuation error.

15. (2) The connecting word *and* turns a run-on sentence into a correct compound sentence. Choices (3), (4), and (5) are grammatically incorrect.

16. (5) The word *hundred* is correctly spelled in Choice (5). Choices (1) and (2) are grammatically incorrect. Choices (3) and (4) would cause punctuation errors.

17. (5) The plural verb *live* agrees with the plural subject. All the other choices are grammatically incorrect.

18. (4) The possessive plural noun *children's* is correct in this sentence. Choices (1) and (2) are grammatically incorrect. Choice (3) would cause a punctuation error. Choice (5) would cause a spelling/usage mistake.

19. (3) The comparative adjective *larger* is correct in this sentence. All other choices are grammatically incorrect.

20. (4) The plural subject pronoun *we* is correct in this compound sentence. All the other choices are grammatically incorrect.

21. (4) The connecting word *since* clearly shows the time relationship between the dependent clause and the main clause in this sentence. All the other choices are incorrect.

22. (3) In this sentence, the contraction *it's* replaces *it is* and should have an apostrophe. Choices (1) and (5) capitalize common nouns, which is incorrect. Choice (2) would result in a run-on sentence. Choice (4) calls for *its'*, which is not a correct word.

23. (1) The dependent clause *when it snows* must be set off with a comma when it begins a sentence. Choice (2) is incorrect because *kids* is used as a plural, not a possessive form. Choice (3) would result in the use of the wrong first-person possessive. Choices (4) and (5) would result in punctuation errors.

24. (3) This sentence requires the third-person plural possessive *their*. Choices (1), (2), and (4) would result in punctuation errors. Choice (5) would result in a spelling error.

25. (4) This paragraph is written in the present tense. Choice (1) would result in a pronoun error. Choices (2) and (3) would result in punctuation errors. Choice (5) would result in a spelling error.

26. (5) The pronoun *she* is correct in this sentence. Choices (1), (2), and (4) are incorrect verb forms. Choice (3) would result in a punctuation error.

WRITING SKILLS REVIEW REFERRAL CHART

When you have completed the Section 3 Writing Skills Review, check your answers against the Answers and Explanations beginning on page 274. On the chart below, circle the items you answered correctly. Then, in the last column on the chart, list the total number of items you answered correctly.

Each item is related to a specific unit of instruction in Section 3 of this book. Use this chart to help you determine your areas of strength and identify areas where your skills need further development. The chart also may be used to help you identify which types of test items you answer best and which are more difficult for you.

SECTION 3: WRITING SKILLS LESSONS	ITEMS	NUMBER OF ITEMS CORRECT
Unit 1: Usage (pp. 140–201)	1, 3, 4, 6, 10, 12, 17, 19, 20, 25, 26	
Unit 2: Sentence Structure (pp. 202–221)	2, 7, 8, 13, 15, 21	
Unit 3: Mechanics (pp. 222–253)	5, 9, 11, 14, 16, 18, 22, 23, 24	

TOTAL: _____ of 26

Do you notice any patterns in the items you did not circle? Try to identify areas where you need more practice. Then review those units in Section 3 of this book. South-Western's *Pre-GED Writing Skills Exercises* book provides you with additional practice opportunities for each Writing Skills lesson in this book.

Writing Skills Posttest

The Pre-GED Writing Skills Posttest is approximately one-half the length of the GED exam. Use it to discover what you have learned. It also will help you identify areas where you need further review. To make the best use of the test, follow these steps. First, review the test-taking tips on page 6. Then take the test. After you finish the test, use the Answers and Explanations section that begins on page 282. Finally, use the Referral Charts on pages 285-286. Completing the Referral Charts is an extremely important part of the test-taking process.

Choose the one best answer for each item. Items 1 to 9 refer to the following paragraph.

(1)His grandfather, as well as other relatives, were the topic of conversation as Eddie searched for his photo album. (2)As he fished around in several drawers, Otis said, "I never knew that your people were immigrants." (3)Eddie wondered if that was because England isn't a place people associate with the word *immigrant* today. (4)It was explained by him that his great-grandparents were poorly paid factory workers in the industrial town of Brighouse. (5)As he spoke, he was examining the shelfs of a closet for the lost photo album. (6)"They came here," he said, "because they weren't able to feed the family there." (7)Otis said that he didn't understand why they had choose New Hampshire. (8)Eddie emerged from the closet; a wide grin was worn on his face and held a thick photo album in his hands. (9)As you'll see from these pictures, he chuckled, "Manchester, New Hampshire, looked an awful lot like home!"

1. Sentence 1: His grandfather, as well as other relatives, were the topic of conversation as Eddie searched for his photo album.

What correction should be made to this sentence?

(1) change *grandfather* to *Grandfather*
(2) omit the comma after *grandfather*
(3) omit the comma after *relatives*
(4) change *were* to *are*
(5) change *were* to *was*

2. Sentence 2: As he fished around in several drawers, Otis said, "I never knew that your people were immigrants."

Which of the following is the best way to write the underlined portion of this sentence? If you think the original is the best way, choose (1).

(1) As he fished around
(2) As he fishes around
(3) As he are fishing around
(4) As his friend fished around
(5) As his friend are fishing around

3. Sentence 3: Eddie wondered if that was because England isn't a place people associate with the word *immigrant* today.

Which of the following is the best way to write the underlined portion of this sentence? If you think the original is the best way, choose (1).

(1) England isn't
(2) England is'nt
(3) england isn't
(4) england is'nt
(5) england isnt'

4. Sentence 4: It was explained by him that his great-grandparents were poorly paid factory workers in the industrial town of Brighouse.

Which of the following is the best way to write the underlined portion of this sentence? If you think the original is the best way, choose (1).
(1) It was explained by him that
(2) He explained that
(3) He explained which
(4) It was explained by him who
(5) It was explained by him which

5. Sentence 5: As he spoke, he was examining the shelfs of a closet for the lost photo album.

What correction should be made to this sentence?
(1) change *spoke* to *had spoken*
(2) remove the comma
(3) replace the comma with a semicolon
(4) change *shelfs* to *shelves*
(5) change *shelfs* to *shelfes*

6. Sentence 6: "They came here," he said, "because they weren't able to feed the family there."

Which of the following is the best way to write the underlined portion of this sentence? If you think the original is the best way, choose (1).
(1) because they weren't
(2) unless they weren't
(3) although they weren't
(4) because they isn't
(5) although they isn't

7. Sentence 7: Otis said that he didn't understand why they had choose New Hampshire.

Which of the following is the best way to write the underlined portion of this sentence? If you think the original is the best way, choose (1).
(1) they had choose New Hampshire.
(2) they had chose New Hampshire.
(3) they had chosen New Hampshire.
(4) they had choosen New Hampshire.
(5) they has chosen New Hampshire.

8. Sentence 8: Eddie emerged from the closet; a wide grin was worn on his face and held a thick photo album in his hands.

Which of the following is the best way to write the underlined portion of this sentence? If you think the original is the best way, choose (1).
(1) Eddie emerged from the closet; a wide grin was worn
(2) Eddie emerged from the closet, a wide grin was worn
(3) Eddie emerged from the closet; he wore a wide grin
(4) Eddie emerged from the closet, he wore a wide grin
(5) Eddie emerged from the closet he wore a wide grin

9. Sentence 9: As you'll see from these pictures, he chuckled, "Manchester, New Hampshire, looked an awful lot like home!"

Which is the best way to rewrite the underlined portion of this sentence? If you think the original is the best way, choose (1).
(1) As you'll see from these pictures,
(2) As you'll see from these pictures;
(3) As you'll see from these picture's,
(4) "As you'll see from these picture's,"
(5) "As you'll see from these pictures,"

Items 11 to 18 *refer to the following essay.*

(1)People often talk about how imagination, courage, and hard work are necessary for success in life. (2)In the real world, these important character traits sometimes shows themselves in surprising ways.

(3)For instance, in 1992 a group of young people in New York City decided to improve part of its run-down neighborhood. (4)Tired of looking at an abandoned fire station that the city had boarded up in 1988. (5)After prying open a door and they entered the station, the young people used shovels, mops, and brooms to clean the building. (6)Along the buildings front side, they hung a sign that said "Youth Center for Ocean Hill Brownsville Youths Determined to Succeed."

(7)Their message were clear and dramatic enough to get the attention of several city officials. (8)The officials criticized the youths' methods, they promised to meet with them about starting a community center in the neighborhood.

(9)These young people deserve a helping hand because they have taken serious the idea that imagination, courage, and hard work are the keys to a successful future.

10. Sentence 1: People often talk about how imagination, courage, and hard work are necessary for success in life.

Which of the following is the best way to write the underlined portion of this sentence? If you think the original is the best way, choose (1).

(1) imagination, courage, and hard work are
(2) imagination, courage, and hard work, are
(3) imagination, courage, and hard work is
(4) imagination, courage, and hard work, is
(5) imagination courage and hard work is

11. Sentence 2: In the real world, these important character traits sometimes shows themselves in surprising ways.

What correction should be made to this sentence?

(1) omit the comma after *world*
(2) change *sometimes* to *sometime*
(3) change *shows* to *show*
(4) change *themselves* to *itself*
(5) change *themselves* to *theirselves*

12. Sentence 3: For instance, in 1992 a group of young people in New York City decided to improve part of its run-down neighborhood.

Which of the following is the best way to rewrite the underlined portion of this sentence? If you think the original is the best way, choose (1).

(1) its run-down neighborhood
(2) it's run-down neighborhood
(3) their run-down neighborhood
(4) there run-down neighborhood
(5) there run-down nieghborhood

13. Sentence 4: Tired of looking at an abandoned fire station that the city had boarded up in 1988.

Which of the following is the best way to write the underlined portion of this sentence? If you think the original is the best way, choose (1).
(1) Tired of looking
(2) He grown tired of looking
(3) They grown tired of looking
(4) He had grown tired of looking
(5) They had grown tired of looking

14. Sentence 5: After prying open a door and they entered the station, the young people used shovels, mops, and brooms to clean the building.

Which of the following is the best way to write the underlined portion of this sentence? If you think the original is the best way, choose (1).
(1) they entered
(2) entering
(3) they entering
(4) entered
(5) they will enter

15. Sentence 6: Along the buildings front side, they hung a sign that said "Youth Center for Ocean Hill Brownsville Youths Determined to Succeed."

What correction should be made to this sentence?
(1) change *buildings* to *building's*
(2) change *buildings* to *buildings'*
(3) change *buildings* to *buildings's*
(4) change the comma to a semicolon
(5) add a comma after *said*

16. Sentence 7: Their message were clear and dramatic enough to get the attention of several city officials.

What correction should be made to this sentence?
(1) change *Their* to *There*
(2) change *Their* to *They're*
(3) change *were* to *was*
(4) change *city* to *city's*
(5) change *officials* to *officiales*

17. Sentence 8: The officials criticized the youths' methods, they promised to meet with them about starting a community center in the neighborhood.

Which of the following is the best way to write the underlined portion of this sentence? If you think the original is the best way, choose (1).
(1) methods, they
(2) methods, but they
(3) methods; but they
(4) methods they
(5) method's they

18. Sentence 9: These young people deserve a helping hand because they have taken serious the idea that imagination, courage, and hard work are the keys to a successful future.

Which of the following is the best way to write the underlined portion of this sentence? If you think the original is the best way, choose (1).
(1) serious
(2) seriouser
(3) seriously
(4) seriesly
(5) less serious

Items 19 to 26 *refer to the following paragraph.*

(1)Four of us has helped LaShan move into her new apartment today—what a horror story! (2)Derrick was the only person with a car; and it made a habit of stalling as we hauled the stuff from her old apartment. (3)Of course, her new place is on the sixth floor, and there no elevator. (4)We were shocked to see that the sink refrigerator and stove hadn't been put in, and there were exposed wires everywhere. (5)Her landlord had promised it would be ready. (6)LaShan was spending a few days at my house until she gets running water and electricity. (7)I don't mind; she's helped me out plenty of times in the passed. (8)It's just a shame that her landlord is causing alot of problems for both of us.

19. Sentence 1: Four of us has helped LaShan move into her new apartment today—what a horror story!

What correction should be made to this sentence?

(1) change *Four* to *For*
(2) change *us* to *we*
(3) change *us* to *you*
(4) omit *has*
(5) change *move* to *moves*

20. Sentence 2: Derrick was the only person with a car; and it made a habit of stalling as we hauled the stuff from her old apartment.

Which of the following is the best way to write the underlined portion of this sentence? If you think the original is the best way, choose (1).

(1) with a car; and
(2) with a car, and
(3) with a car: and
(4) with a car and;
(5) with a car and:

21. Sentence 3: Of course, her new place is on the sixth floor, and there no elevator.

What correction should be made to this sentence?

(1) change *her* to *his*
(2) omit the comma after *floor*
(3) replace the comma after *floor* with a semicolon
(4) change *there* to *their*
(5) change *there* to *there's*

22. Sentence 4: We were shocked to see that the sink refrigerator and stove hadn't been put in, and there were exposed wires everywhere.

Which of the following is the best way to write the underlined portion of this sentence? If you think the original is the best way, choose (1).

(1) sink refrigerator and stove
(2) sink, refrigerator, and stove
(3) sink, refrigerator, and stove,
(4) sink; refrigerator; and stove;
(5) sink—refrigerator and stove—

23. Sentence 5: Her landlord had promised it would be ready.

What correction should be made to this sentence?
(1) change *Her* to *Her's*
(2) change *landlord* to *Landlord*
(3) change *promised* to *promise*
(4) change *it* to *the apartment*
(5) change *it* to *they*

24. Sentence 6: LaShan was spending a few days at my house until she gets running water and electricity.

Which of the following is the best way to write the underlined portion of this sentence? If you think the original is the best way, choose (1).
(1) was spending
(2) is spending
(3) were spending
(4) spend
(5) has spent

25. Sentence 7: I don't mind; she's helped me out plenty of times in the passed.

What correction should be made to this sentence?
(1) omit the semicolon
(2) change *she's* to *she is*
(3) change *me* to *I*
(4) change *me* to *mine*
(5) change *passed* to *past*

26. Sentence 8: It's just a shame that her landlord is causing alot of problems for both of us.

What correction should be made to this sentence?
(1) change *It's* to *Its*
(2) change *It's* to *Its'*
(3) change *is causing* to *have caused*
(4) change *alot* to *a lot*
(5) change *problems* to *problem's*

Writing Skills Essay

Read the following essay topic. Take some time to think about what you want to say. Then organize your ideas, draft an essay, revise it, and edit it.

TOPIC: Many people feel that they have one or two dominant personality traits, such as a sense of humor, generosity towards others, or an easy-going nature. In your opinion, what is your most important personality trait? Why do you feel it is the most important?

► *Answers begin on page 283.*

POSTTEST • Answers and Explanations

Pages 277–278

1. (5) The plural verb *were* should be changed to the singular *was* to agree with the singular subject *grandfather.*

2. (4) The pronoun *he* has an unclear antecedent. You cannot tell who is looking in drawers, Eddie or Otis. Choice (5) contains incorrect subject-verb agreement.

3. (1) The sentence is correct as written. Choices (2), (3), (4), and (5) include incorrect capitalization or punctuation.

4. (2) The active voice is preferable to the passive. There is no compelling reason to change to the passive voice in this sentence. Choices (3), (4), and (5) incorrectly replace *that.*

5. (4) The plural of *shelf* is *shelves.* Choices (1), (2), and (5) will not correct the error in spelling.

6. (1) The sentence is correct as written. Choices (2), (3), and (5) use incorrect connecting words. Choices (4) and (5) contain subject-verb disagreement.

7. (3) The past perfect of *choose* is formed with the helping verb *had* and the past participle *chosen*.

8. (3) The second clause uses the passive voice. It should be changed to the active voice. A semicolon correctly separates the two independent clauses.

9. (5) The underlined words need quotation marks. The comma after *pictures* is correct. *Pictures* doesn't need an apostrophe so Choices (3) and (4) are incorrect.

Pages 279–280

10. (1) The sentence is correct. Commas are used to separate words in a series. The plural verb *are* is needed. Choices (3), (4), and (5) contain errors in subject-verb agreement. Choices (2), (4), and (5) contain punctuation errors.

11. (3) *Traits* is plural, so the verb should be in the plural form. Choices (1), (2), (4), and (5) do not provide subject-verb agreement.

12. (3) The singular pronoun *its* should be changed to the plural pronoun *their*. Choices (2), (4), and (5) contain spelling errors or incorrect pronouns.

13. (5) The original sentence is a fragment. It lacks a subject. Choice (5) supplies the missing subject. Choices (2) and (3) omit the helping verb *had.* Choices (2) and (4) create pronoun-antecedent disagreement.

14. (2) The verbs *prying* and *entered* should be in parallel structure. Changing *entered* to *entering* makes the structure parallel.

15. (1) *Buildings* is plural. The singular possessive, *building's*, is needed. Choices (2), (3), (4), and (5) use incorrect punctuation.

16. (3) The verb should be singular to match the singular subject, *message*. Choices (1), (2), (4), and (5) create spelling or punctuation errors.

17. (2) The original is a run-on sentence. A connecting word should be added after the comma. Choices (3), (4), and (5) contain punctuation errors.

18. (3) *Serious* should be in the adverb form, *seriously*. Choices (1) and (5) are incorrect forms. Choices (2) and (4) are not words.

Pages 281–282

19. (4) The verb should be in the simple past tense. The helping verb, *has*, is not needed. Choice (1) is a misspelling. Choices (2) and (3) use incorrect pronouns. Choice (5) creates subject-verb disagreement.

20. (2) The semicolon should be replaced with a comma. Compound sentences need a comma before the word that joins them.

21. (5) The second clause needs a verb. *There's* is

a contraction of the words *there* and *is*. Using *there's* supplies a verb.

22. (2) Commas should follow all items in a series except for the last.

23. (4) The pronoun *it* has an unclear antecedent. The nouns in the sentence before are *sink*, *refrigerator*, and *stove*.

24. (2) The sentence should be in the present tense, *is spending*.

25. (5) *Passed* should be replaced by the homonym *past*. Choices (3) and (4) contain incorrect pronouns. Choice (1) uses incorrect punctuation.

26. (4) *Alot* should be two separate words, *a lot*.

ESSAY

Essays will vary. Be sure that you followed each of the five steps in your writing.

POSTTEST REFERRAL CHARTS

After you have completed the Posttest, check your answers against the Answers and Explanations on pages 283 and 284. On the following charts, circle the items you answered correctly. Then, in the last columns on the charts, list the total number of items you answered correctly.

Use this first chart to help you identify your areas of strength. You will also see where your skills need to be developed further to be ready to go on to GED-level writing skills material.

SECTION 2: FOUNDATION SKILLS		PART I ITEMS	NUMBER OF ITEMS CORRECT
Foundation Skill 1:	Beginning to Write (pp. 22–31)	3, 5, 6, 10, 15	
Foundation Skill 2:	Writing Sentences (pp. 32–41)	13, 20	
Foundation Skill 3:	Journal Writing (pp. 42–51)	2, 12, 23	
Foundation Skill 4:	Identifying Purpose and Audience (pp. 52–61)	17	
Foundation Skill 5:	Writing a Paragraph (pp. 62–71)	6	
Foundation Skill 6:	Writing to Narrate (pp. 72–81)	7, 14, 19, 24	
Foundation Skill 7:	Writing to Explain (pp. 82–91)	4	
Foundation Skill 8:	Writing to Describe (pp. 92–101)	8, 18	
Foundation Skill 9:	Writing to Persuade (pp. 102–111)	7, 11, 16, 21	
Foundation Skill 10:	Writing an Essay (pp. 112–121)	9, 22, 25, 26	

TOTAL: ____ of 26

Use this second chart in the same way you used the first one. Both charts will help you determine what areas you may need to further review before moving on to the South-Western *GED Writing Skills* book.

SECTION 3: WRITING SKILLS LESSONS	PART I ITEMS	NUMBER OF ITEMS CORRECT
Unit 1: Usage (pp. 140–201)	2, 5, 7, 9, 10, 11, 13, 14, 16, 17, 19, 22, 23, 24	
Unit 2: Sentence Structure (pp. 202–221)	4, 8, 21	
Unit 3: Mechanics (pp. 222–253)	1, 3, 6, 12, 15, 18, 20, 25, 26	

TOTAL: ____ of 26

Glossary

A

abstract noun a noun used to name something not recognized by the senses. (page 142)

Friendship is one of the great joys of life.

action verb a verb that is exact in its meaning in a way that another verb is not. (page 90)

the verb to be The baby was in the crib.

action verb The baby squirmed in the crib.

active voice the form of a verb used when the subject performs the action. (page 78)

(s) (v)
My family threw a surprise party for me.

adjective a word that describes a noun or pronoun. (page 196)

Jon is very likeable. (describes the noun *Jon*)

He is very likeable. (describes the pronoun *he*)

adverb a word that describes a verb, adjective, or another adverb. (page 196)

The child sat happily. (describes the verb *sat*)

He was very nice. (describes the adjective *nice*)

The young athlete swam rather gracefully. (describes the adverb *gracefully*)

antecedent the word to which a pronoun refers. (page 148)

(a) (p)
Henry is fixing the car he bought last week.

audience the person or people for whom something is written. (page 52)

B

body the middle paragraphs in an essay. (page 113)

brainstorm to think intensely about a subject in order to get ideas for writing about it. (page 22)

C

cause-and-effect chain a chain of events in which one event causes another event, which causes yet another, and so on. (page 84)

chronological order order according to time. (page 74)

clause a group of words that contains a subject and a verb. (page 210)

collective noun a singular noun that represents a group of people or things. It seems to be plural, but it takes a singular verb. (page 178)

The audience was laughing throughout the play.

common noun a noun that does not name a particular person, place, or thing. (page 144)

woman town war religion

comparative form the form of an adjective or adverb that compares two things. (page 198)

adjective Silk is smoother than other fabrics.

adverb He smiles less pleasantly than Jane.

complex sentence a sentence containing an *independent or main clause* (which expresses a complete thought) and a *dependent clause* (which does not express a complete thought). (page 210)

(dependent clause) (independent clause)
When the bell rang, I gave my friend the book.

compound object an object made up of one or more nouns or pronouns. (page 206)

The loud crash scared the dog and me.

compound sentence a sentence containing two complete thoughts (each with its own subject and verb) that are related. (page 204)

(s) (v) (s) (v)
Finally the gloomy weather lifted, and we went for a ride.

compound subject a subject made up of more than one noun or pronoun. (page 180)

Ken and Liz know a lot about their town's history.

compound verb two or more verbs sharing the same subject. (page 206)

The door crashed open and slammed shut.

concluding paragraph the last paragraph of an essay. It sums up the main idea. (page 113)

concluding sentence the sentence that ties together the information in a paragraph. (page 66)

concrete noun a noun that names something that can be recognized by the senses (sight, smell, taste, hearing, or touch). (page 142)

I heard a scream. Smoke poured from the window.

continuous tenses verb tenses showing continuous action. (page 166)

present continuous tense I am building a house.

past continuous tense I was building a house.

future continuous tense I will be building a house.

contraction the joining of two words into one. In the process, one or more letters are left out, and an apostrophe replaces them. (page 244)

words: did not *contraction:* didn't

D

dangling modifier a modifier that does not modify any of the words in the sentence where it is located. (page 216)

Driving down the highway, the fields rolled by.

dependent clause a clause that depends on the rest of a sentence for its meaning; also called a *subordinate clause* because it is subordinate to, or less important than, another clause. (page 210)

When the bell rang, I gave my friend the book.

descriptive writing writing that uses details to help the reader get a clear picture of someone or something. (page 92)

draft to put ideas into sentences. (page 26)

E

edit to correct errors in grammar, spelling, and punctuation. (page 30)

end punctuation punctuation that ends a sentence. Three types of end punctuation are the period, the question mark, and the exclamation point. (page 224)

essay a clear and detailed written discussion of a particular topic. (page 112)

explanatory writing writing that explains or informs. (page 82)

G

gender the state of being masculine, feminine, or neuter (such as pronoun "it"). (page 154)

grammar the rules for putting words together to form sentences. (page 22)

H

homonyms two words that sound alike but are spelled differently and have different meanings, such as *passed* and *past.* (page 248)

I

independent clause a clause that expresses a complete thought and could stand alone as a sentence. (page 210)

When the bell rang, I gave my friend the book.

interrupting phrases a group of phrases that can "interrupt a sentence" by taking the place of *and.* These phrases are *along with, as well as, in addition to,* and *together with.* They are always set off by commas. (page 186)

Tina, along with her four sisters, is at a party.

introductory paragraph the first paragraph of an essay, containing the main idea. (page 113)

irregular verbs verbs that do not follow the regular rules for past tense endings. (page 162)

M

misplaced modifier a modifier placed too far from the word it modifies. (page 216)

misplaced modifier The wine in the refrigerator with the green label is Enrico's.

correctly placed modifier The wine with the green label in the refrigerator is Enrico's.

modifier a word that changes the meaning of another word by making it more specific. (page 100)

Jerry's facial expressions can change quickly.

I received a wonderful gift.

N

narrative writing writing that tells a story. (page 72)

noun a word that names a person, place, or thing. (page 142)

Noah keeps an iguana in his apartment.

number singular or plural. (page 154)

O

outline an organizer that shows how information will be presented in an essay. (page 114)

P

paragraph a group of sentences that all focus on a single idea. Paragraphs divide a piece of writing into a series of smaller ideas. (page 62)

parallel structure in a sentence, the wording of compound elements in similar ways. (page 206)

nonparallel	This afternoon I was exercising, eating, and read a book.
parallel	This afternoon I exercised, ate, and read a book.

passive voice the form of a verb used when the subject of the verb receives the action. (page 78)

(s) (v)
A surprise party was thrown by my family.

past participle a verb form made by adding *-ed* or *-en* to the present tense verb. (page 166)

perfect tenses verb tenses showing action that has been completed. (page 167)

present perfect tense	I have finished my work.
past perfect tense	I had finished it.
future perfect tense	I will have finished it.

person first person (the person speaking), second person (the person being spoken to), or third person (any other person, thing, or idea spoken about). (page 154)

personal narrative a story that tells about an experience from your own life. (page 72)

persuasive writing writing that tries to convince a reader to agree with an opinion or take an action. (page 102)

plural the form a word takes when it refers to more than one. (page 142)

dogs copies beaches teeth

possessive noun a noun that shows ownership. (page 144)

the dentist's office; many dentists' offices

possessive pronoun a pronoun that shows ownership. (page 150)

used before a noun	My bicycle was stolen.
used alone	That bicycle is mine.

prefix a group of letters added to the beginning of a word to change its meaning. (page 242)

dis + honor = dishonor

preposition a word such as *for, after, above,* or *with* that shows a relationship. (page 149)

prepositional phrase a group of words that begins with a preposition. (page 186)

(p)
The violin with the dusty neck is mine.

pronoun a word that takes the place of or refers to a noun in the same or another sentence. (page 148)

subject pronoun	Henry is reading the magazine he bought.
object pronoun	I read him a magazine article.

pronoun shift the use of one pronoun to refer to something and then a shift to a different pronoun to refer to the same thing. (page 156)

shift We ate ice cream because it cools you off.

correct We ate ice cream because it cools us off.

proper noun a noun that names a particular person, place, or thing. (page 144)

Alma New York the Vietnam War Islam

purpose why something is written. The purpose can be to tell a story, to explain or inform, to entertain, to describe, or to persuade. (page 52)

R

regular verbs verbs that always follow the same spelling rules for their endings: adding no ending, *-s,* or *-es,* for present tense; adding *-d* or *-ed* for past tense; and showing future tense by putting *will* before the verb and adding no ending. (page 160)

revise to make a piece of writing clearer, tighter, truer, and more detailed. (page 28)

run-on sentence a sentence that runs together two or more complete thoughts. (page 70)

run-on My hands are cold I have no gloves.

correct My hands are cold. I have no gloves.

S

sensory details details relating to any of the five senses (sight, smell, taste, hearing, and touch). (page 94)

sentence a group of words that express a complete thought. A complete sentence contains a subject and a verb, begins with a capital letter, and ends with a punctuation mark. (page 36)

sentence fragment an incomplete sentence lacking either a subject or a verb. (page 38)

no subject Threw the pail over the wall.

no verb The table to the left of the couch.

simple sentence a sentence with one subject and one verb. (page 204)

(s) (v)
The gloomy weather lifted.

simple tenses past tense, present tense, and future tense. (page 166)

singular the form a word takes when it refers to only one. (page 142)

dog copy beach tooth

stressed emphasized when spoken. (page 164)

paTROL MOVEment toDAY YESterday

subject-verb agreement agreement of the subject's number with the verb's number (singular or plural). (page 110)

singular The automobile is parked in the garage.

plural Fifteen automobiles were delivered.

subordinate clause a dependent clause that has no meaning except when joined to the main clause in the sentence. (page 214)

suffix a group of letters added to the end of a word to change its meaning. (page 242)

thought + *less* = thoughtless

superlative form the form of an adjective or adverb that compares three or more nouns. (page 198)

adjective Of the three men, Charles is the tallest.

adverb Of all of us, Joe is the most talkative.

supporting sentences sentences that back up a main idea with details, examples, reasons, or facts. (page 66)

T

tense the form of a verb that tells when the action takes place. (page 80)

present tense I play the lottery almost every week.

past tense Last Friday I played the lottery.

future tense Next Friday I will play the lottery.

timeline a method of putting events in time order. (page 74)

topic sentence the sentence that states the main idea of a paragraph or passage. (page 66)

V

verb a word in a sentence that tells what the subject is or does. (page 160)

Joanne works there six days a week.

INDEX

Acknowledgments

EXCERPTS

From THE ANNOTATED ALICE (ALICE'S ADVENTURES IN WONDERLAND & THROUGH THE LOOKING GLASS) by Lewis Carroll. Copyright © 1960 by Martin Gardner; published by Clarkson N. Potter, Inc. Reprinted by permission of Random House, Inc., page C11.

From WRITING BECOMES ELECTRONIC by Bernhardt J. Hurwood; excerpt by Tom Clancy. Copyright © 1986 by Bernhardt J. Hurwood. Reprinted by permission of Contemporary Books, Inc., page C3.

Reprinted with the permission of Macmillan, an imprint of Simon & Schuster, Inc. from KAFFIR BOY by Mark Mathabane. Copyright © 1986 Macmillan, page C15.

From THE AUTOBIOGRAPHY OF MALCOLM X by Malcolm X, with the assistance of Alex Haley. Copyright © 1964 by Alex Haley and Malcolm X. Copyright © 1965 by Alex Haley and Betty Shabazz. Reprinted by permission of Random House, Inc., page C13.

From JOURNAL OF A NOVEL by John Steinbeck. Copyright © 1969 by the Executors of the Estate of John Steinbeck. Used by permission of Viking Penguin, a division of Penguin Books USA Inc., page C5.

PHOTOGRAPHS

The Bettmann Archive C2; CBS Television Network/Photofest C10; Robert E. Daemmrich/Tony Stone Images, Inc. C4; Gerald L. French/FPG 139 (top), 140-141; Bruce H. Frisch/Photo Researchers, Inc. 139 (bottom), 222-223; Giraudon/Art Resource, NY C7; Richard Hutchings 1; Andy Levin/Photo Researchers, Inc. C8; Blair Seitz/Photo Researchers, Inc. C14; South-Western Publishing 32; Tom Tracy/The Stock Shop C3; Roger Tully/The Stock Shop C2; Bernard P. Wolff/Photo Researchers, Inc. 139 (center), 202-203

ART

Barbara Berasi C3 (bottom), C4, C5, C6 (bottom), C7, C8 (bottom), C11 (center), C12 (right), C13 (top); Lisa Donovan C15; Network Graphics 34, 54, 55, 64, 78, 127, 129, 130, C6 (top), C8 (top), C9, C10, C11 (top & bottom), C12 (left & bottom), C13 (bottom), C14; Carol Porteous C3 (top)

Answer Guide

TECHNOLOGY, PAGES C2–C3

The Writing Connection

Answers will vary. Here is a sample:

I sometimes use a computer at the local library. I use it to write letters to my family or to apply for a new job. I like the computer because my handwriting is sort of sloppy and the computer can check my spelling. I can also rewrite a different sentence easily. However, it is hard to remember what you've typed after it's rolled up on the screen. You have to move back and forth a lot when you're typing something long.

Problem Solver

From 1981 to 1988, the use of computers in the home increased by about 21 million. There were about 26 million more personal computers in American homes in 1992 than there had been in 1982.

EMPLOYMENT, PAGES C4–C5

The Writing Connection

Answers will vary. Here is a sample:

Pros:
- can express personal thoughts and opinions
- can be creative
- tell stories
- could be famous
- work isn't physical

Cons:
- very hard to make a living
- too many hours alone
- I prefer working outdoors
- words aren't as interesting as people

I would not like to write for a living because I am a social person. I like working with people better than working with words.

Problem Solver

A female high school graduate can earn $4,504 more than a woman who did not graduate from high school ($18,042 - $13,538). A woman with a college degree can earn $9,612 more than a woman with a high school diploma ($27,654 - $18,042). There is a difference of $8,176 between the income of a male high school graduate and of a female high school graduate ($26,218 - $18,042).

CULTURES, PAGES C6–C7

The Writing Connection

Answers will vary. Here is a sample:

There is an historical document in my grandmother's scrapbook that is very important to me. This document is an immigrant card. It contains information about my grandmother and grandfather. They came from Ireland to the port of Philadelphia in 1906. The card shows the official stamp that made it possible for them to become American citizens. To me, this document means that my ancestors struggled to make a better life, just as I am doing.

Problem Solver

There are 2,963 years separating the oldest and most recent documents on the map. The oldest document is the *I Ching* in China from about 1100 BCE, and the most recent is the *Emancipation Proclamation* in the United States in 1863. To find the difference, you must know that any date in the BCE is a negative number. Look at the timeline below to see this more clearly. Solve for the difference. (1863 + 1100 = 2963)

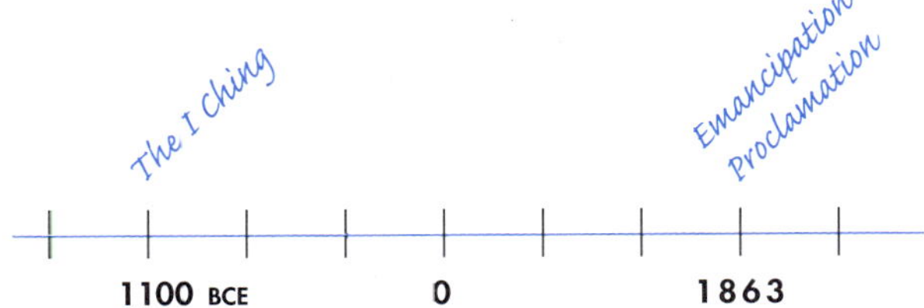

NEWS MEDIA, PAGES C8–C9

The Writing Connection

Answers will vary. Here is a sample:

I watch the evening news on TV and read the daily paper. It seems to me that most of the news reported by the press is bad news or sensational. I rarely see a story of good news. There are times when I turn the news off because I get so tired of bad news. But I think people like to hear bad news. It sells more newspapers and gives TV news programs higher ratings.

Problem Solver

A line chart or bar graph would effectively present this material. A bar graph would be good because it would show visually the huge change between 1925 and 1975. The 1975 circle graph shows the most extreme change in ownership of newspapers.

ENTERTAINMENT, PAGES C10–C11

The Writing Connection

Poems will vary widely. Here is a sample list for a topic:

a poem about	possible shape
my husband Rob	the letter "R"
music	a banjo
love	a heart, two lips
my neighborhood	a house
summer	rays of sunshine

Problem Solver

The puzzle contains 100 squares and 15 of them are orange. That means 15 percent of the puzzle's squares are orange.

LANGUAGES, PAGES C12–C13

The Writing Connection

Answers will vary. Here is a sample:

To improve my reading skills, I would read more. I could read more books, magazines, and news papers. I would try reading about different subjects that interest me such as astronomy, racing, and health. I also would read aloud to my children at bedtime.

Problem Solver

There are not more Chinese speakers than speakers of all other languages combined. You can see at a glance that lining up all the bars of people who speak other languages would give a much longer bar for "Speakers of Other Languages" than the bar for "Chinese Speakers."

HEALTH MATTERS, PAGES C14–C15

The Writing Connection

Answers will vary. Here is a sample:

I suppose everybody hears a lot about AIDS already, but I think there are still people who think they can't be affected by it. I know because I was one of these people. Then one of my friends died. I had known him for nineteen years. He didn't use protection. I didn't either until I found out how he got sick. More people need to know how to fight this disease and more money needs to be spent on finding a cure for it.

Problem Solver

Braille contains 37 more characters than the Latin alphabet (63 - 26). Ideas such as "and" and "with" are used so often in language that it makes sense to have a Braille symbol for each of them. In the six Braille positions, there are many differences in the number and position of the large and small dots.

CONNECTIONS SKILLS ANALYSIS CHART

The CONNECTIONS activities within the lessons of this book and on the theme pages themselves will help you develop your skills. The chart on the following page lists the skill or skills you will build in each CONNECTIONS activity.

UNIT	LESSON ACTIVITY	SKILLS APPLIED
Unit 1 Usage	Lesson 1 (page 146)	recognizing proper nouns
	Lesson 2 (page 152)	writing sentences; using pronouns
	Lesson 3 (page 156)	writing a paragraph; using pronouns
	Lesson 4 (page 164)	writing a paragraph; proofreading for verb-tense errors
	Lesson 5 (page 170)	writing sentences
	Lesson 6 (page 175)	writing a paragraph; proofreading for subject-verb agreement
	Lesson 7 (page 181)	writing a paragraph: proofreading for subject-verb agreement
	Lesson 8 (page 188)	writing sentences; proofreading for subject-verb agreement
	Lesson 9 (page 194)	writing a paragraph; using action verbs
	Lesson 10 (page 200)	writing tongue twisters; using verbs, nouns, adverbs, and adjectives
Unit 2 Sentence Structure	Lesson 11 (page 207)	writing compound sentences
	Lesson 12 (page 214)	writing complex sentences, using braille
	Lesson 13 (page 219)	writing a paragraph; proofreading for sentence errors
Unit 3 Mechanics	Lesson 14 (page 227)	writing a paragraph; proofreading for end punctuation and commas
	Lesson 15 (page 234)	writing dialogue; using correct punctuation
	Lesson 16 (page 238)	writing titles; proofreading for capitalization errors
	Lesson 17 (page 245)	writing sentences; proofreading for spelling errors
	Lesson 18 (page 251)	writing a paragraph; using homonyms and frequently misused words

THEME	THEME ACTIVITY	SKILLS APPLIED
Technology	The Writing Connection (page C3)	write: write a paragraph
	Problem Solver (page C3)	data analysis: interpreting graphs
Employment	The Writing Connection (page C5)	write: write a list
	Problem Solver (page C4)	data analysis: charts
Cultures	The Writing Connection (page C7)	write: write a paragraph
	Problem Solver (page C6)	problem solving: subtraction
News Media	The Writing Connection (page C9)	write: write a paragraph
	Problem Solver (page C8)	data analysis: compare and contrast
Entertainment	The Writing Connection (page C10)	write: write a poem
	Problem Solver (page C11)	number relationships: percents
Languages	The Writing Connection (page C13)	write: write a paragraph
	Problem Solver (page C13)	data analysis: interpreting graphs
Health Matters	The Writing Connection (page C15)	write: write a paragraph
	Problem Solver (page C14)	data analysis: discovering patterns

You can use CONNECTIONS in *two* ways:

- Complete the CONNECTIONS activities that appear in each lesson of Section Three of this book. The lessons containing these activities are indicated below. Answers can be found in the Answers and Explanations section on pages 259–269.

- Turn to the theme pages listed below and complete the *Writing Connection* and *Problem Solver* activities. These activities will focus your energies on two of the most challenging tasks in passing the GED—writing and math problem solving. Answers to these activities appear in the Connections Answer Guide beginning on page A1.

CONTENTS

WRITING WITH MACHINES

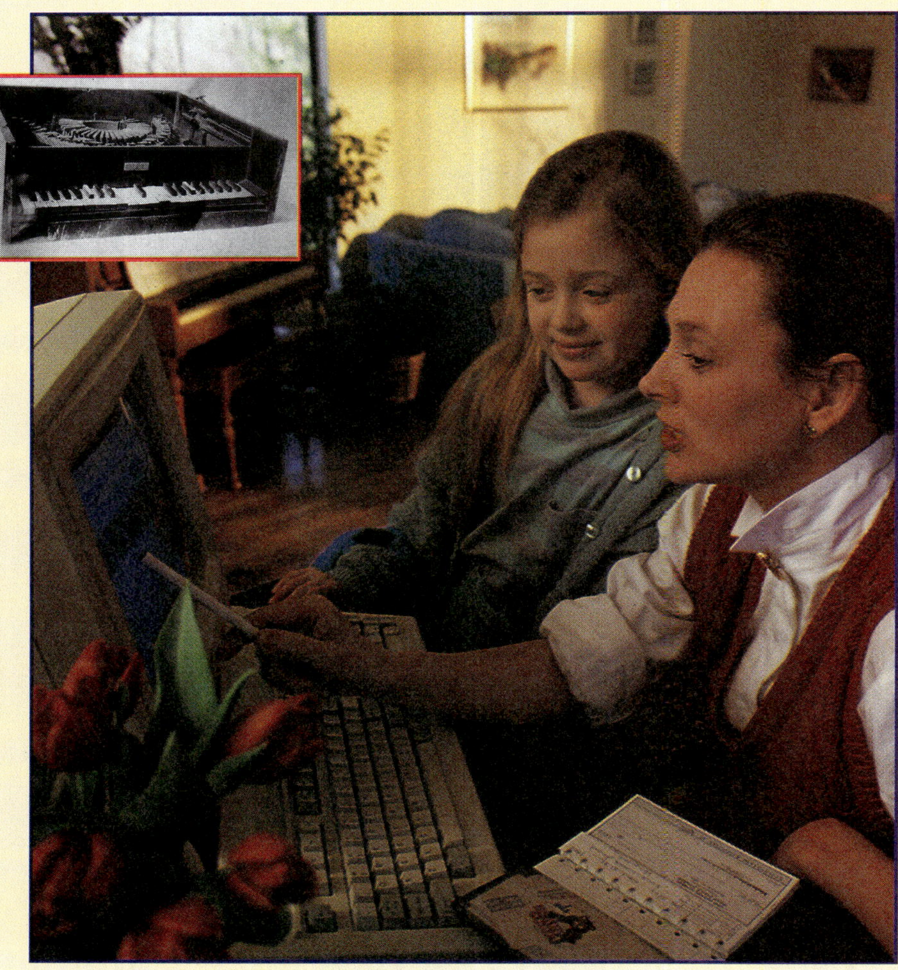

1829
William Austin Burt invents the first typewriter.

1942
The first digital computer is built by John Atanasoff and Clifford Berry.

1952
A computer predicts the winner of U.S. presidential election.

1974
First microcomputers are built.

1976
First portable computer is built.

1981
First laptop computer is built.

1992
Around 29 million personal computers are used in U.S. homes

PERSONAL COMPUTERS **have changed the way people write. Fifty years ago most people handwrote or typed information. Today, however, many turn to personal computers to do their writing. Many children learn to use computers to write in school. Of course, people use their computers for more than writing. They also use computers to balance their checkbooks, organize information, draw pictures, play games, and send messages.**

WORKING WORLD

Computers have important roles in business and industry. They have changed industries, such as publishing and manufacturing, greatly. They have influenced jobs in many fast-growing industries, such as travel or health-care. They have created many job opportunities within the computer industry itself. There were more than 500,000 computer programmers in the United States in 1990. Positions for computer training and service personnel are on the rise.

Problem Solver

Use the timeline and graph to answer these questions: About what was the increase in personal computers in the home between 1981 and 1988? How many more personal computers were in U.S. homes in 1992 than in 1982?

To find the answers, turn to page A1.

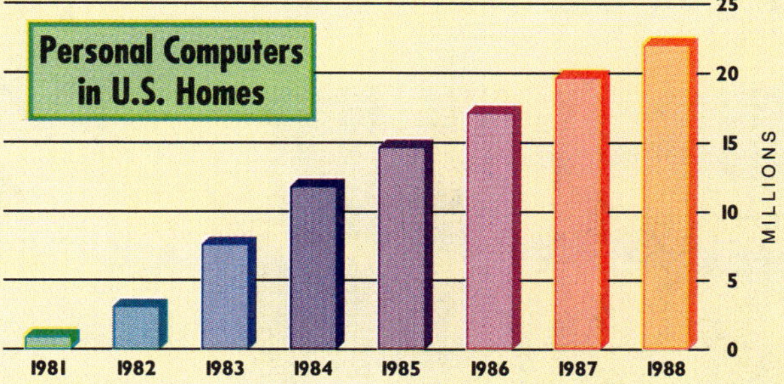

MICROCHIPS

With the invention of the microchip in 1959 computers became faster and smaller. A microchip is a small device that serves as the computer's 'brain.' Today, thanks to the microchip, many people have small personal desktop computers in their homes or carry portable notebook computers. Microchips are also found in microwave ovens, VCRs, and any other device that is 'programmable.'

from *Writing Becomes Electronic*

If anything, using a computer has probably improved my style. You type stuff on paper, and to change anything means retyping a whole page or, in fact, a series of pages. It prevents you from doing the little housekeeping things you'd like to do, like moving a paragraph around or inserting a new thought or character. On a computer it's easy to do that. This morning I wanted to make one of my characters appear to be a little clearer on something that would show up five hundred pages later. And it was just a matter of breaking up a paragraph, fiddling around with a few things and deciding which one I liked, inserting it, punching the SAVE command, and that was that. It's done.

—Tom Clancy, author of *Patriot Games* and *Clear and Present Danger*

the Writing Connection

Read what Tom Clancy has to say about writing on a computer. He represents a positive viewpoint on using computers to write. Other writers may hold different opinions. Some say they feel more creative when they write with a pen or pencil. Others don't know how to use a computer. Have you used a computer or do you think you'd like to? Organize your thoughts, then draft a paragraph describing your opinion. Be sure to include details that explain your opinion.

You can find a sample opinion on page A1.

WRITER'S WORK

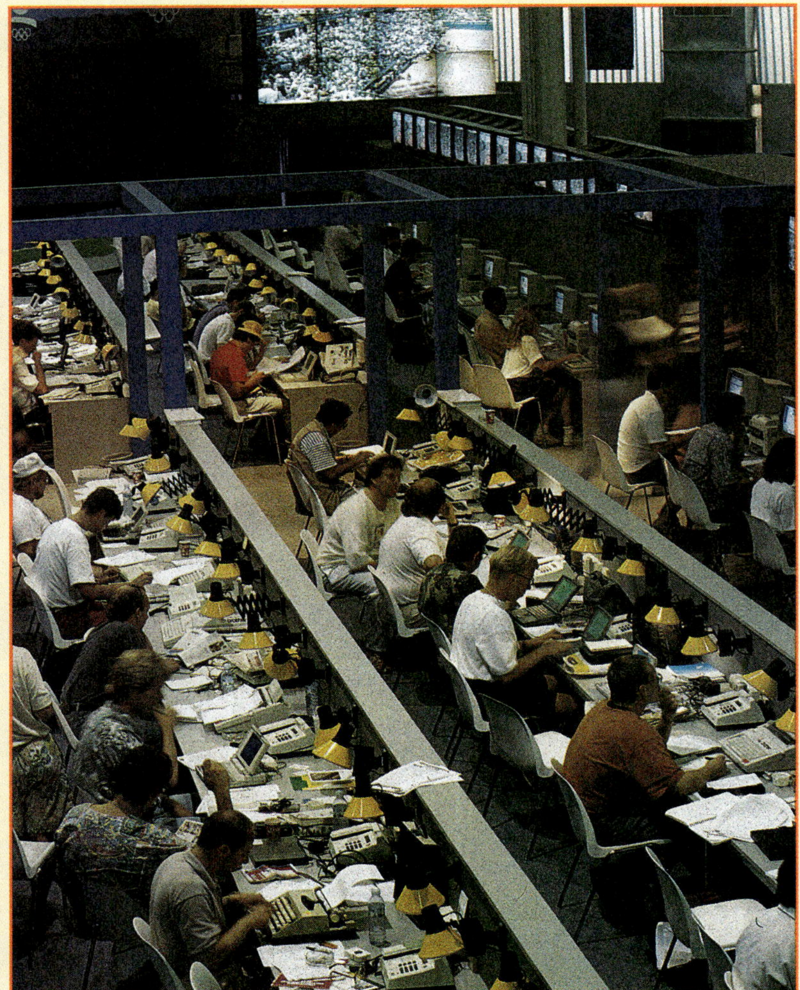

GOOD WRITING SKILLS can lead to a variety of jobs. There are some jobs where writing skills are the most critical skills. In many other jobs writing skills are important. As you complete your education, you will increase your writing skills. This increase in writing skills may lead to increased employment opportunities and often to higher pay.

AVERAGE INCOME
(Persons 25 years and over)

SCHOOL COMPLETED	AVERAGE INCOME Women	Men
Less than 9th grade	$11,637	$16,880
9th to 12th grade (no diploma)	13,538	20,944
High school graduate (includes GED)	18,042	26,218
Some college (no degree)	21,328	31,034
College degree	27,654	39,894

PROBLEM Solver

Look at the table. According to this table:

1. How many more dollars per year can a female high school graduate earn than a woman who attended but did not graduate from high school?
2. How much more can a woman with a college degree earn than a woman with a high school diploma?
3. What is the difference in income between a male high school graduate and a female high school graduate?

To find the answers, turn to page A1.

the WRITING Connection

Read what John Steinbeck has to say about writing. Would you like to write for a living, as Steinbeck did? Or would you like to write advertisements? How about being a technical writer? Make a list of the pros and cons of being a writer. Then write a few sentences explaining why you would or would not like to be a writer.

Turn to page A1 for a sample response.

from *Writers at Work*

"It has been a good day of work with no harm in it. I have sat long over the desk and the pencil has felt good in my hand. Outside the sun is very bright and warm and the buds are swelling to a popping size. I guess it is a good thing I became a writer. Perhaps I am too lazy for anything else. . . .

"On the third finger of my right hand I have a great callus just from using a pencil for so many hours every day. It has become a big lump by now and it doesn't ever go away. Sometimes it is very rough and other times, as today, it is as shiny as glass."

—John Steinbeck

THE "WRITE" JOB

Advertising copywriters write:

- product campaigns
- print advertisements
- radio or TV advertisements
- promotional catalogs and materials

Technical writers write:

- manuals
- business reports
- proposals
- brochures

In some occupations—such as advertising or journalism—a major part of the job is writing. In other occupations, however, writing is not the central focus. It is a skill that can help you do the job well. Some of these occupations include:

- secretary
- nurse
- sales manager
- insurance underwriter
- office manager
- quality control technician
- claims examiner
- data analyst
- social worker
- bookkeeper
- business owner
- community relations worker
- travel agent

WORLD DOCUMENTS

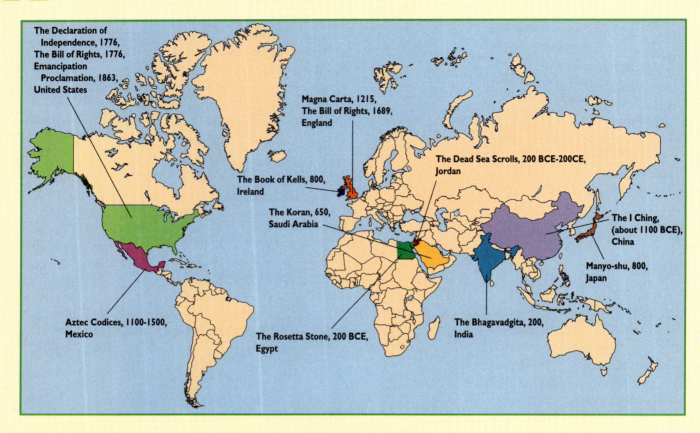

The Declaration of Independence, 1776, The Bill of Rights, 1776, Emancipation Proclamation, 1863, United States

Magna Carta, 1215, The Bill of Rights, 1689, England

The Dead Sea Scrolls, 200 BCE-200CE, Jordan

The Book of Kells, 800, Ireland

The Koran, 650, Saudi Arabia

The I Ching, (about 1100 BCE), China

Manyo-shu, 800, Japan

Aztec Codices, 1100-1500, Mexico

The Rosetta Stone, 200 BCE, Egypt

The Bhagavadgita, 200, India

A CULTURE'S IMPORTANT IDEAS **are recorded in documents that have both practical and symbolic value. The *Magna Carta*, or "Great Charter," of England is one example. This document, written in 1215, limited the power of the king and established people's rights. Other cultures have documents that hold a similar importance. For example, the *Bhagavadgita* in India (200 CE), *The Book of Changes* (or *I Ching*) (about 1100 BCE) and *The Book of Documents* (or *Shu Ching*) in China, the *Manyo-shu* in Japan (800 CE), and the *Declaration of Independence* (1776) in the United States are cultural, historical treasures.**

PROBLEM Solver

As you can see on the map, the world's important cultural documents differ in age. How many years separate the oldest and the most recent documents represented on this map?

To find the answers, turn to page A1.

from *the Emancipation Proclamation*

"...Now, therefore, I, Abraham Lincoln, President of the United States, by virtue of the power in me vested as Commander-in-Chief of the Army and Navy of the United States...do order and declare that all persons held as slaves within said designated States and parts of States are, and henceforward shall be, free; and that the Executive Government of the United States, including the military and naval authorities thereof, will recognize and maintain the freedom of said persons...."

—Abraham Lincoln (1863)

the Writing Connection

The Emancipation Proclamation granted freedom to three million African Americans. The document became a symbol of African American freedom.

Is there a historical document or a family document that is especially important to you? Why is it special? Organize your ideas, then draft a paragraph describing the document and why it is important to you.

Turn to page A1 for a sample response.

AZTEC CODICES

The Aztec people, who lived in Mexico from the 1100s to the 1500s, created sacred documents called *codices*. An Aztec scribe painted symbols and pictures on deerskin or paper to make the codices. The Aztec civilization used these documents to record their history, to predict the future, and to describe religious and cultural ceremonies.

Working World

Important cultural and historical documents such as the ones described on these two pages are usually kept (and often exhibited) in museums and libraries. Museums and libraries offer a variety of employment opportunities at many levels. These range from historians and librarians to security guards to office workers to movers and installers of art exhibitions.

THE WRITTEN WORD

SINCE 1920, when about 2,400 daily newspapers were published in the United States, the number of different daily newspapers has been steadily declining. One reason for this dramatic change is that "media giants" have emerged and swallowed up hundreds of small independent publishers. Big companies now own and manage the majority of the country's newspapers.

Percentage of Newspapers Owned Independently or by Chains

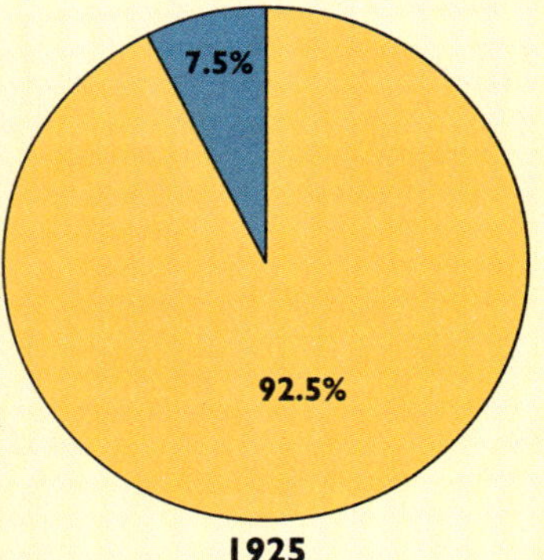

1925

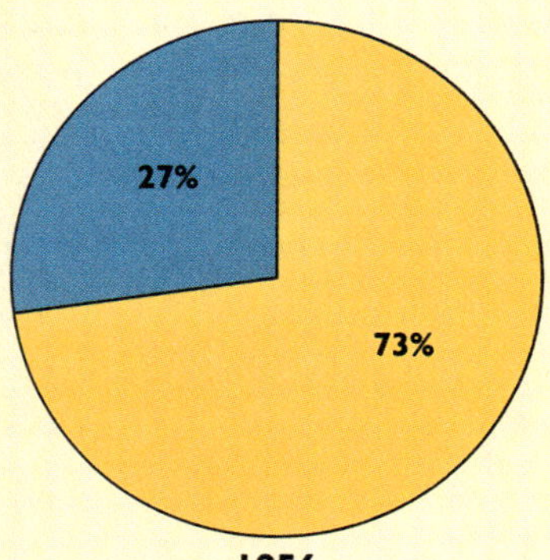

1956

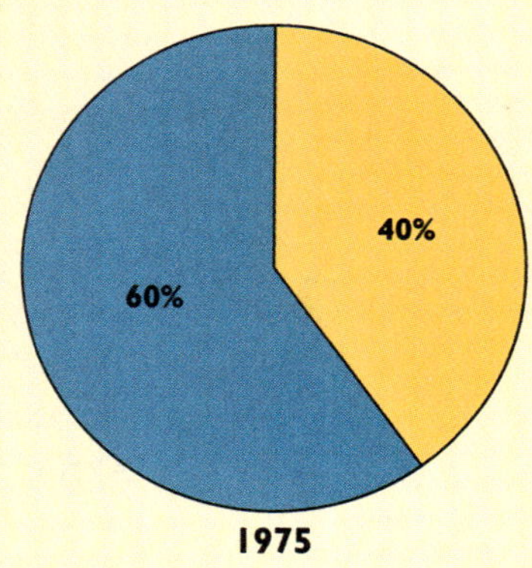

1975

- newspapers owned by chains
- newspapers owned by independent companies

PROBLEM Solver

Look at the circle graphs on the right. As you can see, the percentage of independent daily papers in the U.S. has dropped sharply since 1925. How else could you communicate this information? Would a bar graph be a good way to present this material? Why or why not? Was the increase in chain-owned newspapers greater between 1925 and 1956 or between 1956 and 1975?

To find the answers, turn to page A1.

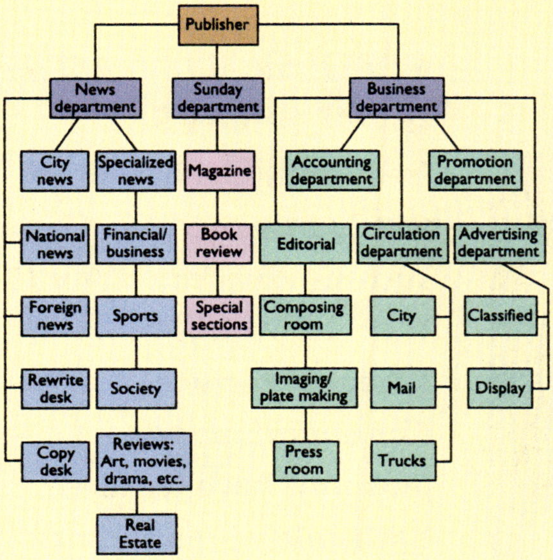

Publisher

News department
Sunday department
Business department

City news
Specialized news
Magazine
Accounting department
Promotion department

National news
Financial/business
Book review
Editorial
Circulation department
Advertising department

Foreign news
Sports
Special sections
Composing room
City
Classified

Rewrite desk
Society
Imaging/plate making
Mail
Display

Copy desk
Reviews: Art, movies, drama, etc.
Press room
Trucks

Real Estate

HOW A NEWSPAPER PUBLISHES THE NEWS

A newspaper is delivered at your door or you pick it up at the newsstand. How was it produced? The diagram above shows the different departments of a large city newspaper and how they work together. You, the reader, are the most important force that impacts this industry. Newspapers, like other businesses, depend on sales.

WORKING WORLD

Many cities with populations of 35,000 or more have a variety of media. They may boast at least one television station, several radio stations, and at least one newspaper. There are many career opportunities in news production. There are jobs for:

- audio and video technicians
- reporters
- printers
- truck drivers
- data entry operators
- advertising copy writers
- sales people
- graphic artists
- writers
- editors
- accountants

the WRITING Connection

Although the quotes in Views on the Press are all more than forty years old, many people's opinion of the press has not changed much. Almost everybody has something to say about the way the press does its job. Many people feel the press favors some politicians or political parties. Other people say that the press focuses on sensational news. Write four sentences on your opinion of the press. Then draft a paragraph that includes details that help explain your feelings.

Turn to page A1 for a sample response.

VIEWS ON THE PRESS

"A free press can of course be good or bad, but, most certainly, without freedom it will never be anything but bad."

—Albert Camus, French writer

"A newspaper is a device for making the ignorant more ignorant and the crazy crazier."

—H.L. Mencken, American writer and editor

"It is very difficult to have a free, fair, and honest press anywhere in the world.... As a rule, papers are largely supported by advertising, and that immediately gives the advertisers a certain hold over the medium which they use."

—Eleanor Roosevelt, First Lady of the United States, 1933–1945

WORD GAMES

POPULAR TELEVISION GAME SHOWS **frequently are based on words or word play. Games such as *What's in a Word?*, *Word for Word*, *Password*, *Wheel of Fortune*, *Concentration*, and *Jeopardy!* have featured both celebrities and non-celebrities playing for prizes. *Wheel of Fortune* and *Jeopardy!* have survived for many years and have set records for popularity in the 1980s and 1990s.**

WORKING WORLD

Word games such as crossword puzzles can increase and sharpen your vocabulary and make you a more confident person in conversation and in writing. Good conversational and writing skills can increase employment opportunities for you.

CROSSWORD PUZZLES

Crossword puzzles are published in thousands of newspapers and magazines today. Yet they were unknown until 1913, when the New York World published a "word-cross" created by journalist Arthur Wynne. In the 1920s crosswords became very popular in the United States and England, and today they remain the most widely enjoyed word game. Word games are also popular in the form of board games such as Scrabble and Boggle.

3000 BCE

REBUSES ***(Egypt)***

combinations of pictures, symbols, and letters that make up a word

spells BESIDE.

500 BCE

RIDDLES ***(Babylonia)***

puzzles that take the form of questions

300 BCE

PALINDROMES ***(Greece)***

words and phrases that are spelled the same backwards and forwards

MOM and MADAM

200 BCE

ACROSTICS ***(Roman Empire)***

take letters from a set of words and rearrange them to form a message

50 BCE

PUNS ***(Roman Empire)***

jokes based on the intentional misuse of words

1200

ANAGRAMS ***(Palestine)***

words or phrases whose letters can be rearranged to make other words or phrases

DIET and TIDE

1700s

CHARADES ***(England)***

a game in which words and phrases are acted out

Entertainment

the WRITING Connection

One of the most famous writers associated with word games or word play was Lewis Carroll. His book, *Alice's Adventures in Wonderland*, contains an example of a "shaped" poem. The poem takes the shape of a mouse's tail. Try writing a shaped poem. See if you can make the shape of the poem relate to its content. Remember, it doesn't have to rhyme. For example, a sad poem could be shaped like a tear.

Turn to page A2 for a sample response.

'Fury said to
a mouse, That
he met in the
house, "Let
us both go
to law: *I*
will prose-
cute *you*.—
Come, I'll
take no de-
nial: We
must have
the trial;
For really
this morn-
ing I've
nothing
to do."
Said the
mouse to
the cur,
"Such a
trial, dear
sir, With
no jury
or judge,
would
be wast-
ing our
breath."
"I'll be
judge,
I'll be
jury,"
said
cun-
ning
old
Fury:
"I'll
try
the
whole
cause
and
con-
demn
you to
death".'

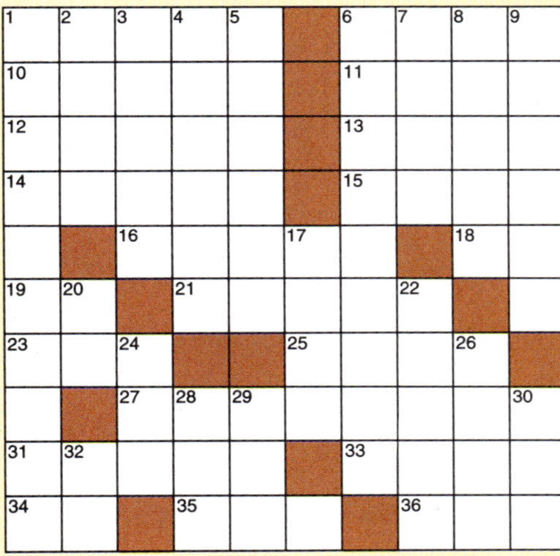

PROBLEM Solver

Look at the crossword puzzle. How many squares does this puzzle contain? How many of these squares are orange? One way to judge a puzzle's difficulty is to find the percent of orange squares. What percent of this puzzle's squares are orange? The more orange squares, the easier the puzzle is.

To find the answers, turn to page A2.

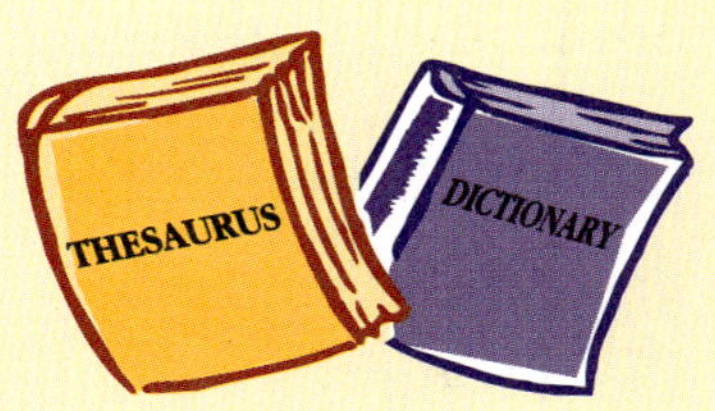

1800s

TONGUE-TWISTERS
(England)

phrases that are hard to say quickly

"She sells seashells by the seashore."

1913

CROSSWORD PUZZLES
(United States)

games using definitions, synonyms, antonyms, and abbreviations

1930s

SCRABBLE
(United States)

board game that became extremely popular in 1952 and remains so today

1950s-present

TELEVISION WORD GAMES
(United States)

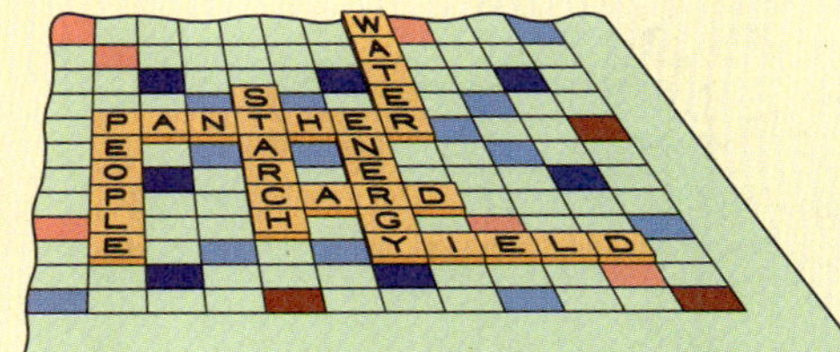

1980s

SCATTERGORIES AND BOGGLE
(United States)

games featuring word plays

ALPHABETS

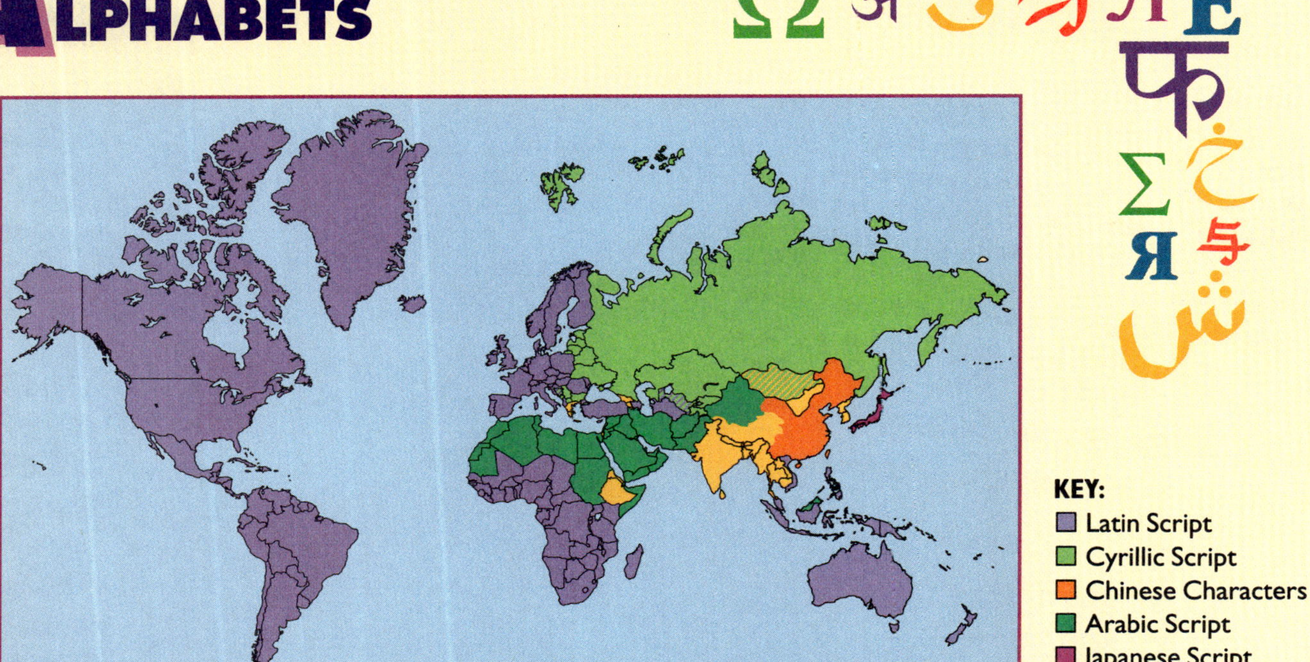

PEOPLE SPEAK **more than 4,000 languages around the world today. However, there aren't 4,000 different alphabets. In fact, there are fewer than four dozen! Many languages use the same alphabet. For example, people in France, Mexico, Germany, Tanzania, Turkey, Finland, and Canada use the Latin alphabet. The map above shows the alphabet used in the major newspapers of different countries. As you can see, the Latin, Cyrillic, and Arabic alphabets are used in more geographic areas than others. However, newspapers published using the Chinese alphabet have the most readers.**

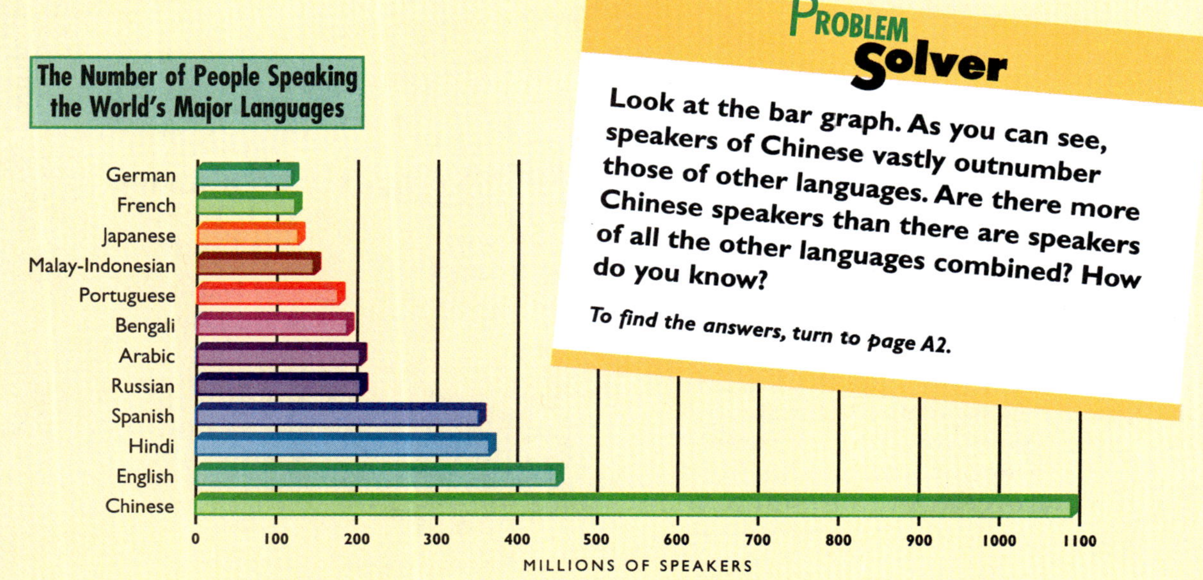

PROBLEM Solver

Look at the bar graph. As you can see, speakers of Chinese vastly outnumber those of other languages. Are there more Chinese speakers than there are speakers of all the other languages combined? How do you know?

To find the answers, turn to page A2.

3 TYPES OF ALPHABETS

There are three basic types of alphabets used in the world today—those containing:

- ideograms
- phonetic symbols
- and syllabic symbols.

森 An *ideogram* is a symbol that stands for an object or an idea. For instance, *forest* would be represented by the ideogram or picture for *forest* instead of the letters. The Chinese language is written in ideograms.

R A *phonetic symbol* corresponds to one particular sound. Unlike an ideogram, a letter symbol does not usually stand for a whole object or idea. A group of phonetic symbols used together stand for an object or idea. English, Spanish, and Arabic all use phonetic alphabets.

च *Syllabic symbols* correspond to more than one sound—usually one consonant and one vowel. The Hindi language uses Devanagari script, which consists of syllabic symbols. Here is a Devanagari consonant as it is written with the vowel *a* (pronounced *uh*).

the WRITING Connection

Read what Malcolm X had to say about his discovery of the power of writing. During a prison term, he taught himself thousands of new words by studying a dictionary and reading as much as possible. Malcolm X appreciated both reading and writing. Draft a paragraph describing what you could do to improve your reading skills, writing skills, or handwriting. Be sure to include details that help show why you feel as you do. Revise and edit your work.

Turn to page A2 for a sample response.

from *The Autobiography of Malcolm X*

I saw that the best thing I could do was get hold of a dictionary—to study, to learn some words. I was lucky enough to reason also that I should try to improve my penmanship. It was sad. I couldn't even write in a straight line. . . . In my slow, painstaking, ragged handwriting, I copied into my tablet everything printed on that first page, down to the punctuation marks. I believe it took me a day. Then, aloud, I read back, to myself, everything I'd written on the tablet. Over and over, aloud, to myself, I read my own handwriting.

—Malcolm X (as told to Alex Haley)

WORKING WORLD

In ancient times many people did not know how to write, and so writers or scribes were respected. Although some people are still unable to read and write, most people in the United States today know how to read or write in English or another language. Being able to write in English is a valuable skill that is necessary for many jobs. Being able to read and write more than one language can lead to opportunities interpreting and translating. It may lead to work overseas.

A HEALTHY RESPECT FOR LANGUAGE

"Braille" written in Braille

Braille is the alphabet used by blind persons all over the world. Invented by Louis Braille in 1824, the alphabet consists of 63 symbols, each of which is made of one to six dots. These dots are embossed, or raised, on paper and are read with the fingertips. A person can write in Braille using a device called a stylus.

PROBLEM Solver

Look at the chart. Braille symbols differ from other alphabets. How many more symbols (or "characters") are there in Braille than in the Latin alphabet? Why do you think some symbols represent whole ideas and others represent sounds? What patterns do you see in the different arrangements of the six Braille positions?

To find the answers, turn to page A2.

LANGUAGE PLAYS an important role in everyone's life. Unfortunately, some people have difficulty reading or writing because of vision problems; others have difficulty listening or speaking because of hearing problems. Some people cannot respond properly to the printed word because of nervous conditions.

Language and communication also play a role in the quality of health care people receive. Some people have almost no opportunity for appropriate *health care* because of race, sex, or economic conditions. Writing or speaking about health care issues may cause improvements to be made.

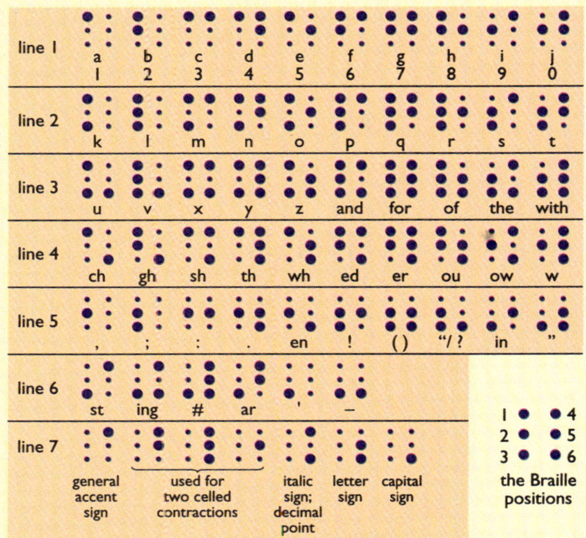

TREATING DYSLEXIA

Dyslexia is one of the most common learning disabilities. A dyslexic person has difficulty recognizing and writing letters and words. Letters will often appear confusingly jumbled, backwards, or upside down, as in the illustration. Although dyslexia can be diagnosed, its cause is still not clear. The treatment of dyslexia involves teaching the use other senses to help people read and write and providing them with emotional support.

The Way a Dyslexic Person Might Write a Sentence

The bop saw wiet anb drown.

The dog was white and brown.

WORKING WORLD

Health care offers a wide range of employment. Language skills and communication are extremely important in health care jobs. Public and private hospitals, as well as other institutions, hire people for jobs such as:

- nurses' aides
- receptionists
- physical therapists
- x-ray technicians
- medical records transcribers

the WRITING Connection

In the excerpt below, South African tennis player Mark Mathabane discusses the health care black citizens received under apartheid. Is there a health care issue you would like to bring to the public's attention? Draft a paragraph describing the issue and your suggestions about it. Have someone else edit your work.

Turn to page A2 for a sample response.

from *Kaffir Boy*

A week or so after I came back from the National Tournament, my eyes began to hurt. At first I paid little attention to the pain, attributing it to fatigue. I had had many ailments in my life from sore teeth to migraines to pneumonia—but because medical attention was sought only in life-and-death situations by many blacks, I had simply waited for nature to take its course. I did the same with my sore eyes.

They got worse. They swelled and ached to the point where I could hardly read or keep them open for long, especially in light. My mother became alarmed. . . .

Three weeks later on a Friday my mother gave me part of her monthly wage, and I went to the clinic. I found the place overcrowded with black women, men and children seeking treatment for all kinds of diseases and injuries. I waited on the long line; it became afternoon; still I was not attended to. By the time I was through with the paper-work many doctors had gone, and those that remained were giving priority to emergency cases. Apparently the fact that I was going blind was not considered an emergency; there were dying people around me.

—Mark Mathabane

ANATOMY OF A PARAGRAPH

The topic sentence usually appears at the beginning of a paragraph. It tells the reader what the paragraph is about.

A paragraph is made up of related sentences. Each sentence must be complete and must end with either a period, a question mark, or an exclamation point.

In general, the verbs in a paragraph are in the same tense. In this paragraph, the verbs are in the present tense.

I enjoy reading, and I wish I had more time to spend doing it. Reading allows a person to take a rest from all the noise of the world. When I read, I am allowed to be by myself with my own thoughts. Yet, in another way, reading is like having a trusted companion nearby. I have my own thoughts, but I also hear about the writer's thoughts. For me, reading is peaceful whether I am reading a newspaper on the bus or a mystery novel in bed. I would like to read more often because every time I really slow down and let myself relax with something to read, I get a rich reward.

Connecting words help the reader see the relationship between ideas in a paragraph. Here, the word *yet* signals a contrast between two thoughts. The word *because* signals a cause-and-effect relationship between two ideas.

Sentences that give supporting details about the subject follow the topic sentence. Here sentences give specific information about why the writer enjoys reading.

The concluding sentence appears at the end of a paragraph. It summarizes the ideas of the paragraph and restates the topic sentence in a fresh way.